## THIS WRITING GUIDE IS IDEALLY SUITED FOR THE PERSON WHO:

- Is new to the art of writing (and understanding) Army Efficiency Reports.
- Wants his/her top performers to have a competitive edge in "passing" selection boards at all levels.
- Doesn't like to continually start writing performance appraisal narratives from scratch.
- Doesn't quite know how to word or document performance and potential.
- Wants to submit good, effective write-ups to impress the "boss."

**THIS GUIDE CAN BE USED BY**:  Anyone who evaluates the performance of others.  It will be used by those who are serious about getting the "jump" on the competition.

## HIGHLIGHTS OF THE BOOK

The book *Writing Guide for Army Efficiency Reports*  *(Third Edition)* was developed to aid in the drafting of:

** INDIVIDUAL RECOGNITION WRITE-UPS

** PERSONAL AWARDS

** ARMY EFFICIENCY REPORTS (SUPERIOR & SUBSTANDARD)

### Plus, the book contains:

** 2,000 WORD DICTIONARY - Alphabetical listing of 2,000 of the most used ADJECTIVES, NOUNS, & VERBS on PERSONAL PERFORMANCE/PERSON-ALITY TRAITS in the English language (with definitions).

** 2,000 WORD THESAURUS - The dictionary words are grouped in unique, easy-to-use sections by SUPERIOR -TO-SUBSTANDARD performance, AND, by PERFORMANCE and PERSONALITY TRAIT sections.

** 2,500 BULLETS-PHRASES - Ready to use, FAVORABLE & UNFAVORABLE Sections

** SPECIAL "PHRASE, THOUGHT, OR IDEA" SECTION filled with example statements for use in any letter or documentation.

**\* THE PEOPLE WHO USE THIS GUIDE HAVE A DEFINITE AND DECIDED ADVANTAGE OVER NON-USERS.**

\* 30 DAY MONEY-BACK GUARANTEE if not completely satisfied

See advertisements & order forms within this book, or call in credit card orders. Government Purchase Orders Accepted.  Write or Call:

### PROFESSIONAL MANAGEMENT SPECTRUM, INC.
### P. O. BOX 30330
### PENSACOLA, FL  32503
### PHONE:  1-800-346-6114 FAX: (850) 432-3908
### WEB: www.servicebooks.com

# WRITING GUIDE FOR ARMY EFFICIENCY REPORTS

## Third Edition

ISBN 0-9623673-2-X

The words "he," "him," and "his" in the Guide are used to communicate ideas, and are not intended to discriminate against anyone.

PRINTED IN THE UNITED STATES OF AMERICA

# TABLE OF CONTENTS
## PERFORMANCE APPRAISALS

## FAVORABLE APPRAISALS
### FAVORABLE PERFORMANCE THESAURUS

### FAVORABLE BULLETS/PHRASES

## UNFAVORABLE APPRAISALS

## PERFORMANCE DICTIONARY

## SENTENCE SUBJECTS

# PERFORMANCE APPRAISALS

The sample write-ups provided in this guide reflect several writing styles. They give the reader a variety of ideas on how subject material can be written. When drafting performance appraisals, remember you are writing to "sell" the evaluee to selection boards by covering that individual's performance, ability, and potential. All writing styles in this guide accomplish this objective.

There is enough material available in this guide to form a sound base in the construction of hundreds of individual write-ups, each with its own uniqueness and individuality.

The material in one chapter can be used with the subject matter of other chapters.

**REMEMBER:**

* If you do not know how to draft a performance appraisal, you don't know how to read one--your own included.

* If you cannot author a good narrative, you are hurting the careers of those individuals working for you who deserve to be promoted.

**FREQUENT USE OF THIS GUIDE WILL INCREASE YOUR ABILITY TO UNDERSTAND AND WRITE PERFORMANCE APPRAISALS.**

# INTRODUCTION

Every large organization has some means to evaluate the performance of its members. Administrators call this evaluation process "performance appraisal."

## PRIMARY OBJECTIVES OF GIVING PERFORMANCE APPRAISALS

1. To identify promotion, retention, and future duty potential.

2. To select, promote and retain the best qualified personnel.

3. To provide feedback to the evaluee.

## PERFORMANCES MEASURED

1. **PERSONAL TRAITS** - How something is done (for example, the leadership, initiative, etc. used or applied to accomplish something).

2. **JOB PERFORMANCE** - What and how much is done.

3. **JOB BEHAVIOR** - Appearance, adaptability, behavior, etc.

## OBJECTIVE AND SUBJECTIVE ANALYSIS

**OBJECTIVE ANALYSIS** should be used whenever possible to document an individual's performance. Objective analysis means to quantify performance results. How much was done? What was done? Use hours, time, percent, dollars, etc.

**SUBJECTIVE ANALYSIS** is the evaluator's perceptions, beliefs, or thoughts on how something was accomplished. This is an analysis of a person's "inner" qualities (or personality) and must be based on observations over a period of time. Subjective analysis is used to describe what prompted or caused an individual to do something (personal traits such as leadership, imagination, etc.).

# PREPARATION CHECK-LIST

The more knowledge and tools an evaluator has at his/her disposal the better. The following information should be reviewed PRIOR to committing a subordinate's performance to print.

1. All performance appraisals should be handled discretely. They should be worked on in private.

2. Rough copies of past performance appraisals might be retained on file for reference for the next reporting period.

3. Insofar as practicable, reporting seniors should grade all performance appraisals of the same competitive category at one time. This will facilitate comparative grading.

4. Endeavor to obtain a just and equitable spread in the marks assigned to a comparative group.

5. Do not gravitate toward either a gratuitously high or rigidly severe policy of grading. The military is plagued by general over-assessment of average performers and occasional under assessment of "top performers." This serves to reduce the promotional opportunities of the "best qualified."

6. Exercise care to mark objectively, avoiding any tendency which might allow general impressions, a single incident or a particular trait, characteristic, or quality to influence other marks unduly.

7. When uncertain, due to limited observation, as to the appropriate evaluation of any rating area, mark the "Not Observed" block rather than assign a "middle-of-the-road" mark.

8. Avoid marking a new person somewhat lower than he/she deserves in order to reflect improved performance in subsequent performance appraisals. This malpractice can result in unjust advancement or assignment actions.

9. Before beginning to write, check over available performance data and determine which category you are going to place an individual being reported on:
    a. Head and shoulders above his contemporaries--promote early/now.
    b. Above many contemporaries--promote above most.
    c. Good performer--promote with majority of contemporaries.
    d. Behind peer group performance--do not promote.

When a decision has been reached, write a performance appraisal that will support and justify your position.

10. The "head and shoulders" performers should be immediately identified at the start of the narrative. The remaining write-up must justify and reinforce your position.

11. Ensure realistic marks are assigned to individuals whose performance of duty has been manifestly unsatisfactory. Impersonal grading and concise statements of fact best serve overall interests under such circumstances.

12. Conversely, ensure that due consideration is accorded when an individual demonstrates truly outstanding or exceptional professional competence and potential. In such cases accentuate the positive. State all major accomplishments that have been achieved. More importantly, comment constructively on capacity or potential for future increased responsibility or promotion.

13. If the command has made an outstanding performance during the reporting period, an individual's personal contribution to this effect should be included. Of course, the converse is true.

14. After completion of a performance appraisal, review previous worksheets on the same person, if available, to ensure that any changes in the marks on the current report are intended. Any significant shift of marks in reports signed by the same reporting senior should be substantiated in the narrative.

15. When making subsequent reports on the same person, guard against repetitive phraseology, as this will reflect lack of thought on your part and it will not help an individual's promotion chances.

16. Before submitting a smooth performance appraisal, analyze the narrative to make sure that what is meant to be said is, in fact, actually being said. Give careful thought not only to what the chosen words mean to the evaluator, but also how they may be construed by a selection board.

17. When the performance appraisal is finished, review it to ensure that:
    a. All parts are consistent (marks & narrative agree).
    b. The trend in performance (increase or decrease) is correctly conveyed.
    c. All spelling and grammatical errors are corrected.

18. Bear in mind that performance appraisal narratives reflect the degree and extent in which evaluators measure up to their moral obligation. And, an evaluator's write-up may be used to judge his/her performance.

19. Words are both valuable and dangerous tools. Choose them carefully.

20. Words mean what they say. Review the following:

## POTENTIAL  CAPACITY  ABILITY

To indicate that an individual has these qualities without supporting evidence will register to a selection board as "insufficient data." A person can have POTENTIAL, CAPACITY, or ABILITY and yet accomplish nothing. Write how these qualities were demonstrated.

## TRIES  STRIVES

Someone can TRY or STRIVE without accomplishing anything. As above, note how these qualities were positively demonstrated.

## ACCEPTS  ASSIGNED  NORMALLY  GENERALLY

Simply ACCEPTING assignments does not show initiative. Performing ASSIGNMENTS does not show initiative. NORMALLY and GENERALLY mean less than always.

## AVERAGE ABOVE  AVERAGE  EXCELLENT OUTSTANDING

These words have "canned" meanings and understandings. ABOVE AVERAGE is generally assumed to mean less than EXCELLENT or OUTSTANDING. AVERAGE means less than ABOVE AVERAGE, etc. If you are going to place someone's performance in one of these categories, be sure to choose the correct word(s).

# "DO" Check List:

-DO submit performance appraisals -DO write performance appraisals directed on time and in correct format.

TO selection boards.

-DO write on how someone contributed above or below what is normally expected.

-DO write to express, not impress.

-DO be fair, honest, and objective.

-DO comment of growth potential and qualifications for promotion and future duty assignments.

-DO write on hard, pertinent facts, not "faint praises" without substance.

-DO use short, concise phrases or complete sentences with proper grammar.

-DO use underline to highlight key areas only.

# "DON'T" Check List:

-DON'T assign marks that are inconsistent with the narrative.

-DON'T write performance appraisals directed TO the individual.

-DON'T assign exceptionally high/low marks without comments in the narrative that clearly distinguish the performance.

-DON'T include minor, isolated, or insignificant imperfections which do not affect performance.

-DON'T use glittering generalities which go on and on without saying anything useful.

-DON'T use long words when shorter words will do.

-DON'T be verbose or redundant.

**-DON'T** restate the job description in the narrative. That space is too valuable.

**-DON'T** write "during the period of this report" or words to that effect. It is understood, unless otherwise stated, that all actions and events in a performance appraisal occurred during the reporting period being covered. Again, narrative space is too valuable.

**-DON'T** start too many sentences with the same: He... He... His... etc.... Reading becomes sluggish and boring and shows lack of attention or ability on the part of the drafter.

**-DON'T** use a person's name without associated rank. For example, do not write "Jones is..."; instead, it should be "LT Jones is..."; A performance appraisal is an official document and an individual's rank should always accompany his/her name.

**-DON'T** use the term "ratee." It is too impersonal and impresses no one.

# PERFORMANCE APPRAISALS

## DRAFTING THE NARRATIVE

1. **OBJECTIVE**. Performance appraisals should be drafted with two objectives in mind. These objectives are:

    a. To document, in SPECIFIC terms, what an individual contributed to command, and department/division effectiveness and accomplishment; and,

    b. To document the subjective "inner" qualities demonstrated by an individual on how performance was accomplished.

2. **GUIDANCE.**

    a. **BE POSITIVE**: Any shortcoming or deficiency mentioned in the narrative should be significant, either in terms of performance or potential. At any level in an organization some occasional, routine guidance is necessary. If the comment is made that someone requires occasional instruction or guidance, that means he/she requires more instruction or guidance than would normally be expected. In effect, comments on minor deficiencies are automatically magnified when they are included in the narrative.

b. **BE CORRECT**: A direct, hard-hitting write-up is better than an elegant one--concentrate more on content and specific accomplishments.

c. **BE FACTUAL**: Quantify individual achievements and accomplishments when possible.

d. **BE SPECIFIC**: A few well worded phrases or sentences on individual accomplishment and achievement mean much more than pages on billet description, command employment, etc...

e. **BE OBJECTIVE**: To the maximum extent possible, comment on quantifiable "objective" accomplishments, not on "subjective" personal notions.

# OPENING FORMAT

The most closely read sentences in a performance appraisal are the opening sentences. The opening should be a powerful and persuasive statement--an "attention getter" to immediately capture the attention of the reader. The opening format can be limited to four themes:

(1) Overview of best attributes/performance (or the converse for substandard performers);

(2) Organizational ranking (for top performers);

(3) Potential (for top performers); and,

(4) Awards or other forms of recognition received. The opening format sets the "theme" for the remaining narrative.

# OPENING FORMAT SAMPLES

... (Name) is an exceptionally well qualified . . . Extremely well organized, mission-oriented and empathic with his subordinates and work environment. Infused (organization) with enthusiasm and dedication. Unlimited potential. Awarded... Medal for...

... (Name) professional talents, dedication, and aggressive work habits are an asset to the (organization). Virtually unlimited potential. Awarded Letter of Commendation for...

... (Name) is an outstanding manager and organizer. Willing to accept any assignment regardless of scope. Boundless potential. Selected as ... of the Year.

... (Name) is an energetic, industrious, and conscientious individual who has proven himself time after time to be a top performer. (Potential...Awards)

... (Name) has continually proven himself to be a (peer group) of exemplary character and outstanding ability. (Potential...Awards)

... (Name) professional knowledge, self-motivation, and determined, tireless efforts have made excellent contributions to the efficient functioning of (organization). (Potential...Awards)

## CLOSING FORMAT

The CLOSING FORMAT is another good place for a drafter to "sell" an individual to a selection board. : Top notch performers' performance appraisals might close with one of the following:

...Virtually unlimited potential.

...Limitless potential.

...Unbounded potential.

...Extraordinary growth potential.

## SUMMARY

Performance appraisal systems are relatively easy to understand. To properly draft one of these performance appraisals, simply refer to and follow the appropriate instruction for administrative and procedural guidance. However, today there is keen competition for the limited number of available promotion slots. Writing a performance appraisal that just meets the instructional requirements by no means assures success or promotion. Proper use of the material available in this book should enhance promotion competitiveness.

## NARRATIVE STRUCTURE EXAMPLES
### (In Bullet/Phrase Format)

(Name) is well read, with good working knowledge of the English language. Written reports clear and concise. Oral presentations command complete attention of a listening audience.

(Name) is ready for positions of increased responsibility and trust now. Recommended for (.....) duty and for a billet as (.....). (Name) is most strongly recommended for immediate selection to (.....).

(Name) rare and successful blend of leadership coupled with superior management and administrative abilities assure success in virtually any assignment. Stays with a job until it is completed, regardless of the time of day or night. During the past three months worked over 100 off-duty hours re-outfitting and organizing (.....). Unlimited ability and potential. Highly recommended for (.....).

(Name) career continues to be underscored by pride, self-improvement and accomplishment. Initially assigned the primary duties of ..., found time to assume other, equally demanding tasks. Filling in as the ..., organized the monumental task of ... In the area of training, personally planned and scheduled ... Volunteered to assume increased and diverse duties of ... In this capacity managed successful efforts to ...

(Name) most outstanding (peer group). Top notch leader. Well versed in all facets of professional specialty. Energetic and resourceful. Always plans ahead. Self-starter with great desire for professional challenge. Firm, fair, unbiased leader. Demands high standards of performance from self and subordinates. Effectively capitalizes on subordinate strengths and improves weaknesses. A highly talented front-runner in peer group. Promote early.

The wide and varied technical background (name) brought to this job were instrumental in starting the successful operation of ... Being undermanned, the job was particularly demanding and time consuming. Working with others in a unified and cohesive manner is a particularly strong asset of (name). Ability to immediately establish and maintain excellent rapport with subordinates on all levels. Much of this is due to the fair, open, and unbiased manner of leadership style. Each person knows that they will be given an equal opportunity commensurate with capabilities in all assignments, and that all will be given the opportunity to learn. He personally counsels each newly reporting person, setting forth organizational requirements and what the individual can expect in return. Communicates thoughts and ideas with ease and clarity. Written reports are brief, concise, and to the point. Conduct and appearance beyond reproach. Demonstrating a continuing great personal pride in self with uniform proudly worn. Instills this same pride in others.

(Name) is an industrious and versatile individual who approaches any task enthusiastically and with dispatch. A skillful manager with proven ability to attain a high standard of performance in any endeavor. Directs watch team with firm but fair hand, and provides a unified purpose and sense of direction without dulling initiative. Readily adaptable to changes in policy, procedure, or assigned workload. Always gives a personal contribution as a special effort to ensure cohesiveness and uniformity. Established good rapport with subordinates and does not hesitate to provide personal or professional assistance, encouraging their trust through genuine interest in their problems. Accomplishments include: ...

(Name) watch team operational effectiveness graded at (.....) during (event) earning the highest grade in (organization). Received verbal and written praise from (name/title/billet) for the outstanding work and effort put into job as (job name). A proponent of physical fitness, (name) actively participates in various sporting events and maintains a trim physique. Conduct and appearance, on and off duty, are model worthy of emulation by entire ... community.

(Name) fully enjoys military life, is quick to point out career benefits. Will not tolerate open dissent toward command policies or procedures. Personally responsible for convincing others to take initial or additional off-duty educational courses.

(Name) is the most productive and versatile (peer group) at (organization). Proven top quality organizer, administrator, and manager whose potential for increased responsibility and authority is boundless. Supplying much of the early leadership and planning, proved to be a major force in the successful ... Has a great deal of energy, is highly industrious, and doesn't believe in idle time. These rare qualities, coupled with his friendly personality and quick wit, allow him to establish and maintain an atmosphere of pride and professionalism in any organizational environment. A partial listing of personal accomplishments include...

(Name) is eager to stay abreast of the latest changes in management, technology, and operations. Currently enrolled in ... To accomplish these and other varied tasks (name) routinely reports to duty early and remains later than contemporaries. (Name) is a steadying and guiding influence to subordinates and peer group.(Name) is ready now to meet increasingly more responsibility and challenge. Most strongly recommended for promotion ahead of peer group.

A poised and mature (peer group) with a thirst for knowledge and a desire for challenge. Soft spoken with an authoritative manner and commanding presence. A positive motivator who displays compassion, decisiveness, and determination. Intelligent and articulate, runs an orderly and highly productive organization.

(Name) is a self-starter whose great personal initiative and leadership skills identify him as being "head and shoulders" above contemporaries.

(Name) is a top performer. Unlimited potential. Totally professional, poised, mature, and dedicated. A self-starter. Intelligent. Always volunteers for additional responsibility. Rising superstar of boundless ability. Does not believe in idle time or unfinished projects. Manages own time and that of others to best possible advantage. Possesses managerial and organizational expertise rarely observed in contemporaries. Completes large volume of work each day, frequently working extra hours. Neat, trim, and fit. Immaculate "recruit poster" quality appearance. Articulate in speech, polite in manner. Submits timely, accurate staff work. Enjoys loyalty, cooperation, and total support of subordinates.

(Name) ready for promotion now. Possesses superior management and leadership abilities. Extremely knowledgeable, industrious, totally resourceful. Performance of all duties singularly and collectively outstanding. Head and shoulders above contemporaries. Original thinker, thrives on challenge and responsibility. Articulate self-expression. Proven competence and unparalleled ability. Particularly adept at gaining immediate support and loyalty of others. Compassionate, demanding leader.

(Name) absolute quality performer. A high achiever with unlimited growth potential. Concerned counselor, tactful leader. Reliable, responsive, and articulate. Adds more to job than expected. Places duty ahead of personal interests. Continually alert for ways to increase personal and professional knowledge. Personable and outgoing. A real morale booster.

(Name) is work-aggressive and highly productive. Unlimited potential for professional growth. Volunteers for additional tasking. Has a knack for administrative detail. Provides strong, positive leadership. Enthusiastic, "take charge" attitude. Cheerful and personable, promotes high morale and works well with superiors.

Excellent all-around (peer group). Conscientious and totally dependable. Professional, "can-do" attitude. Unbound personal initiative. Enthusiastic leadership. In tense or trying situations can always be counted on to provide appropriate spark of leadership, humor, or energy.

(Name) proven ace performer with endless potential and ability. Energetic, industrious, and conscientious. Outstanding performance contributed significantly to high level of readiness and efficiency. Has knack for getting the job done where others fail. Punctuality and strong sense of duty highlight daily performance. Exceptional military attitude and bearing. Commanding presence. Infectious, cheerful personality elicits maximum support and cooperation. Promote now.

(Name) is my number one (peer group). Promote ahead of all others. Dedication to duty and attention to detail without equal. Energetic self-starter. Demands and receives only top quality performance. Deep sense of personal responsibility and pride of duty. Special talent for organizational detail. Ready sense of humor and a pleasant personality. Fosters high morale throughout the ranks.

(Name) an exceptional leader, manager, and organizer. Demonstrated performance as a leader significantly improved overall performance and readiness. Pride, personal involvement, and job accomplishment underscore daily performance. Industrious and creative, enjoys finding viable solutions to complex situations. Possesses unbounded initiative and potential. Actions well planned, organized, and executed. Dynamic, compassionate leader, knows how to motivate subordinates.

# WORD PICTURE PERSONALITY

Documenting exactly what a person accomplishes in a performance appraisal is both useful and necessary. Work accomplishment alone, however, does not give a complete description or "picture" of an individual. The careful use of a few well chosen "word picture" adjectives can describe a person's inner qualities--what possesses a person to do something--what a person "IS."

By combining what a person accomplishes and putting to print along with those accomplishments a person's personality characteristics, a complete "picture" of an individual is possible. Take, for example, the following:

"(Name) is energetic, resourceful, and self-reliant. He (go on to list exactly what he accomplished)."In the above example, a selection board will know what was accomplished. More importantly, the board will gain valuable insight to the individual's "inner" qualities, capabilities, and potential-- "energetic, resourceful, and self-reliant."

Selection boards do not promote people simply because they do a good job in their present pay grade. The potential to successfully discharge the greater duties of higher pay grades must be clearly in evidence. Potential must be documented in performance appraisals.

By using the appropriate "word picture personality" characteristics listed on the following pages, selection boards can "see" and evaluate the full worth and potential (or lack thereof) of an individual.

# FAVORABLE APPRAISALS
## PERSONALITY

The following list of words express, define, state, or describe FAVORABLE personality characteristics, traits, performance, or results.

## ADJECTIVES

| | | |
|---|---|---|
| ACE | ADEPT | ADMIRABLE |
| ADROIT | AFFABLE | AGILE |
| ALERT | ALL-AROUND | AMIABLE |
| | | |
| AMICABLE | APPEALING | ARTISTIC |
| ASSERTIVE | AUSPICIOUS | BENIGN |
| BLITHE | BRISK | CANDID |
| | | |
| CHARISMATIC | CHARMING | CHEERFUL |
| COMPOSED | CONGENIAL | CONSONANT |
| CORDIAL | COURAGEOUS | COURTEOUS |
| | | |
| DAUNTLESS | DETERMINED | DEVOTED |
| DEXTEROUS | DIPLOMATIC | DISCREET |
| DISCRIMINATING | DISTINGUISHED | DYNAMIC |
| | | |
| EAGER | EFFERVESCENT | ELEGANT |
| ENERGETIC | ENGAGING | ENTERPRISING |
| ENTHUSIASTIC | ETHICAL | EXCEPTIONAL |
| | | |
| EXPERIENCED | EXPERT | EXUBERANT |
| FAIR-MINDED | FEARLESS | FESTIVE |
| FIRST-STRING | FORTHRIGHT | FORWARD-LOOKING |
| | | |
| FRANK | FRIENDLY | GALLANT |
| GENEROUS | GENTEEL | GLAD |
| GOOD-HUMORED | GOOD-NATURED | GRACIOUS |
| | | |
| GREGARIOUS | GUNG HO | HIGH-MINDED |
| HONEST | HONORABLE | HUMOROUS |
| IMPOSING | INDUSTRIOUS | INFLUENTIAL |
| | | |
| INNOVATIVE | INQUISITIVE | INSPIRED |
| INTREPID | INSPIRING | INTREPID |
| JOCOSE | JOCULAR | JOLLY |

| | | |
|---|---|---|
| JOVIAL | JOYFUL | JUDICIOUS |
| LARGE-MINDED | LEADING | LEVELHEADED |
| LIGHTHEARTED | LIMPID | LIVELY |
| | | |
| LOYAL | MANNERLY | MASTERFUL |
| MASTERLY | MATURE | MERRY |
| METICULOUS | MORALISTIC | NOBLE |
| | | |
| OPEN-EYED | OPENHANDED | OUTGOING |
| PEERLESS | PERSONABLE | PERSUASIVE |
| PLEASANT | PLEASING | PLEASURABLE |
| | | |
| POLISHED | POLITE | PREDOMINANT |
| PREEMINENT | PRESTIGIOUS | PROFICIENT |
| PROGRESSIVE | PROMINENT | PROUD |
| | | |
| PROVIDENT | PRUDENT | PRUDENTIAL |
| RADIANT | REFINED | RELIABLE |
| RELIANT | RENOWNED | REPUTABLE |
| | | |
| RESERVED | RESOLUTE | RESOURCEFUL |
| RESPECTABLE | RESPONSIBLE | RIGHTEOUS |
| SAPID | SCRUPULOUS | SELF-COMPOSED |
| | | |
| SINCERE | SKILLED | SKILLFUL |
| SNAPPY | SOCIABLE | SOCIAL |
| SOLITARY | SPIRITED | STALWART |
| | | |
| STELLAR | STERLING | STUDIOUS |
| SUAVE | TACTFUL | TEMPERATE |
| THANKFUL | TIDY | TRUSTWORTHY |
| | | |
| TRUTHFUL | UNASSUMING | UNFLAPPABLE |
| UNINHIBITED | UP-AND-COMING | UPRIGHT |
| VERACIOUS | VERSATILE | VERSED |
| | | |
| VIGOROUS | VIRTUOUS | VIVACIOUS |
| WELL-ADVISED | WELL-BRED | WELL-CONDITIONED |
| WELL-DISPOSED | WELL-GROOMED | WHOLESOME |
| | | |
| WILY | ZEALOUS        ZESTY | |
| ZIPPY | | |

# PERSONALITY - NOUNS

| | | |
|---|---|---|
| ACCLAIM | ACCOLADE | ACHIEVER |
| AGILITY | AMITY | ANIMATOR |
| A1 | APLOMB | ADEPT |
| | | |
| BENEVOLENCE | CHARISMA | CHARMER |
| COMPETITOR | COURAGE | DETERMINATION |
| DEXTERITY | DIGNITY | DIPLOMACY |
| | | |
| DIPLOMAT | EAGER BEAVER | EAGERNESS |
| EARNEST | ELEGANCE | ENTHUSIASM |
| ENTHUSIAST | EPITOME | ESPRIT DE CORPS |
| | | |
| ESTEEM | ETIQUETTE | EUPHORIA |
| EXCITER | EXPERTISE | FELICITY |
| FERVOR | FINESSE | FLAIR |
| | | |
| FORTE | FORTITUDE | FRIENDLY |
| GIFT | GLORY | GOOD FAITH |
| GOODWILL | GRIT | GUSTO |
| | | |
| HERO | HONESTY | HONOR |
| HUMOR | INDUSTRY | INFLUENTIAL |
| INITIATIVE | INSPIRATION | INTEGRITY |
| | | |
| INTESTINAL FORTITUDE | | JACK-OF-ALL-TRADES |
| JOURNEYMAN | | JOY |
| KINDLINESS | | KINDNESS |
| | | |
| LAUREL | LIVELINESS | LOYALTY |
| MASTERMIND | MATURITY | MOTIVATION |
| PARAGON | PATHFINDER | PATRIOT |
| | | |
| PATRIOTISM | PEP | PILLAR |
| PINNACLE | POISE | PRESTIGE |
| PRIDE | PROFESSIONAL | PROFESSIONALISM |
| | | |
| PROMINENCE | PROPRIETY | PROWESS |
| PRUDENCE | RENOWN | REPERTOIRE |
| RESOURCE | RESPECT | SANITY |
| | | |
| SELF-ASSURANCE | | SELF-CONFIDENCE |
| SELF-CONTROL | | SELF-DETERMINATION |
| SELF-DISCIPLINE | | SELF-ESTEEM |

SELF-IMPROVEMENT          SELF-RELIANCE
SELF-RESPECT    SELF-RESTRAINT    SELF-SACRIFICE
SELF-STARTER    SELF-WILL    SINCERITY

SPECIALIST    SPARTAN    SPIRIT
STALWART    STANDARD-BEARER
STANDOUT    STAR    STIMULATOR

TACT    TEMPERANCE    TROUBLE-SHOOTER
VERACITY    VERVE    VIGOR
VIM    VIRTUE    VITALITY

WHIZ    WINNER    WORKHORSE
WELL-BEING    ZEAL    ZEALOT
ZEALOTORY    ZEST    ZESTFULNESS

## PERSONALITY VERBS

ACCLAIM    ADMIRE    CHAMPION
CHARM    CORUSCATE    EFFERVESCE
ENCHANT    ENCOURAGE    ENGENDER

ENHANCE    ENTRUST    EPITOMIZE
EXALT    EXCEL    EXEMPLIFY
FLOURISH    GRATIFY    INSPIRE

MOTIVATE    OUTCLASS    OUTDO
OUTMATCH    OUTSHINE    OVERSHADOW
PERSONIFY    POLISH    PRAISE

PREDOMINATE    PREVAIL    RADIATE
RESPECT    SOCIALIZE    SPARKLE
SPIRIT    ZIP

# OF OR WITHIN THE MIND

The following list of words express, define, state, or describe **FAVORABLY** individual intellect. Intelligence, knowledge, wisdom, or reasoning.

## ADJECTIVES

| | | |
|---|---|---|
| ABLE | ACCOMPLISHED | ACUTE |
| AGILE-MINDED | ALERT | ANALYTIC |
| ANALYTICAL | APT | ARTFUL |
| | | |
| ASTUTE | AWARE | BRIGHT |
| BRILLIANT | CALCULATING | CAREFUL |
| CLAIRVOYANT | CLEAR-HEADED | CLEAR-SIGHTED |
| | | |
| CLEAR-WITTED | CLEVER | COGENT |
| COGNIZANT | COMMON SENSE | COMPREHENSIBLE |
| CONCEIVABLE | CONCENTRATING | CONCEPTIVE |
| | | |
| CONCEPTUAL | CONSCIOUS | CRAFTY |
| CREATIVE | CULTIVATED | CULTURED |
| CUNNING | CURIOUS | DEDUCTIVE POWER |
| | | |
| DEEP-THINKING | DELIBERATING | DEXTEROUS |
| DISCERNIBLE | DISCERNING | DISCREET |
| EDUCABLE | EDUCATED | ENLIGHTENED |
| | | |
| ERUDITE | FARSEEING | FARSIGHTED |
| FORESIGHTED | FECUND | FERTILE |
| FREE-SPOKEN | GIFTED | IDEAL |
| | | |
| IDEALISTIC | IDEALIZE | IMAGINABLE |
| IMAGINARY | IMAGINATION | IMAGINATIVE |
| INCISIVE | INNATE | INFORMED |
| | | |
| INGENIOUS | INSIGHTFUL | INSPIRATION |
| INTELLECTUAL | INTELLIGENT | INVENTIVE |
| JUDICIAL | JUDICIOUS | KEEN |
| | | |
| KEEN-WITTED | KNOWING | KNOWLEDGEABLE |
| LEARNED | LEGERITY | LETTERED |
| LEVELHEADED | LITERARY | LITERATE |

LOGICAL             MATURE              MENTAL
MENTOR              METHODICAL          MINDFUL
NIMBLE              OMNISCIENT          PENETRATING

PERCEPTIVE          PERSPICACIOUS       POLITIC
PONDERABLE          POWERFUL            PRAGMATIC
PRESENCE OF MIND    PROFICIENT          PROFOUND

PRUDENT             PUNGENT             QUICK
QUICK-THINKING      QUICK-WITTED        RATIONAL
REASONABLE          RECEPTIVE           RETENTIVE

SAGACIOUS           SAGE                SANE
SAPIENT             SCHOLARLY           SELF-TAUGHT
SENSIBLE            SHARP               SHARP-WITTED

SHREWD              SKILLFUL            SLY
SMART               SPECULATIVE         STUDIOUS
TALENTED            THINKABLE           THINKING

THOUGHTFUL          VIVID               WELL-GROUNDED
WELL-INFORMED       WELL-READ           WELL-VERSED
WIDELY-READ         WISE                WITTED
WITTY               WORLDLY-WISE

## OF OR WITHIN THE MIND - NOUNS

ABSTRACT            THOUGHT             ACUITY
ACUMEN              ACUTENESS           APTITUDE
APTNESS             ARTISTIC  IMAGINATION

AWARENESS           BOLD IMAGINATION
BRAINCHILD          BRAIN TRUST
CLAIRVOYANCE                            BRILLIANCE
                                        CLEVERNESS

COGITATION          COGNIZANCE          COHERENCE
COMMON SENSE                            COMPREHENSION
CONCEPTION                              CONSCIOUSNESS

CONSTRUCTIVE-IMAGINATION                CRAFTINESS
CREATIVE ABILITY    CREATIVE IMAGINATION
CREATIVENESS                            CREATIVE POWER

CREATIVE THOUGHT CREATIVITY
CUNNING CURIOSITY DEDUCTION
DEDUCTIVE POWER DEXTERITY EDUCATOR

ENLIGHTENMENT ERUDITION EXPERIENCE
EXPERTISE FACILITY FACULTIES
FACULTY FERTILE MIND FORESIGHT

FORESIGHTEDNESS FREETHINKER
GENIUS GUMPTION HEADWORK
HIGHER EDUCATION HIGHER LEARNING

HINDSIGHT IDEA IMAGINATION
INGENUITY INSIGHT INSPIRATION
INTEGRATIVE POWER INTELLECT

INTELLECTION INTELLECTUAL
INTELLECTUAL FACULTY INTELLECTUAL GRASP
INTELLECTUAL POWER INTELLIGENCE INVENTION

INVENTIVENESS INVENTOR JUDGMENT
KEENNESS KEEN-WITTEDNESS KNOW-HOW
KNOWLEDGE LEARNING LEVELHEADEDNESS

LITERACY LITERATE LIVELY IMAGINATION
LOGIC LOGICAL THOUGHT MASTERY
MENTAL ALERTNESS MENTAL CAPACITY

MENTAL FACULTY MENTALITY MENTAL PROCESS
ORIGINALITY OUTLOOK PENETRATION
PERCEPTION POSTULATOR POWER OF MIND

POWER OF REASON POWER OF THOUGHT
PRACTICAL KNOWLEDGE PRACTICAL WISDOM
PRODUCTIVE IMAGINATION PROFICIENCY

PROFOUND KNOWLEDGE PRUDENCE
QUICKNESS QUICK THINKING QUICK WIT
RATIONALE RATIONAL FACULTY

RATIONALISM RATIONALITY READY WIT
REASON REASONING REASONING FACILITY
RECALL RESOLUTION RESOLVE

RETENTIVITY
SAGE
SEASONED UNDERSTANDING

RICH IMAGINATION
SCHOLAR
SENSIBILITY

SHARPNESS
SHREWDNESS      SMARTNESS
SOUND UNDERSTANDING

SHARP-WITTEDNESS
SOUNDNESS
SPECULATION

STRAIGHT THINKING  TALENT
THINKER         THOUGHT
UNDERSTUDY      VISION

TECHNIQUE
UNDERSTANDING
VISUALIZATION

VIVID IMAGINATION
WISDOM          WISENESS
WITS            WITTICISM

VOCABULARY
WIT

## OF OR WITHIN THE MIND - VERBS

COGITATE        COMPREHEND      CONCEIVE
CONCENTRATE     CONCEPTUALIZE   CONTEMPLATE
CREATE          DIFFERENTIATE   DISCERN

ENLIGHTEN       ENTERTAIN IDEAS ENVISION
FABRICATE       FORESEE         IMAGE
IMAGINE         INVENT          IRRADIATE

KNOW            LEARN           MEDITATE
ORIGINATE       OUTTHINK        OUTWIT
PENETRATE       PERCEIVE        PICTURED

PONDER          POSTULATE       PRODUCE
RATIONALIZE     REASON          RE-EXAMINE
RESOLVE         RETHINK         REEVALUATE

SAVVY           SPECULATE       TEACH
THINK           THINK-UP        UNDERSTAND
VISUALIZE       VISION

The following list of words express, define, state, or describe FAVORABLY an individual's ability or capacity to convey information and thoughts to others through the mastery of the English language.

# ADJECTIVES

| | | |
|---|---|---|
| ARTICULATE | CLEAR-CUT | CONCISE |
| CONVERSANT | ELABORATE | ELOQUENT |
| EMPHATIC | EXPLICIT | FAIR-SPOKEN |

| | | |
|---|---|---|
| FLUENT | IMPLICIT | INFORMATIVE |
| LUCID | PERSPICUOUS | POLYGLOT |
| SILVER-TONGUED | | SMOOTH-SPOKEN |

| | | |
|---|---|---|
| SMOOTH-TONGUED | | SUCCINCT |
| TACIT | TACITURN | TALKATIVE |
| TERSE | VOLUBLE | WELL-SPOKEN |

# SPEAKING & WRITING - NOUNS

| | | |
|---|---|---|
| CLARITY | DICTION | DISCOURSE |
| ELOQUENCE | FORUM | LUCIDITY |
| ORATOR | QUIP | SAVOIR-FAIRE |

| | | |
|---|---|---|
| VERBALISM | VERBALIST | WORDING |
| WORDPLAY | WORDSMITH | |

# SPEAKING & WRITING - VERBS

| | | |
|---|---|---|
| CONFUTE | EDIT | EDITORIALIZE |
| EDUCATE | ELUCIDATE | EMPHASIZE |
| ENUNCIATE | EXPOUND | INSINUATE |

# HUMANE QUALITIES

The following list of words express, define. or describe how an individual inter-relates with others.

## ADJECTIVES

| | | |
|---|---|---|
| BENEVOLENT | BIG-HEARTED | COMPASSIONATE |
| CONGRUOUS | EMPATHETIC | EMPATHIC |
| FEELING | FERVENT | FORGIVING |
| | | |
| GENIAL | GENTLE | GOOD-HEARTED |
| GREATHEARTED | HARMONIOUS | HEARTFELT |
| HEARTY | HOSPITABLE | HUMANE |
| | | |
| KIND | KINDLY | MERCIFUL |
| NICE | OPENHEARTED | PENSIVE |
| POIGNANT | REGRETFUL | RESPECTFUL |
| | | |
| SELFLESS | SENSITIVE | SENTIMENTAL |
| SYMPATHETIC | TENDER | TENDERHEARTED |
| THOUGHTFUL | TRUSTFUL  TRUSTING | |
| UNSELFISH | WARM | WARMHEARTED |

## HUMANE QUALITIES - NOUNS

| | | |
|---|---|---|
| AMENITY | COMPASSION | CONSONANCE |
| COURTESY | EMPATHY | FAIR PLAY |
| FORGIVENESS | HARMONY | HUMANITARIAN |
| | | |
| MERCY | NICETY | PITY |
| SENSITIVITY | SOLACE | SOLICITUDE |

## HUMANE QUALITIES - VERBS

| | | |
|---|---|---|
| EMPATHIZE | FORGIVE | SYMPATHIZE |

# POSITIVE - ACTIVE

The following express FAVORABLE, positive, active words.

## ADJECTIVES

| | | |
|---|---|---|
| ABSOLUTE | ACCOMPLISHED | AGGRESSIVE |
| AGOG | ANXIOUS | ARDENT |
| ARDUOUS | AUDACIOUS | AVID |
| | | |
| BANNER | BOLD | CHALLENGING |
| COMPELLING | COMPETITIVE | COMPLEX |
| COMPLICATED | COMPREHENSIVE | COMPULSIVE |
| | | |
| CONSUMMATE | CONTAGIOUS | CONVINCING |
| CRISP | CRITICAL | CRUCIAL |
| DECISIVE | DIVERSE | DOMINANT |
| | | |
| DOMINEERING | DRAMATIC | DRASTIC |
| EFFICIENT | ELATED | ELEVATED |
| EMINENT | EMOTIONAL | ENGROSSING |
| | | |
| ENVIABLE | ENVIOUS | ESSENTIAL |
| EXACT | EXACTING | EXCEEDING |
| EXCELLENT | EXCITABLE | EXCITING |
| | | |
| EXCLUSIVE | EXEMPLARY | EXPEDIENT |
| EXPEDITIOUS | EXPLOSIVE | EXTENSIVE |
| EXTRA | EXTRANEOUS | EXTRAORDINARY |
| | | |
| EXTREME | EXULTANT | FABULOUS |
| FANTASTIC | FAR-REACHING | FASCINATING |
| FAULTLESS | FEISTY | FEVERISH |
| | | |
| FIDUCIARY | FIERCE | FIERY |
| FINE | FIRST-RATE | FIVE-STAR |
| FLASHY | FLUID | FOOLPROOF |
| | | |
| FORCEFUL | FORCIBLE | FOREMOST |
| FORMATIVE | FORTHWITH | FOUR-STAR |
| FRANTIC | FREQUENT | FRESH |

| | | |
|---|---|---|
| FRUITFUL | FULL-FLEDGED | GLORIOUS |
| GRANDIOSE | GRATIFYING | GRUELING |
| HANDS-ON | HASTILY | HASTY |
| | | |
| HEADLONG | HECTIC | HIDDEN |
| HIGH-FLYING | HIGH-POWERED | HIGH-PRESSURE |
| HIGH-SPIRITED | HURRIED | HYPER |
| | | |
| IDEAL | ILLUSTRIOUS | IMAGINABLE |
| IMMACULATE | IMPASSIONED | IMPECCABLE |
| IMPORTANT | IMPRESSIBLE | IMPULSIVE |
| | | |
| INCISIVE | INCREDIBLE | IN-DEPTH |
| INERRANT | INEXHAUSTIBLE | INEXTINGUISHABLE |
| INFALLIBLE | INFECTIOUS | INSATIABLE |
| | | |
| INSTANTANEOUS | INSTINCTIVE | INSTRUMENTAL |
| INTEGRAL | INTENSE | INTERESTED |
| INTRICATE | IRREPRESSIBLE | JUBILANT |
| | | |
| LAUDABLE | LAUDATORY | LETTER-PERFECT |
| LONG-RANGE | MARVELOUS | NOTABLE |
| OUTSTANDING | PARAMOUNT | PARLOUS |
| | | |
| PERFECT | PERPETUAL | PERSISTENT |
| POSITIVE | POSSESSIVE | POTENT |
| POWERFUL | PRECISE | PREVAILING |
| | | |
| PREVALENT | PRIME | PROLIFIC |
| PROMPT | PROSPEROUS | PROVOCATIVE |
| PROVOKING | PUNCTILIOUS | PURPOSEFUL |
| | | |
| QUICK | QUIZZICAL | REFRESHING |
| REGENERATE | RELENTLESS | REMARKABLE |
| RENASCENT | RESILIENT | RESOUNDING |
| | | |
| RESURGENT | ROBUST | ROSY |
| SERIOUS | SEVERE | SHIPSHAPE |
| SHREWD | SIMPLISTIC | SINGLE-HANDED |
| | | |
| SPONTANEOUS | SPEEDY | SPLENDID |
| SPOTLESS | STAGGERING | STIMULANT |
| STRENUOUS | STRICT | STRINGENT |

| | | |
|---|---|---|
| STRONG | STRONG-MINDED | STRONG-WILLED |
| STUPENDOUS | SUBSTANTIAL | SUCCESSFUL |
| SUPERB | SUPERFINE | SUPERIOR |
| | | |
| SUPERLATIVE | SUPPORTIVE | SUPREME |
| SURPASSING | SWIFT | TENACIOUS |
| TERRIFIC | THRIFTY | TOUGH |
| | | |
| TOUGH-MINDED | TRENCHANT | ULTIMATE |
| UNBEATABLE | UNBOUNDED | UNEQUIVOCAL |
| UNERRING | UNFAILING | UNPARALLELED |
| | | |
| UNQUESTIONABLE | UNRIVALED | UNYIELDING |
| UNSTOPPABLE | VALUABLE | VIGILANT |
| WELL-DEFINED | WELL-DONE | WELL-FOUNDED |
| | | |
| WELL-HANDLED | WELL-MEANING | WELL-KNOWN |
| WELL-OFF | WELL-ROUNDED | WELL-TIMED |
| WIDE-RANGING | WONDROUS | WORTHFUL |
| WORTHWHILE | WORTHY | YOUTHFUL |

## POSITIVE, ACTIVE - NOUNS

| | | |
|---|---|---|
| ACHIEVEMENT | ACME | ACTIVATION |
| AGITATOR | ALACRITY | ANXIOUSNESS |
| APEX | AROUSAL | ASPIRATION |
| | | |
| ASSET | AVERSION | BRAINSTORM |
| CAMARADERIE | CATALYST | COMMENDATION |
| COMPLEXITY | COMPLIMENT | CONTRIBUTION |
| | | |
| CONTROVERSY | CRISIS | DIEHARD |
| DRIVE | EMBODIMENT | EMULATION |
| ENCHANTMENT | ENCOURAGEMENT | ENDEAVOR |
| | | |
| ENERGY | ENJOYMENT | ENTERPRISE |
| EXCELLENCE | EXCITEMENT | EXPECTATION |
| EXPEDIENCE | EXPERIENCE | EXPEDIENCY |
| | | |
| EXUBERANCE | FASCINATION | FEAT |
| FIRST | FIRST CLASS | FOCUS |
| FORCE | FRENZY | GIMMICK |

| | | |
|---|---|---|
| GRANDEUR | GRAVITY | HEADWAY |
| IDEAL | IMMEDIACY | IMPETUS |
| IMPORTANCE | INCITEMENT | IMPROVEMENT |
| | | |
| IMPROVISATION | INCENTIVE | INDUCEMENT |
| INFLUENCE | INNOVATION | JEST |
| JESTER | KEYNOTE | KILTER |
| | | |
| KINK | KUDO | LANDMARK |
| LIFE BLOOD | MANIPULATION | MASTERY |
| MAXIM | MERIT | MIGHT |
| | | |
| MOTIVE | NURTURE | ORDEAL |
| PARADOX | PASSION | PASSIONATE |
| PECULIARITY | PERFECTION | PERSEVERANCE |
| | | |
| PERSONIFICATION | PERSUASION | PLAUDIT |
| PLEASURE | POTENCY | POWER |
| POWERHOUSE | PRECISION | PREMIUM |
| | | |
| PREPAREDNESS | PREPOTENCY | PROGRESS |
| PROMOTER | PROMPTITUDE | PROPONENT |
| PROPOSAL | PROSPERITY | PROTOTYPE |
| | | |
| PUNDIT | QUALITY | QUERY |
| QUEST | QUIRK | RADIANCE |
| REDRESS | RESILIENCE | RIVAL |
| | | |
| SACRIFICE | SCRUTINY | SELF-ASSERTION |
| SELF-EXAMINATION | SELF-IMAGE | SEVERITY |
| SIMPLICITY | SPARK | SPEARHEAD |
| | | |
| SPECTACLE | STIMULUS | STRENGTH |
| SUCCESS | SUPERLATIVE | SUPPORTER |
| SUPREMACY | SWIFTNESS | TASKMASTER |
| | | |
| TENACITY | THRIFT | VITALIZATION |
| WONDERWORK | | |

# ACTIVE, POSITIVE - VERBS

| | | |
|---|---|---|
| ABET | ACHIEVE | ADVOCATE |
| ANIMATE | AGITATE | ANALYZE |
| ANTICIPATE | APPLAUD | AROUSE |
| | | |
| ASPIRE | ASSERT | AVOID |
| BOLSTER | CAPITALIZE | CIRCUMVENT |
| COMMEND | COMPEL | COMPLICATE |
| | | |
| CONCEIVE | CONFRONT | CONTRIBUTE |
| CONTRIVE | CREATE | CULTIVATE |
| DELVE | DETER | DEVISE |
| | | |
| DOMINATE | ELICIT | EMERGE |
| EMBODY | EMULATE | ENDEAVOR |
| ENERGIZE | ENFORCE | ENRICH |
| | | |
| ENTHUSE | ENTICE | ERADICATE |
| ERUPT | ESCALATE | ESTABLISH |
| EXCEED | EXCITE | EXHORT |
| | | |
| EXPAND | EXPEDITE | EXPLOIT |
| EXPLORE | EXPOSTULATE | FABRICATE |
| FACILITATE | FINE-TUNE | FORMULATE |
| | | |
| FORTIFY | FULFILL | GENERATE |
| GLORIFY | GRIND OUT | HASTEN |
| HONE | HURDLE | IGNITE |
| | | |
| ILLUSTRATE | IMMERGE | IMMERSE |
| IMPEL | IMPOSE | IMPRESS |
| IMPROVE | IMPROVISE | INCITE |
| | | |
| INDUCE | INFECT | INFUSE |
| INITIATE | INNOVATE | INSPIRIT |
| INSTIGATE | INSTILL | INTEGRATE |
| | | |
| INTERFUSE | INTRIGUE | INVIGORATE |
| JOSH | JUGGLE | KINDLE |
| KNUCKLE DOWN | LAUNCH | MINGLE |

29

| | | |
|---|---|---|
| MANIPULATE | NOURISH | ORGANIZE |
| ORIGINATE | OUTLAST | OVERCOME |
| OVERSEE | OVERWHELM | PERPETUATE |
| | | |
| PERPLEX | PERSEVERE | PERSIST |
| PERSUADE | PREPARE | PROD |
| PROLIFERATE | PROMOTE | PROPAGATE |
| | | |
| PROPEL | PROPONE | PROSPER |
| PROVOKE | PURGE | QUANTIFY |
| QUICKEN | RALLY | RECTIFY |
| | | |
| REDRESS | REFINE | REFORM |
| REFUTE | REHABILITATE | REJUVENATE |
| RENEW | RENOVATE | REORGANIZE |
| | | |
| RESURGE | REVIVE | SCRUTINIZE |
| SPARK | SPEARHEAD | SPURT |
| STIMULATE | STRENGTHEN | STRIVE |
| | | |
| STOKE | SURPASS | THRIVE |
| TRANSFORM | ZENITH | |

# BULLETS/PHRASES

What is a "bullet/phrase?" A bullet/phrase is a statement that may or may not have a verb, object, or subject. Bullets/Phrases serve to reduce the amount of space required to make a statement. Thus, using bullets/phrases allows more material to be covered in the same space, or the same amount of material in less space, than in formal sentence structure.

## EXAMPLE OF FORMAL SENTENCE STRUCTURE:

"He is highly intelligent, possesses a stimulating imagination, and routinely provides sound advice and recommendations for anticipated problems."

## EXAMPLE OF BULLET/PHRASE:

"Highly intelligent, stimulating imagination, provides sound advice and recommendations."

The samples in this chapter are in bullet/phrase form. They can be combined or used independently. The samples can be either shortened more, or they can be turned into complete sentences.

The sample bullets/phrases are broken down into three basic categories to allow for ease of use. Although categorized into specific trait areas, many have universal application.

## BULLET PHRASES - FAVORABLE

## PERSONAL, PERSONALITY TRAITS

...Perceptive and alert
...Courteous nature
...Composed and calm

...Energetic spirit
...Great mental grasp
...Optimistic outlook

...Cheerful, helpful personality
...Interesting, convincing speaker
...Projects air of dignity

...Great raw ability and talent
...Talented and charismatic
...Stimulating intelligence

...A quick thinker
...Exceptional orator
...Personal magnetism

...Sincere and uncommonly likable
...Always enthusiastic
...Friendly and cheerful

...Strong moral fiber
...Emotionally stable
...Impeccable character

...Sound judgment
...Thoughtful and caring by nature
...Mentally alert

...Quick to learn
...Mental sharpness
...Bold, forward thinker

...Amiable, good natured
...Agreeable, pleasant personality
...Creatively inclined
...Admired courage

...Firm and resolute
...Pleasing personality

...Never gives up
...Frank and forward
...Capable of independent decision

...Advanced knowledge
...Presence and poise
...Matchless ingenuity

...Highly motivated
...Good common sense
...Extensive knowledge

..."Can do" enthusiasm
...Analytical mind
...Boundless energy

...Calm and affable manner
...Interesting conversationalist
...Thirst for knowledge

...Broad and varied intellect
...Powerful, influential figure
...Alert, energetic personality

...Humorous and witty personality
...Sound of mind and judgment
...Sensitive and understanding

...Open minded
...Quick to perceive and act
...Determined and dedicated

...Honest, respectful reputation
...Contributes innovative ideas
...Intrepid, resolute drive

...Great personal drive
...Keen sense of ethical conduct
...Sharp mental keenness
...Exercises sound judgment

...Clear, orderly self-expression
...Resilient, resolute personality

...Resourceful and dedicated
...Honest and faithful
...Innovative and imaginative

...Spirit of inquiry and drive
...Optimistic outlook and attitude
...Correct mental approach

...Personal vision and courage
...Unlimited learning capacity
...Quick, penetrating mind

...Dominating spiritual force
...Cleverness and guild
...Stands behind principles

...Intellectual courage
...Thinks and plans ahead
...Exceedingly articulate

...Sound, prudent judgment
...High ethical principles
...Endless zeal and courage

...Relentless drive and ambition
...Well-calculated actions
...High personal integrity

...Briskly alert and energetic
...Keen rational powers
...Retentive mind

...Persuasive talker
...Great self control
...Matchless desire

...Unflagging zeal
...Keen sense of humor
...Self-motivated

...Great personal courage
...Organized and industrious
...Exercises sound judgment

...Stimulating imagination
...Full of energy and vitality
...Warm, friendly personality

...Unequaled personal demeanor
...Has pride and self-assurance
...Well-adjusted personally

...Grasps essentials quickly
...Unyielding fair-mindedness
...Great verbal dexterity

...Shows courage under pressure
...Resilient and energetic
...Composed under pressure

...Proper personal behavior
...Clear in thought
...Strong will of mind

...Even tempered
...Industrious nature
...Firm, caring attitude

...Engenders trust
...Well organized
...Brilliant, lively wit

...Emotionally stable
...Mentally and physically able
...Has vision and foresight

...Shrewdly astute and alert
...Adapts with uncommon ease
...Relentless drive and desire

...Confident of abilities
...Strong spirit and character
...Discriminating mind

...A pillar of strength
...Emotionally mature
...Inquisitive mind

...Sparks excitement
...Strongly motivated
...Results oriented

...Probing personality
...Mental courage
...A winning spirit

...Great foresight
...Mentally alert
...Articulate speaker

...Thoughtful of others
...Kind in manner
...Energetic personality

...Boundless analytical ability
...Personal devotion to duty
...Radiates energy and enthusiasm

...Genuine concern for others
...Unwavering self-reliance
...Impeccable moral character

...Competitive, winning spirit
...Elegant and cultivated manner
...Convincing, persuasive talker

...Confident of abilities
...Acute, thorough thinker
...Good-natured and friendly

...Creative writing ability
...Keenly analytical individual
...Firm, resolute character

...Versatile, multi-disciplined
...Loyal, devoted subordinate
...Dynamic, energetic personality

...Proper and correct manner
...Full of energy and ability
...Alert, energetic personality

...Mentally artful and skillful
...Effervescent personality
...Unselfish and trusting

...Kind, amiable disposition
...Forthright, confident manner
...Erect, trim in carriage

...Develops logical priorities
...Friendly, cooperative attitude
...Meticulously well groomed

...Self-motivated and resourceful
...Commands large vocabulary
...Boundless enthusiasm and energy

...Inspiring imagination
...Cheerful readiness
...Ingenious nature

...Refined personality
...Vision for the future
...Eager and capable

...Forward-thinking
...Skilled innovator
...Positive attitude

...Engaging personality
...Intellectually gifted
...Highly motivated

...Commanding presence
...Never loses temper
...A self-starter

...Strong initiative
...Creatively inclined
...Sound character

...Cordial and affable
...Exudes optimism
...Clear discerning wit

...Exacting nature
...Vibrant personality
...Good academic aptitude

...Friendly and sociable
...Fighting enthusiasm
...Strength of character

...Sense of propriety
...Dares to dream
...Eager willingness

...Powerful figure
...Fresh, new ideas
...Forward-thinking

...Performs with aggressiveness of a zealot. Always ahead of the action.
..."Can do" attitude and amicable personality booster morale.
...Progressive outlook, resilient and resolute personality.

...Discriminates between fact and fiction, never caught off guard or loses
      sight of important events or developments.
...Analytical mind, adaptable to changing situations. Gives quality results
      in any endeavor or situation.
...Good Samaritan, dedicated to helping others.

...Few people work harder or have more innate talent.
...Intellectually gifted, technically experienced, and always highly
      motivated.
...Articulate in self-expression and innate ability to think logically.

...Probing personality, quick to pick up on things.
...Extremely friendly and sociable nature.
...Can view situation as a whole in terms of its component parts, sort out
      pertinent facts, and come to realistic conclusion.

...Effective in relating point of view and in winning an unbiased listener.
...Possesses mental courage to stand on principles.
...Dedicated, results-oriented individual.

...Has high ideals, morals, and ethics.
...Acts responsibly in all situations.
...A relentless drive and dedication evidenced in all endeavors.

...A superb speaker who can stoke the first of teamwork and cooperation
      among all willing listeners.
...Unshakable, unyielding character.
...Indestructible sense of humor.

...Good ability to learn and understand, and then put that information to
      good use.
...Sound in thought, good in judgment.
...Unlimited capacity for solving difficult problems.

...A proper blend of personal candor and sound professional judgment.
...Exercises mature judgment and meticulous precision to detail.
...Clear and logical in thought.

...Skilled, eloquent speaker and writer.
...Strongly motivated to succeed.
...Has courage of character to challenge and forge ahead into new areas.

...Exceptional professional competence and intellectual capacity.
...Possesses finest personal qualities and moral strength.
...Long-standing record of creditability, loyalty, and dedication.

...Drives to success by self-motivation and strong sense of purpose.
...Uses common sense to tackle problems.  Logical in decision making
　　　process.
...Intelligent, inquisitive, and confident.  At ease in any situation.

...Originates well thought ideas and does not await direction or guidance to
　　　organize and proceed with task at hand.
...Noteworthy demeanor and presence.
...Highly motivated achiever.

...Demonstrates understanding and genuine concern for health and
　　　welfare of subordinates.
...Presents succinctly and eloquently prepared briefs.
...Has presence of mind to act correctly during critical and short-fused
　　　situations.

...Exceptional personal drive and energy.
...Analytical thought process knows no bounds.
...Daily actions marked by efficiency and practical logic.

...Remains flexible and cooperative under any conditions.
...Earned wide reputation for warm personality, friendly disposition, and
　　　total professionalism.
...Confident, easy-going mannerism. Displays an air of dignity.

...Impressive ability and motivation.
...Never shows despair or resignation in  ace of seemingly insurmountable
　　　odds or problems.
...Fosters friendly goodwill.

...Articulate, well groomed, without equal in personal demeanor.
...A pillar of high moral purpose and strength.
...Individual drive and motivation is refreshing.

...Innate ability to get to crux of any problem and provide correct fix.
...Fully capable of meeting new situations in resourceful manner.
...Great intellectual energy and capacity.

...Has practical knowledge and skill, and the ambition to put to good use.
...Strength of character to tackle any assignment.  Ability to succeed.
...Irrepressible curiosity and ability to fix things.

...Abundant energy and enthusiasm.
...Has the will and courage to succeed, despite the tasking.
...Continually exhibits the highest standards of loyalty, integrity, and personal behavior.

...Intellectually active. Not restrained in ideas by conventional thought processes.
...Converts ideas into positive action.
...Possesses good judgment and foresight.

...Possesses mental capacity to properly weigh and evaluate complex matters.
...Unmatched capacity and appetite for learning.
...Strong desire and ability to learn.

...Has ability to see through problem areas and provide fruitful solutions.
...Positive mental attitude and outlook.
...Polished, persuasive speaker.

...Innate ability to grasp and understand perplexing matters.
...Kind, benign disposition.
...Thorough in nature, exercises sound and logical judgment.

...Inspires self-improvement in subordinates through sterling personal example.
...Possesses unrestrained enthusiasm.
...Faces demanding challenges head-on, with courage of conviction and high sense of professional pride.

...Energetic, resilient personality.
...Highly perceptive intellect.
...Talented and charismatic with a terrific sense of humor.

...Bubbling enthusiasm permeates entire organization.
...Ethical, honest personality.
...Expressed thoughts and opinions routinely prevail at meetings and informal gatherings.

...Imaginative skill and mental dexterity always produce quality results.
...Thoughts are well written and orally expressed. Never in doubt or confused.
...Mentally quick and resourceful.

...High ethical principles, and sound, sensible judgment.
...Abundant initiative and personal drive.
...Rational, logical, and responsive to all tasking.

...Amicable, friendly disposition.
...Discriminates between important and inconsequential matters.
...Enthusiasm and demeanor noteworthy.

...Clear and positive in self-expression.
...Original, imaginative thinker.
...Refined presence and dignified manner.

...Great intellectual awareness.
...Demonstrates sound, mature judgment.
...Articulate and precise in speech and the written word.

...Learning ability and growth potential unlimited.
...Innovative and productive. Pursues new ideas with success.
...Friendly, radiant personality.

...Innovative, always coming up with something better or improved.
...Enjoys mental challenge of resolving complex problems and situations.
...Friendly, enchanting personality.

...Originates highly accurate and professionally written reports and
        correspondence.
...Fully developed sense of loyalty.
...Stimulating, persuasive conversationalist.

...Unending drive and urge for success.
...Boundless enthusiasm and capacity for work.
...Not limited or restrained by conventional thought.

...Perceptive. Explores all situations and possibilities and then makes best
        use of available resources.
...Possesses great moral strength, personal drive, and energy.
...Amicable personality spiced with good wit and humor.

...Thrives on pressures of immediacy and responds resourcefully with
        innovative suggestions.
...Interesting speaker, convincing conversationalist.
...Continually exhibits highest standards of loyalty, integrity, and personal
        behavior.

...Cheerful and good-natured.
...Extremely energetic and enthusiastic.
...Influential, persuasive personality.

...Stays calm and collective. Keeps composure under pressure.
...Positive attitude is profound. Displays exceptional energy and drive.
...Curious and inquisitive nature.

...Courteous and respectful manner.
...Stands above contemporaries in personal commitment to
        professionalism and excellence.
...Boundless enthusiasm and energy. Always a willing volunteer.

...Wide diversity of personal and professional talent.
...Resourceful, respected, and inspired.
...Great mental agility and skill.

...Has endless zeal and courage. Feeds on adverse conditions that others
        would shun if given the opportunity.
...Engaging and engrossing personality.
...Capable of independent decision and action.

...Outstanding attitude and good humor are major morale builders.
...Cooperative, cheerful personality.
...Clear, analytical mind.

...Impeccable personal moral character and behavior.
...Imaginative and inventive mind.
...Steadfast, loyal dedication to duty and superiors.

...Polished, persuasive speaker with an agreeable manners.
...Firm and fair. A strong advocate of equal opportunity.
...Has creative thinking and innovative problem solving techniques.

...Written products are clear and cogent.
...Fair and without prejudice. Readily embraces precepts of equal
        opportunity.
...Well mannered with pleasant personality.

...Mind is quick, innovative, and decisive.
...Excellent ability to enunciate new ideas verbally and in writing.
...Keen intellectual perception.

...Composed, not easily excited under stress or pressure.
...Possesses highest personal integrity.
...Eager and interested in all professional matters, with a deep sense of
    responsibility.

...Mentally quick and active, capable of complex reasoning.
...Unequaled academic abilities and accomplishments.
...Strong, positive drive toward professional excellence.

...A constant source of innovative, workable ideas.
...Intelligent and mentally stable with an orderly mind.
...Personable, professional, and highly respected for point of view.

...Selects logical and correct courses of action.
...Especially skilled at painting vivid word picture in written and oral form.
...Unquenchable thirst for knowledge.

...Capable of good spontaneous judgment and decision making.
...Unbeatable character and personality.
...Contributes many innovative, workable solutions to complex problems.

...Mentally skillful, unhesitant in action.
...Decisive and efficacious.  Of impeccable character.
...Honest.  High morality and ethical principles.

...Refreshing, lively personality.
...Possesses the utmost degree of accuracy and attentiveness.
...A take charge attitude with great personal industry.

...A ready wit and an outgoing personality.
...Has practical, prudent wisdom.
...Even, steadying temperament.

...Capable of orderly and rational reasoning.
...Stable in character, resolute in action.
...Calm and composed in stressful situations.

...Has high moral principles and personal values.
...Quick in mind.  Alert and responsive.
...Continually seeks personal growth and development.

...Methodical and highly conscientious.
...Readily takes initiative for additional responsibilities.
...Work is marked by initiative, integrity, and excellence.

...Dependable and reliable with uncompromising principles.
...A pillar of moral strength and courage.
...Possesses an impressive breadth of experience and knowledge, and
      knows how to use both to best advantage.

...Dignified in presence and appearance.
...Completely self-reliant with vast intellectual capacity.
...An innovative and creative mind and manner.

...High ambition and achiever.
...Creative and artistic nature.
...Well rounded individual with a diversity of talents and interests.

...Demonstrates ability to cope with stress-filled circumstances.
...Possesses high personal moral standards.
...Endless energy, initiative, and positive spirit.

...Continually strives for, and achieves, self-improvement and professional
      development.
...Tremendous personal courage and self-discipline.
...Endless constructive mental energy.

...Highly developed sense of responsibility.
...Keen sense of fair play, and intense advocacy of individual and human
      rights.
...Communicates ideas and thoughts with ease and clarity.

...Fair, open-minded, and unbiased in reason and action.
...Has a friendly personality and a quick wit.
...Displays compassion, decisiveness, and determination.

...Great personal initiative and drive for success.
...Capable of independent thought and action.
...Possessed of fine sense of moral prudence.

...Thoughtful and caring by nature.
...Stable, well-adjusted personality.
...Graceful in manner, commanding in presence, a dominant personality.

...Prompt in response.  Cheerful in nature.
...Mentally alert, physically ready.  Quick and decisive in action.
...Makes independent decisions that have merit and substance.

...Affable, pleasant personality.
...Studious, perceptive, active mind.
...Mannerly, courteous, and polite.

...Great inter-discipline. Has emotional stability and strength.
...Unafraid of rendering decisions despite some personal risks.
...Plans ahead. Has vision for the future.

...Has special talent for areas requiring intellectual challenge.
...Intense, eager performer.
...Logical and coherent mind.

...Possesses unselfish dedication to duty and matchless ingenuity.
...Has positive attitude, good common sense, and thorough professional
     knowledge.
...Intellectually productive.

...Persuasive, convincing speaker.
...Fully developed purpose and sense of pride.
...Exercises sound judgment in practical matters.

...Has the mental faculty and attitude to lead others with great success.
...Exhibits confident composure under stress.
...Firmness of mind in face of difficulty.

...Will, determination, and sense of purpose for job accomplishment
     without equal.
...Decisive in mind, determined in action.
...Has strength of mind and character to accept and meet challenges
     beyond the scope and range of contemporaries.

...Benevolent interest and genuine concern for others.
...Shows courage and determination in the face of adversity.
...Possesses intellectual courage and proven capacity to lead.

...Has strong will, desire, and ability to succeed.
...Extremely self-confident of abilities without being cock- sure.
...Personal integrity is unassailable.

...Actions and plans are calculated and well thought out in advance.
...Strong will of mind and commanding presence.
...Relentless drive and dedication.

...Pleasant manner and personality.
...Demonstrates considerable finesse and diplomacy.
...Immensely rational, logical, and responsive to tasking.  A front runner.

...Always proper in manner and behavior.
...Strong loyalty and sense of duty.
...Positive, cooperative spirit.

...Full of courage and compassion.
...Sensitive to needs and desires of others.
...Amicable personality with social grace.

...Excellent foresight ability.
...Has great moral strength and courage.
...Straightforward and above board.  Others always know where they stand.

...Will not accept status quo.  Uses own initiative to get things going in
        positive direction.
...Pleasing, sincere personality.
...Calm and controlled personality.

...Sincere manner and caring nature.
...Possesses requisite competence and aptitude to accomplish the most
        demanding tasks.
...Always presents the proper mental attitude.

...Ingrained strong pursuit of excellence.
...Affects others with own enduring enthusiasm, pride, and
        professionalism.
...Has inquisitive mind and exacting nature.

...Possesses abundance of zeal, enthusiasm, and exuberance.
...An intelligent and inquisitive mind.
...Full of vigor and ability.

...Magnetic charm and appeal.
...Keen, enthusiastic desire for success.
...Great initiative and persistence.

...Discriminates between important and unimportant and then gets the job
        done correctly and timely.
...Well informed sense of judgment.
...Poised, adept, and well adjusted mentally.

...Friendly and good-fellowship highlight personal traits.
...Mentally quick and resourceful.
...Energetic with no wasted motions or actions.

...Strong personality and will.  Willing to stand up for principles and beliefs.
...Never lacking in spirit or exuberance.
...Ideas and suggestions well organized and thought out and have
considerable substance.

...Ceaseless personal devotion to duty always in evidence.
...Blessed with good sense of humor and compassion.
...Seasoned arbitrator.  Can bring disagreeing parties into agreement and
harmony.

...Spoken and written word punctuated by correctness and exactness.
...Takes minor setbacks in full stride, keeps a clear mental picture of what
is ahead.
...Completely without bias or prejudice.

...Polite, elegant, and graceful in manner.
...Impressive posture and appearance.
...Does not panic when faced with temporary or minor obstacles.  Charges
ahead.

...Effervescent and enchanting personality.
...Judicious, sound decision making facilities.

# FAVORABLE

## LEADERSHIP, MANAGEMENT, & ADMINISTRATION

...Sound management procedures
...Inspires others
...Stirs the imagination

...Spreads infectious enthusiasm
...Creative management initiatives
...Exemplifies ideal leader

...Firm, resolute leader
...Bolsters spirits
...Always an inspiration

...Prompt, diligent administrator
...Inspires performance
...Astute money manager

...Skillful, direct leadership
...Promotes harmonious atmosphere
...Positive motivator

...Firm, yet fair leader
...Real morale booster
...Accomplished leader

...Respected by others
...Leads by example
...Uncommon leadership

...Inspires greatness
...Morally fair and just
...Uncommon leader perceptiveness

...Encourages professional pride
...No-nonsense leader
...Agile leadership

...Watchful, discerning manager
...Interested in others
...Impressive leader

...A real motivator
...Arouses and excites interest
...Molds character and courage

...Composed leader
...Fosters goodwill
...Good organizer

...Promotes sound leadership
...Accomplished counselor
...Takes charge, a real leader

...Exciting leader
...Firm, sympathetic leader
...Natural team leader

...Astute, experienced leader
...Adroit administrator
...Spirited, determined leader

...Inspires and encourages
...Unparalleled leadership
...Motivates and leads others

...Instills pride and purpose
...Well-rounded leadership skills
...Recognizes top performer

...Meticulous administrator
...Actively promotes human rights
...Stirs up enthusiasm

...Charismatic leader
...Knows success is team effort
...Concerned, caring leader

...Inquisitive leader
...Has personal leadership magic
...Sensitive to needs of others

...Inspires confidence
...Unifying presence
...An accomplished counselor

...Has "follow me" confidence
...Propagates goodwill and trust
...Aggressive management acumen

...Motivates others
...Stirs the imagination
...Inspires subordinates

...Impressive leadership record
...Engenders trust and confidence
...Instills loyalty and pride

...Tactful leader and motivator
...Enforces subordinate development
...Supports self-dignity and worth

...Engenders self-development
...Capacity to successfully lead others
...Exercises sound leadership principles

...Frank, direct leader
...Solid material manager
...Selfless leader

...Imposing presence
...Positive influence
...Team leader

...Vigorous leadership style
...Promotes esprit de corps
...Innate managerial skills

...Runs cohesive organization
...Fully taxes subordinates
...Inspires the imagination

...Generates self-confidence

...Exuberant, enthusiastic leader
...Polished, mature leader, thinks and acts rationally.
...Has outstanding rapport with subordinates and is able to extract the
        most from each individual by tailoring leadership to the person and
        task at hand.
...Careful, exact planner who gets positive results.

...An exceptional leader, manager, and organizer.
...Has strong leadership attributes, strong desire to excel.
...Inspires zeal and obedience.

...Displays genuine sincerity and concern for subordinate career planning
        and work development.
...Has ability to inspire others to act decisively under stressful situations.
...Establishes and enforces firm, sound management practices.

...Generates positive attitude and spirit throughout the ranks.
...Manager extraordinary.
...Varied background and experience with ability to make correct decisions
        in even the most stressful situations demonstrate top candidate for
        increased and more demanding positions of leadership.

...Alert, perceptive, prompt-to-act manager.
...Experienced, knowledgeable manager.
...Energetic personality, stimulating leader.

...Extremely accurate and careful about administrative detail.
...Genuinely and warmly respected by all subordinates for technical
      knowledge, leadership qualities, and dedication to duty.
...Prudent, economical use of resources.

...Has inspiring enthusiasm and spirit.
...Skillful employment of personnel resources.
...Has a special flair for expert management of assets.

...Individual vitality and "can do" spirit has permeated entire organization,
      both up and down the ranks.
...A "leader by example" who obtains superior results.
...Helps individuals recognize self-dignity and worth through strong and
      effective personal counseling and leadership.

...Displays uncommon leadership, enthusiasm, and initiative.
...Extremely perceptive and hard working, takes charge and makes
      positive things happen.
...Charismatic leader, wins support and maximum effort of others.

...Molded efficient, smooth-running organization.
...Dedicated to betterment of subordinates.  They know it and always
      contribute maximum effort and energy.
...Organization enjoys high morale and unusually low discipline rate.

...Invigorating supervisor and leader.
...Always contributes 110% to team effort.
...Excites and arouses others to action.

...Leadership style elicits productive vigor and fosters complete harmony
      and team work.
...Possesses sound listening skills.  Able to assist subordinates solve
      personal problems and develop sound technical knowledge.
...Exceptionally fine administrator.

...Promotes harmony and team work.
...A dynamic, motivating leader who achieves maximum success.
...Sets positive, realistic expectations and standards.

...Strict, firm and fair disciplinarian.
...Unified and coherent management philosophy.
...Animating leader, arouses enthusiasm and interest in others.

...Subordinates come together in common purpose and action.
...Breathed new life into a declining organization.
...Demonstrates strong aptitude for administrative work.

...Has firm grip on organizational management procedures.
...Meticulous record keeping and timely submission of reports.
...Encourages striving for excellence among subordinates.

...Equitable and impartial leadership.
...Establishes an exciting and professional work environment.
...Exhibits high trust level in subordinates.  Confidence is returned.

...An extremely perceptive, hard working individual who takes charge and
        gets the job done.
...Consistently the leading element in planning and implementing new
operational and management procedures.
...Consistently places mission first, personal interest second.

...Keen managerial abilities evident in exceptional manner in which tasking
        is always based on available resources. Reaches maximum
        efficiency without stretching too thin.
...Supervises and directs subordinates with goal of improving each
        individual's professional skills.  Unqualified success.
...Can quickly identify problem, formulate solution, direct action, and take
        corrective follow-up action without outside direction or assistance.

...Instills pride and dignity in others.
...Provides calm, patient leadership to more junior personnel.
...Met every diverse demand and challenge though exceptional ability to
        lead and motivate others.

...Through personal, individual counseling, and proper recognition for a job
        well done, has heightened career awareness and self development.
...Strong, decisive leader.
...A personal morale builder to every member of the organization.

...A dynamic leader and vigorous worker.
...Exhibits genuine concern for welfare of subordinates.
...Dedicated to mission purpose, and displays firm and caring attitude
        toward subordinates.

...Direct, hard-line leader with unyielding character.

...Sets example anyone would do well to follow.

...Does not hesitate to provide assistance to those in need and to encourage trust through genuine interest in personal and professional problem areas.

...Potent, productive leader.

...Artful management of resources.

...Vigorous leadership, superb material management, and comprehensive knowledge contributed directly to improving mission readiness and accomplishment.

...Capitalized on individual strengths and provided training and counseling in weak areas.

...Epitome of tactful leadership.

...Stimulates subordinate professional growth.

...Intense, compassionate leader.

...Invigorating, successful leader.

...Successfully researched projects and staff work.

...Applies strict application of discipline and control.

...Brings out best in subordinates.

...Gives loyalty and leadership support to chain of command.

...Accomplished manager, attains all desired ends.

...Alert, astute manager, can turn negative situations to profitable advantage.

...The personification of a dynamic and caring leader.

...Ideally suited for top management and leadership positions.

...Positive attitude generates enthusiasm at all levels.

...Provides corrective counseling in positive, fruitful manner.

...Achieves unusually high standards of performance from others

...Industrious manner and ability to get a job done correctly inspires great trust and confidence in others.

...Skillful manager with proven ability to get things done.

...Unique ability to reach a troubled person and provide sound counseling and guidance.

...Strong professional attitude radiates to subordinates and causes them to respond with their full, best effort

...Calm, sincere, and constructive counseling techniques.

...A good sense of organization, spontaneous propensity to leadership, and a reputation for dependable results.
...Informed leader who genuinely cares about the well-being of others.
...Sets stringent, achievable performance standards for subordinates.

...Concerned, caring leader.
...Able leader, adept counselor.
...Consistently demonstrated outstanding professional and supervisory ability, and unwavering self-reliance in daily performance of duties.

...Extremely versatile leader, adapts leadership style to changing personnel and situations.
...Earned personal trust and confidence of each subordinate.
...Economically sound management practices.

...Good leader, creates excitement and enthusiasm for the job at hand.
...Establishes and pursues precise, clear-cut goals.
...Performed multitude of administrative tasks with enviable punctuality and error free productivity.

...Possesses unique ability to quickly and effectively train and direct inexperienced personnel.
...Fair, impartial, and honest treatment of others.
...Treats others with dignity and self-respect. Treatment returned in kind.

...Compassionate, caring leader.
...Considerate for the feelings of others.
...Continually provided calm and methodical leadership, creating a solid confidence that spread throughout the ranks.

...Skillful direction and counseling ensure few problems need go to superiors for satisfactory solution and resolution.
...Concerned for the welfare and interest of others.
...Exceptionally adept at fine-tuning administrative matters.

...Thoroughly proficient and efficient manager.
...Serious minded. Keeps organization on an even keel.
...Provides vital, life-giving leadership.

...Artfully leads and controls subordinates.
...Skillful in leading others to desired goals.
...Leadership merits special praise and gratitude.

...Provides inner drive to others that moves them to positive action.
...Nurtures subordinate professional development.
...A catalyst of team work and high morale.

...Earns the admiration and respect of subordinates.
...Embodies finest qualities of leadership.
...Ability to create and maintain confidence and respect throughout the
   ranks.

...Always willing to share time and considerable talent with others.
...Consistently demands and receives only the best from subordinates.
...Professional competence enhanced by adept ability to interact
   harmoniously with others.

...Gives others strong sense of direction without dulling their initiative.
...Possesses unending ability to generate enthusiasm.
...Actively enforces equal opportunity programs and goals.

...Humane concern for others tempered by professional concern to fulfill
   organizational commitments.
...Quick to offer positive advice to subordinates on ways to increase
   professional worth and growth.
...Successfully couples strong professional drive for excellence with
   sincere concern for welfare of subordinates.

...Displayed aggressive and imaginative management acumen.
...A forceful figure, others actively fall in behind the able and capable
   leadership and guidance provided.
...Admirable blend of tact and direct leadership.

...Potent and productive supervisor, overcomes difficulties.
...A demanding leader who gets impressive results.
...Many personal accomplishments are impressive and foster unity and
   spirit of pride throughout the ranks.

...Possesses well developed, positive counseling techniques.
...Fosters unparalleled productivity.
...Provides valuable solutions to complex problems.

...Regularly worked long hours.  Worked longer hours when necessary.
   Inspired subordinates to exhibit similar pride and dedication.
...Personal contributions to morale have been a welcomed shot in the arm.
...Calm and stable leader in crisis situations.

...Arouses interest and maximum effort in team efforts.
...Engenders trust and confidence throughout the ranks.
...Demonstrates superb leadership and unbridled enthusiasm.

...Provides vigorous and work-aggressive leadership.
...Astute manager of assets.
...A radiant, confident leader.

...Highly respected leader and organizer.
...Contributed immeasurably to high morale and performance by unique combination of direct leadership and humane compassion.
...Superb leadership resulted in unequaled performance throughout organization.

...Ability to immediately establish and maintain excellent rapport with others.
...A guiding and steadying influence on subordinates.
...A master at providing direction and tactful leadership.

...Management expertise, organizational insight, and skilled leadership principles are personal trademarks.
...A proven leader of unbounded ability.
...Bold and imaginative leadership techniques.

...Provided commendable results in many stressful leadership situations.
...Instituted rigorous training program that proved tremendously successful.
...Establishes and maintains atmosphere of pride and involvement and accomplishment.

...Poised and mature leader with an authoritative manner and presence.
...Attains positive results regardless of tasking difficulty.
...Detailed planning and intensive coordination with all concerned assured positive results.

...Provides positive guidance that improves subordinate skill level.
...Demonstrates superior knowledge of operations and administrative matters.
...Provides energizing, stimulating leadership.

...An assertive and considerate leader who gets results.
...Dominating influence in any organization.
...A proponent of strong, solid leadership.

...Great faculty for exercising command and control.
...Provides skillful direction to subordinates.
...Impressive ability to motivate subordinates.

...Ignites the human spirit and provides assertive, positive leadership
...Concerned, caring leader, allows subordinates to grow in new directions.
...Persuasive and tactful leader.

...Possesses innate managerial skills and ingrained aggressive pursuit of
   excellence.
...Can quickly grasp management principles and concepts involved in
   correct function of any operations.
...Leads with intensity, force, and energy.

...High morale and exceptional enthusiasm demonstrated on a daily basis
   by subordinates attest to leadership powers.
...Displays quality leadership and unstinting commitment to job
   accomplishment and excellence.
...Instituted rigid accountability in all areas of training. Resulted in early
   and complete qualification of all critical positions.

...Subordinates stand head and shoulders above peers in terms of
   performance and professionalism. They are the standard bearers.
...A highly motivated leader whose commitment to job accomplishment
   consistently results in productive output of highest quality.
...Compiled impressive record over a broad range of management and
   administrative matters.

...Astute and close scrutiny of assets ensured most effective use of scarce
   personnel and equipment resources.
...Doesn't get entangled in day-to-day individual problems. Sets and
   achieves multiple long-range goals and objectives.
...Made visible impact on intangible areas of pride, morale and positive
   attitude.

...Spent extensive hours during high tempo operations assessing
   personnel capabilities and limitations. Follow-up actions produced
   immediate and lasting positive results.
...Knows and understands worth and dignity of subordinates and
   successfully integrates this human element in daily leadership.
...Great ability to plan and direct group operations and activities of any
   scope or size.

...Stimulates creative effort and work of others.

...Delegates responsibility wisely and successfully.

...Provides timely recognition for superior performance.

...Rewards superior performance. Corrects substandard performance.

...Develops subordinates at a rapid pace.

...Makes optimum use of assigned personnel.

...Encourages off-duty education and professional growth.

...Keen sense of fair play and intense advocacy of individual and human rights.

...A personal and professional inspiration to each member of the command.

...Firmly and fairly enforces rules and standards.

...Equitable treatment of each subordinate optimized morale and increased command effectiveness.

...Always active, but never too busy to listen to personal problems and provide sound advice.

...Personal leadership has measurably improved overall organizational performance and readiness.

...An individual who commands the fullest respect and support of others.

...Fosters high morale and a total winning attitude and spirit.

...Built a corps of supervisors who take pride in "taking charge" and working together in cohesive, productive manner.

...Instills constructive loyalty up and down the ranks.

...Demonstrated outstanding success as a negotiator, group leader, and arbitrator. Extremely well liked and respected.

...Displayed unique ability to grasp not only broad scope of responsibilities, but also to manage the incredible number of details associated with job.

...Characteristic courage and coolness under pressure provide steadying influence to peers and subordinates.

...Knows how to lead people, and more importantly, knows where to take them.

...A quality leader. A person who inspires others to join in on a common effort and team goal.

...A natural instructor with exceptional ability to make even the most difficult principle easily understandable.

...Unique ability to coordinate group efforts toward attainment of common goals far exceeds requirements of assigned duties and position.

...Led organization to an unparalleled high level of performance.

...Responsive to needs of others. Popular among peers. Friendly, congenial, and cheerful. A real morale booster.

...Demonstrates unwavering support and endless ability in meeting mission requirements and objectives.

...Takes personal interest in welfare and well-being of subordinates.

...Creates favorable attitude and work environment toward a successful career.

...Instills motivation in others by own willingness to listen and learn.

...Provides valuable resolutions to wide range of problems through successful use of available resources.

...Has positive and distinctive leadership qualities that help mold any organization into cohesive, productive unit.

...Establishes and enforces clear-cut goals. Demands positive results.

...When in charge, successful conclusion never in doubt.

...Serves as focus of loyalty to chain of command.

...A take-charge individual. Displays strong initiative and infectious enthusiasm.

...Strength of character and natural team leader traits are the mainstay of a well rounded leadership style.

...Leads unified, enduring, and proud team of professionals.

...Has the leadership spirit and faith to lead people into action.

...Personifies leadership by example.

...Organizational leadership contributes immeasurably to morale.

...Enriches team spirit and pride in accomplishment.

...Persistent and exceptional efforts were important factors in steadily improving organization quality and efficiency.

...Repeatedly demonstrated exceptional leadership and initiative that served as forerunner in organization and led to unsurpassed excellence.

...Bearing, professional expertise, and personal involvement are cornerstones of individual leadership and management success.

...Gives subordinates helping hand and a pat on the back when most needed.

...Diligent efforts and resourcefulness inspired others and greatly contributed to mission accomplishment.

...Early identification of deficiencies and shortcomings in organization led to incalculable savings in manpower and money.

...A dynamic individual whose cheerful attitude and strong loyalty to subordinates ensures their complete zeal, obedience, and support.
...Subordinates consistently demonstrate that they are the best trained and most professional team in existence.
...Remains stable and calm during crisis situations.

...Well known and thought of throughout organization for putting mission accomplishment and desires  of superiors ahead of own personal interests.
...Demonstrated outstanding managerial talent in organizing watch team second to none.
...Knows key to quality performance is people.

...Instills loyalty, drive, and desire to excel in subordinates.
...Recognizes and rewards top performers.  Subordinates work to earn a personal "well done."
...Fully exploits subordinate capabilities.

...Authoritative in action with commanding presence. Gets results.
...Unencumbered by superfluous material.  Gets to the heart of problem areas and provides satisfactory solution.
...Aggressively reorganized and revitalized organization and established team "can do" spirit throughout.

...The many documents called upon to originate are properly staffed and researched, and submitted in a correct, concise, and timely manner.
...An expert at drafting smooth official correspondence and directives.
...Leadership determination and experience leads peer group.

...Ignites enthusiasm throughout the ranks.
...Effective leadership qualities executed in exemplary manner.
...The personification of the model leader:  Self-motivated, enthusiastic, and has willing support and cooperation of subordinates.

...Unflagging zeal and dedication demonstrated in fulfilling myriad responsibilities earned the trust and confidence of superiors and subordinates alike.
...Impressive manager and leader.  Receptive to, and solicits constructive criticism.

...Unfailing devotion to duty and all-around ability instrumental in establishing and then maintaining high state of morale and readiness.

...Improves subordinate weaknesses and effectively capitalizes on strengths by evaluating individual limitations and capabilities.
...Personal leadership motivates others to a higher level of individual performance.
...Understands leadership means getting a common vision and purpose to subordinates.

...Knows that you lead people and manage things.
...Gained the respect and admiration of subordinates by using frank and fair leadership.
...Thorough management and staff work, leaves nothing to chance.

...Truly representative of the highest caliber of talent and leadership available.
...Demonstrates keen understanding of command objectives. Establishes goals with exacting effort and coordination in support of objectives.
...A master of positive leadership. Truly cares about people.

...A leader of dynamic character and stamina, and an unlimited capacity for challenge.
...Met or exceeded all tasking with unique managerial skills and ability to foresee and plan for problem areas before fully developed.
...A leader in counseling subordinates with personal and professional problems.

...Deep concern and care for subordinate development.
...Created and maintained excellent work environment.
...Cultivates team work and a winning professional attitude.

...Established new highs in team harmony and unity.
...Applied managerial skills to good advantage and purpose.
...Can apply knowledge and skill to any situation without waiting for specific guidance or approval.

...Secures the energy and spirit of subordinates through innovative and imaginative leadership.
...Makes things happen and is not content with anything less than maximum effort.
...Arouses interest and excites competitive spirit of others.

...Daily planning and long-range strategy based on sound leadership and management principles.

...Highly capable leader. Always receives willing and spontaneous support of subordinates.

...Radiant personality and confident manner quickly wins willing support of others.

...Sparks a spirit of job excitement and self-sacrifice in subordinates.

...Propagates goodwill and an unmistakable drive and desire for excellence.

...Unquestionable commitment to equality and equitable treatment of subordinates.

...Quality leader. Gives praise when most deserved or needed.

...Own radiant energy and zeal quickly picked up by others.

...Potent, productive leader.

...Provides balanced blend of strong leadership and personal compassion.

...Ensures each individual's capabilities are fully taxed. Highly effective in training others to assume more challenging and demanding positions of authority and responsibility.

...Successfully faces challenges of leadership rarely afforded contemporaries.

...Pleasing, sincere personality blends well with eminent administrative abilities to produce a consistently uniform and quality of excellence.

...Ideally suited to work with today's young professionals. Takes personal interest in each subordinate, providing necessary guidance and direction to instill sense of belonging and individual worth.

...Continually searches for ways to improve procedures and raise efficiency. Many suggestions have been incorporated at management level and are proving highly beneficial and successful.

...Enlightened leadership technique arouses interest and participation.

...Accomplished counselor. Evaluates and documents behavior and uses this information to best possible advantage.

...Exudes spirit of well being, confidence, and determination toward others.

...Innovative and decisive style of leadership provided impetus in maintaining professional work environment.

...Employs open and direct manner in supervising personnel and is highly successful in obtaining maximum results regardless of situation.

...Careful preparation and planning led to achieving outstanding level of performance in a broad operating spectrum.

...Exercises sound leadership fundamentals with care and concern for subordinates.
...Concerned and caring leader, keenly aware of personal side of leadership.
...Provides the electricity, the spark of action that drives subordinates in a positive, constructive direction.

...Exemplary management acumen and personal performance considerably enhanced organizational readiness and reputation.
...A unifying presence to any organization.
...Leadership instilled new sense of pride and purpose in others.

...Possessed of sound judgment and management acumen.
...Projects indelible image of strong, steady leader.
...A real motivator.  Knows how to stir the imagination of others.

...Exceptionally effective in personnel leadership and management.
...Remarkable ability to plan and manage diverse operations.
...Effective application of sound management practices and principles.

...Dedicated leader.  Standards of integrity and bearing are of highest quality.
...Concerned for welfare and well being of all personnel.
...Actively takes lead in backing new organizational programs.

...Personalized style of leadership highly respected and effective.
...Personally encourages each subordinate to set high goals and personal standards.
...Own enthusiasm infiltrates the ranks.

...Intolerant of mediocre performance.
...Leads each subordinate to desired level of performance.
...Organizational harmony and cohesiveness without equal.

...A real leader:  Gives 100%, demands subordinate best, and looks out for their interests and needs.
...Contributes significantly to betterment of morale.
...Exceptionally well organized and perceptive to the problems and needs of others.

...Demonstrates visible concern for the welfare and well being of others.

...Personal achievements and ability to lead, in any organizational environment, contributed immeasurably to sustained superior performance.

...Undertook exacting managerial duties with keen sense of direction and well-defined goals.

...Accepts each task with positive and cooperative spirit.

...Inspires high morale and esprit de corps among others.

...Well liked and respected by peers, always contributes the maximum to group effort.

...Quickly grasped the intricacy of new assignment and established and enforced a strong chain of command link.

...Persuasive and tactful in conveying ideas.

...Gives others responsibility. Lets them grow and creates team spirit and unity.

...A person of common sense. A leader of uncommon perceptiveness.

...Helps subordinates grow and develop skills through timely advise, guidance, and counseling.

...Solicits others for their thoughts and ideas. Encourages maximum participation in a variety of administrative and management matters.

...Has special knack for bringing out the very best effort of each individual.

...Eager and capable of doing superior leadership job across broad range of responsibilities.

...Recognizes that success is a team effort. Gets others involved so that they can learn and grow professionally.

...Action oriented. Not content with anything less than maximum effort and results.

...Solid leader and manager. Steers straight and direct course of action.

...Down-to-earth individual. Others find it easy to converse on personal matters.

...Recognizes and rewards top performers. Takes correct and decisive action on substandard performers.

...Encourages professional development at every opportunity.

...Individual productivity and personal desire for excellence have significantly contributed to organization efficiency and effectiveness.

...Personal time management concepts and leadership ability resulted in exceptional performance by subordinates.
...Repeatedly demonstrated impressive ability to motivate subordinates in any work or operational environment.

...Unique ability to coordinate group efforts toward common goal in any given situation.
...Organization functions like a well oiled machine.
...Optimistic outlook and "can do" enthusiasm radiates in all directions and inspires others to put forth their own best effort.

...Projects positive leadership by own exciting and vibrant enthusiasm for any and all challenges.
...Knows how to reach an objective. Not diverted from task at hand by artificial barriers.
...Tactful leader. Considerate of others and uses restraint while obtaining desired results.

...Infectious positive attitude and steadfast devotion to duty are without equal.
...Has continuing willingness to lend a helping hand. Routinely goes out of way to assist others.

# FAVORABLE

## PERFORMANCE

...Totally committed to excellence
...Enterprising, intense performer
...Competitive spirit

...Stands above peers
...Reaches new heights
...Sound professional judgment

...True team player
...Takes wise courses of action
...Unparalleled success

...Stands above contemporaries
...Dramatic and exciting
...Highest standards of excellence

...Prompt and proper
...Exhibits professional accuracy
...Considerably advanced

...High achiever
...Unblemished record
...Seeks challenging assignments

...Acts decisively under pressure
...Smooth and flawless
...Delivers wholehearted support

...A top professional
...In-depth technical knowledge
...Ace technician

...Head and shoulders above peers
...Emerging as premier performer
...Decisive in action and deed

...Superior to others
...Highly respected by superiors
...Reliable and dependable

...Gives full effort
...Hard-working
...Finds and fixes problems

...Plans carefully and wisely
...Intense dedication to duty
...Always volunteers

...Work free from mistake
...Exceptional ability
...Maintains high standards

...Steadfast dedication
...Positive, fruitful future
...Constant vigil

...Great technical curiosity
...Adds extra dimension
...Strong professional pride

...Proficient and industrious
...A benchmark of excellence
...A role model

...Up and coming star
...Sets professional example
...Accustomed to success

...Overcomes all obstacles
...A standard bearer
...Impressive accomplishments

...Thrives on diversity
...Prompt in response
...Steady, faithful service

...Unblemished record
...Gives extra effort
...Clear cut goals

...Unrelenting work habits
...Always achieves desired ends
...Enjoys stressful situations

...Perceptive and hard working
...Capacity to meet challenges
...Proficient in all ventures

...Performs at peak intensity
...Prompt and proper action
...Meets diverse challenges

...Quick to take positive action
...Captures the imagination
...Keen technical abilities

...Reached full potential
...Technically capable
...Makes good things happen

...Decisive, action oriented
...Total, complete professional
...Comprehensive technical skill

...Impressive performer
...Springs into action
...Stellar performer

...Abundantly productive
...Uncommon excellence
...Quick to respond

...Dominating force
...Action oriented
...Tireless worker

...Highest caliber work
...Mission oriented
...Makes things happen

...Gets results
...Bright, on the ball
...Work-aggressive

...Uses time wisely
...A driving force
...Without equal

...Multi-disciplined
...Hard charger
...Banner performer

...Durable and adaptable
...Promising newcomer
...Prolific performer

...Tough competitor
...Thoroughly proficient
...Extremely zealous

...Responsive to seniors
...Exerts total effort
...Skillful undertaking

...Promotes new ideas
...Prompt and responsive
...Responsibilities discharged superbly, without fail, and always consistent
     with command policy.

...Past performance, full-time dedication, and future ambitions all positive
     assets.
...Provides    unequivocal    commitment    and    support    to    mission
     accomplishment.
...Ability to accomplish diverse tasking is without peer.

...Dedicated, highly competent individual.

...Approaches each endeavor with positive attitude and works to learn the most from each situation.

...Possesses the natural talent and acquired proficiency to accomplish the most demanding tasks.

...Will not necessarily "follow the pack," unafraid of setting and steering new course of thought or action.

...Enthusiastically tackles any project or tasking. Achieves positive results.

...Contributed greatly to mission accomplishment by accepting additional responsibility and by applying vast and varied personal skills effectively.

...Superlative contributions and achievements.

...Contributes maximum effort.

...Provides timely advice and guidance.

...Highly competent and dedicated.

...Absolute quality performer in any tasking.

...Consistently exhibits perfection in all technical aspects of job.

...Established long history of devotion to duty and self-sacrifice.

...Ability to bring into focus the pertinent parts of any tasking.

...Exemplary support of chain of command provides an extremely beneficial example for others.

...Demands and receives quality performance.

...Continues to improve on an already impressive record of accomplishments.

...Exemplifies true meaning of "pride and professionalism" in every facet of personal and professional lifestyle.

...Starts earlier, works smarter and harder than peers. Always a step ahead of the others.

...Punctuality and strong sense of duty highlight daily performance.

...Successfully faced all challenges and assignments with vim, vigor, and strong desire to succeed.

...A hard working individual who takes charge and makes positive things happen.

...Functions particularly well independent of supervision and direction.

...Flexible and cooperative in dealing with superiors. Shows respect for the individual.

...Flexible and cooperative in dealing with seniors. Shows respect for subordinates.

...Superlative contributions and actions in every respect.

...Resilient and energetic. Others routinely draw on abundance of inspiration.

...An energetic and highly motivated achiever.

...A bold, straight line of dedication and inspiration.

...Strong capabilities and abilities across the board.

...Duties performed with uncommon quality and timeliness. A real mainstay to the organization.

...Possesses unusually high level of technical expertise.

...Actively seeks additional responsibility.

...Flawless support and backing of organizational policies and goals.

...Astute management of monetary and equipment assets.

...Can adjust or adapt to any situation with quality results.

...Pursues tasks with a spirit of confidence and relentless drive.

...Recognizes opportunities to excel and refuses to be satisfied with anything less than full effort.

...Clearly demonstrated ability and desire to assume duties broader in scope and magnitude.

...Highly motivated and hard-working individual whose efforts are reflected in the superior performance routinely displayed.

...Thrives on important responsibility and maximum action environment.

...Keen technical insight, efficient performance, and pleasant manner highlight daily performance.

...Always gives unrestrained support to superiors.

...Intense, highly capable. Always gives 100%.

...Diligent and persistent worker.

...Aggressively tackled many demanding challenges and routinely met with success.

...Performs well under external stress and pressure.

...Work highlighted by profusion and variety.

...Quality performer with bright future.

...Good, steady performer. Jobs completed on or ahead of schedule.

...Possesses sufficient skill and resource to accomplish most difficult tasking.

...Hurdles or bulldozes over obstacles, always gets the job done and doesn't let things get in way.
...Has insatiable appetite for increased responsibility.
...Highly self-motivated with successful job accomplishment always the number one priority.

...Demonstrates time-tested ability and capacity to perform beyond the range and scope of contemporaries.
...Ensures all work performed with exacting quality and finest technical skill available.
...Day-to-day performance routinely exceeds highest professional standards.

...Epitomizes those qualities most highly sought in model, career person.
...Built superior record of accomplishment based on sound technical expertise and proven leadership principles.
...Exhibits the skill, temperament, appearance, and reliability of true professional.

...Dynamic and positive approach to everyday problem solving.
...Sets the course and speed for peers. A front-runner in every category.
...Demonstrated impressive breadth of experience within technical specialty.

...Performs well in all situations and uses sound judgment and logic to solve difficult problems or situations.
...Devotion to duty and professional performance without peer.
...Meets or exceeds requirements in every facet of assigned responsibility.

...Considers no job too difficult. Every assignment taken as a challenge and is completed with remarkable reliability.
...Trains for readiness and the unexpected. Always ahead of the action.
...Has uncanny ability to find and fix problem areas.

...A high achiever, always attains desired results.
...Takes corrective action while others ponder and discuss.
...Made substantial, quality contributions to organizational effectiveness.

...A quality performer. Always on the ball and ahead of the others.
...Does what has to be done without awaiting guidance or instruction.
...Relentless drive and motivation without peer.

...A "hot runner" with unlimited potential.
...A true team player with enormous professional capabilities.
...Invariably hand-picked for difficult and complex assignments.

...Takes necessary degree of personal risk without awaiting orders.

...Displays selfless devotion and utmost professionalism.

...Steadfast performance and dedication to duty.

...Able to rapidly acquire in-depth knowledge of intricate systems and varied operational evolutions.

...Unsurpassed devotion to duty highlighted by aggressive assumption of more and more responsibilities with continued quality success.

...Has ability to bring together divergent views and devise viable and valuable solutions to any problem at hand.

...Takes advantage of every opportunity to improve already high level of personal and team technical expertise.

...From the onset, aggressively acted to put principles of "pride and professionalism" on the front burner. Paid handsome dividends.

...Enthusiastic and proper response to dynamic and critical events routinely leads to successful conclusion or resolution.

...Exceeds highest expectations for performance in any difficult assignment.

...Always delivers wholehearted cooperation and support.

...Attention to detail, reliability, and thoroughness to assigned projects are most impressive.

...Excelled in every endeavor and consistently sought more and more challenging assignments.

...Epitomizes the highest standards of a well-rounded professional.

...Exhibits exceptional degree of accuracy and professionalism in each undertaking.

...Pursues chosen profession with boundless enthusiasm, knowledge, and raw ability.

...Filled a most challenging, visible and responsible position in finest sense of the word "professional."

...Rare ability to radiate enthusiasm for menial and complex tasking.

...Maintains busy and active civic community interests without detracting from professional performance.

...Energetic personality, positive "can do" attitude, and a deep pride in job accomplishment highlight daily performance.

...Performs beyond professional abilities and boundaries of contemporaries.

...Effort and dedicated action achieved exceptional results across the board.

...Learns equipment and systems quickly and retains and uses that knowledge to maximum advantage.

...Performance far exceeds that of others of comparable training and experience.

...Met all stated objectives and put into practice a long list of new initiatives which, singularly and collectively, increased overall operational effectiveness.

...Experienced journeyman in technical specialty.

...At the pinnacle of professional excellence.

...The standard bearer for pride and professionalism.

...Works without prompting or prodding.

...A zealot in performing any assignment.

...Pursues all assignments with eager and ardent interest.

...Acts with full, complete, and deliberate interest and attention.

...Takes pride in always doing best job possible.

...Gets things done by taking the initiative.

...Great sense of responsibility for quality of workmanship.

...Vast experience further enhanced by intelligence and technical know-how.

...Made major contributions of considerable and lasting value.

...Totally reliable. Completes any tasking in truly professional manner.

...An irreplaceable source of professional knowledge and sound judgment.

...Symbolizes the top quality professional.

...Career underscored by pride, self-improvement, and accomplishment.

...Sets standards by which excellence is measured.

...Executes tasks expediently and correctly.

...Possesses an infectious positive attitude.

...Great resource for coping with difficult, trying situations.

...Responsive to short-fused tasking and special assignments.

...Forward-looking individual who has demonstrated traits most desirable of a person in positions of high trust and responsibility.

...Gives complete, optimistic, and energetic support to superiors.

...Demonstrated overwhelming willingness and ability to strike out in a new
    direction. Achieved quality results.
...Enhances and improves morale.
...Impressive record of accomplishments.

...Diligent, persistent worker with refined, skillful workmanship.
...Introduces progressive ideas that work.
...Exhibits technical excellence.

...Stimulates harmony and high spirit.
...Keen technical abilities.
...Unsurpassed devotion to duty.

...Always sets the example.
...Dedicated to mission purpose.
...Vast technical experience.

...Initiates sound new ideas.
...Always provides whatever assistance required.
...Routinely contributes to higher standards of performance excellence.

...Compiled impressive list of individual accomplishments.
...Top professional in every respect. Clearly exceeded all established
    standards of excellence.
...Coordinates diverse events with uncommon success and accuracy.

...Sets and achieves high personal standards.
...Surmounts problems, gets results.
...Highly industrious and doesn't believe in idle time.

...Aggressive and meticulous in completion of assignments.
...Intolerant of mediocre performance.
...Performance regularly exceeds job requirements.

...Highly skilled in all phases of job.
...Aggressive in seeking out answers to developing problems.
...Always productively employed.

...Accepts challenges with alacrity.
...Unfailing performance to duty.
...Achieves quality results.

...Unyielding drive and desire for success.
...Enjoys total professional diversity.
...Puts forth unrelenting effort.

...Always puts job ahead of personal desires and interests.
...Workload is correctly balanced and prioritized.
...Maintains an exceptionally high level of performance.

...Quick to provide personal effort on special occasions and projects.
...Plans and completes ambitious workload.
...Top achiever in any task assigned or assumed.

...Knows job completely and excels in every facet of its complex parts.
...Job aggressiveness, dedication, and cooperation exhibited in all tasks are commendable.
...Professional contributions noteworthy, in addition to being a highly respected technical specialist.

...Carries out responsibilities of demanding position in highly capable and professional manner.
...Invariably submits timely and perceptive solutions to personal, operational, and staff problems.
...Forward-minded, aggressive performance of nonpareil competence.

...Can always be relied upon to give all of considerable talent and effort to task at hand.
...Exceptionally well organized.
...Performance always exceeds expectations.

...Uncompromising professionalism.
...Proven top quality organizer.
...Performance stands out prominently from peers.

...Exudes emotional confidence and spirit.
...Sets the pattern and example for peers.
...Takes difficult and hard to accomplish assignments in full stride.

...Enterprising, intense performer.
...Succeeds despite any adversity.
...Deeply devoted to chosen profession.

...Confident of personal and professional abilities.
...Accumulated a long list of impressive accomplishments.
...Aggressively pursues difficult challenges.

...Demonstrates remarkable versatility and capability.
...Prompt, quick, and correct in action.
...Possesses degree of excellence rarely observed within peer group.

...A real competitor. Takes pride in equaling or exceeding accomplishments of others.
...Self-sacrificing, a real team player.
...Pursues, with success, ultimate standards of excellence.

...Tackles difficult tasking with joyous exuberance.
...Plans well organized and designed, not artificial. Achieves and accomplishes more than others.
...Intense emotional drive and determination.

...Plunges into all assignments, unafraid of hard, long work.
...Aspiring performer, sets and achieves high goals.
...Persevering and enduring in completing any assignment.

...Always timely. Places a premium on punctuality.
...Always ready, never caught off guard or unprepared.
...Accepts added responsibility and vigorously tackles any assignment.

...Completes all assignments with accuracy and dispatch.
...Proven technical specialist and successful manager.
...Discharges responsibilities with complete professionalism.

...Exemplifies highest standards of dedication and determination.
...Accepts all challenges and responsibilities without wavering.
...Self-starter with natural ability and aptitude for technically oriented tasks.

...Carries out assignments to complete satisfaction and ensures superiors are kept aware of matters requiring their attention.
...Inspired with a sense of purpose and urgency.
...Unswerving allegiance to duty.

...Unrivaled professionalism.
...Determined and dedicated with a fruitful career ahead.
...Work routinely receives high acclaim and praise.

...Attains quality performance in any endeavor.
...Highly skilled and well trained.
...Frequently sought out for expert opinion.

...Boundless energy and great strength of character set highest standards of excellence.
...Eagerly accepts work assignments others would avoid. Adapts to varying circumstances and situations with uncommon ease.
...Articulate in self-expression and ability to think logically.

...Intense dedication and enthusiasm.
...Has well defined plans and goals.
...A model for all to emulate.

...Extremely energetic and helpful.
...Stimulates productive activity.
...Always vigorous in pursuit of excellence.

...Actions and deeds always conform to precise standards.
...A first-rate professional.
...Established reputation for meeting challenges with professional
    excellence and a winning spirit.

...Recognized flaws and discrepancies and took immediate, positive action
    without waiting for guidance or direction.
...Consistently puts forth that extra degree of effort required in fast-paced
    environment.
...Steadfast in dedication. Results are always immediate and impressive.

...Resourceful and dedicated in fulfilling a variety of collateral duties.
...Always has a personal commitment to quality and performance.
...Clearly demonstrated capacity to meet challenges head-on.

...Forward-thinking. Aggressive in assumption of additional responsibility.
...A multi-disciplined individual with a promising future.
...Proficient and industrious in performance of duty.

...Has long-standing record of credibility, loyalty, and professional
    dedication.
...Will not retreat in the face of adversity.
...Technical ability and skill know virtually no bounds.

...Uses time wisely. No wasted effort or energy.
...Seeks opportunities to grow professionally.
...Consistently produces outstanding results.

...Every goal met timely and correctly the first time.
...Displays keen interest and ability in all tasking.
...Actions well planned and smoothly executed.

...Attains results regardless of complexity or magnitude of tasking.
...Anticipates future tasking and with prior planning doesn't need to push a
    deadline.
...Always gives serious and determined effort.

...Completes all assignments with dispatch.
...Integrity, skill, and accomplishment are personal keynotes to success.
...Rates first against any competition.

...Almost infinite growth potential.
...Tremendous capacity for professional growth.
...Committed determination to achieve high goals.

...At the zenith of technical specialty.
...Anticipates problem areas and plans accordingly.
...Makes decisions after weighing pertinent facts.

...Adamantly supports all regulations and superiors.
...Ingrained ability to work for and achieve positive results.
...Endures and succeeds under stress and pressure.

...Refuses to give up in face of opposition or difficulty.
...Works hard to make jobs of others easier.
...Achieves highest level of performance and effectiveness.

...Well rounded and professionally knowledgeable.
...Maintains superior rapport at all organizational levels.
...Achieves uniformly outstanding results.

...Possesses all attributes required to excel in any tasking.
...Always in harmony and accord with orders of superiors.
...Has complete, concise technical understanding of specialty.

...Gives total support to seniors.
...Supports and enforces all rules and orders.
...Formulates productive plans that contribute to excellence.

...Top performer in every respect.
...Performs all duties without prompting.
...Makes positive, supportable decisions.

...Decisive response to any tasking.
...Demonstrates superlative professionalism with an abundance of personal dedication and self-sacrifice.
...Epitomizes standards by which all others should be measured.

...Carried out multitude of assigned and assumed duties and demonstrated a rare breed of reliability and dedication.

...Perseverance and total dedication to all tasking ensured complete and
continued success.
...Promptly executes all orders.

...Unblemished record of proven performance.
...Unselfish devotion to duty.
...High technical ability and curiosity.

...Sets and achieves high goals.
...Comprehensive and complete technical knowledge.
...At the forefront of peer group.

...Set a standard of performance standards unparalleled in recent memory.
...Can be counted on to take whatever independent action is required to
get the job accomplished.
...Maintains a punishing and productive work schedule.

...Unquenchable thirst for knowledge.  Realizes success requires sacrifice
and dedication.
...Always busy and involved in something constructive.
...Especially strong and effective in the execution of demanding tasks.

...An individual of decisive and positive action.
...Highly skilled in all facets of technical specialty.
...Personal talent and commitment rivaled by few and exceeded by none.

...Enthusiasm, dedication to task at hand, and long hours are key
ingredients to successfully meeting multiple challenges.
...Can readily shift time and talent to short-fused matters with admirable
results.
...Adapts to new work environment particularly rapid.

...Intense dedication, unexcelled efficiency and cheerful enthusiasm are
cornerstones to success.
...Demonstrates superior knowledge of duties and consistently gives
quality performance.
...Job-aggressive, a hard charger.

**The following pages contain bullets/phrases without an ending. This allows a drafter to select an appropriate beginning or add whatever ending is desired.**

...Did a masterful job in/as...
...Without equal in ability to...
...A top specialist in the field of...

...Has tremendous natural ability for...
...Indispensable performance in/as...
...Achieved impressive results in/by...

...Rejuvenated and put new life into...
...Performance goes beyond limits of...
...The leading force and influence in...

...Actively supports and encourages.
...Advanced education and skill in...
...Gives full spirit and support to...

...Ever-energetic, looks forward to.
...Exhibits all essential features of a...
...Firmly established as the top...

...Routinely prevails over others at...
...Has the natural flair and ability to...
...Impressive accomplishments include...

...Praiseworthy characteristics include...
...Represents the embodiment of...
...Takes exceptional pride in...

...Achieved resounding success in/by...
...Successfully carried out...
...Maintains highest standards of...

...Quality leader. Knows value of...
...Prompt and proper in response to...
...Provided masterful insight into...

...Maintains high standards in/of...
...Displays intense dedication in/to...
...Conforms to exacting standards of...

...A foremost authority on/in...
...Preeminent in ability to...
...Excels in ability to...

...Successfully carried out...
...Widely respected for ability to...
...Great mental aptitude for...

...Furthers technical specialty...
...Gives wholehearted support to..
...A strong advocate of...

...A perfect example of...
...A remarkably skilled...
...Inexhaustible source of...

...Masterful ability to...
...Developed a landmark...
...An accomplished, proficient...

...Rare, extraordinary ability to...
...Has substantial knowledge of...
...Routinely hand picked to...

...Played vital role in...
...An acknowledged expert in...
...Has natural gift for ability to...

...Has special talents for...
...Skilled in art of...
...The driving force behind...

...Has positive, clear view of...
...Has natural aptitude for...
...Thoroughly understands...

...Observes chain of command...
...Stresses importance of...
...Highly specialized in...

...Held in high esteem for ability to...       ...Maintains sharp edge in...
...Has extensive knowledge in/of...            ...An absolute master at...
...Especially skilled and adept in/at...       ...Has excellent talent for/in...

...Contributed to vital interests by...        ...Made marked improvement in...
...Widely recognized for ability to...         ...An indispensable member of...
...Freely spends many off-duty hours...        ...Articulate in ability to...

...Stands above peers in ability to...         ...Uniquely skilled to...
...A recognized expert in field of....         ...Has veracious appetite for...
...Won over subordinates by/with...            ...A dominating force in...

...Remarkable talent/ability for/to...         ...Has a natural curiosity for...
...A champion in the field of...               ...Has a fine touch for...
...Instills loyalty and a drive to...          ...Unlimited capacity to/for...

...Achieved total success in/by...             ...No end to potential for/to...
...Inspires confidence by...                   ...Unblemished record of...
...Inspires and encourages other by...

...Top performer.  Merits serious consideration for...
...Displays special skill and knowledge in field of...
...Surpasses peers in sheer ability to...

...Has full insight and understanding of...
...Has the knowledge and competence to...
...Transformed below average organization into...

...Totally immersed and involved in successful effort to...
...Established new standards of excellence in...
...Extremely high degree of excellence in...

...Unlimited potential with capacity for...
...Made significant progress and gain when/on...
...A fundamental, essential ingredient to the successful...

...Routinely receives high compliment and praise when...
...Enjoys the especially difficult and complex job of...
...Has acquired the necessary attributes to...

...Cheerfully devotes off-duty time working on...
...Devised procedures that carefully weighed time, personnel, and financial
          procedures that resulted in...
...Assumed greatly expanded responsibilities with/when...

...Personal sacrifice and uncompromising standards of conduct provided impetus for...

...Strong leadership, acute management acumen, and technical competence resulted in...

...Totally mastered each and every aspect of...

...Spearheaded self-help project to/that...

...Simplified and streamlined procedures for...

...Impressively managed diverse and complex...

...Established and enforced strict controls on...

...Through acute awareness, perseverance, and personal diligence...

...Produced commendable results in/as...

...Successfully managed wide and varied programs in/on...

...Instrumental in successful completion of...

...Personal drive and ambition hastened progress and development of...

...Earned high praise and acclaim by/for...

...Open minded. Can accommodate wide variety of...

...Quickly surged ahead of contemporaries by/in...

...Fully experienced in practical application of...

...Successfully fused together all elements of...

...Performance reached a peak of intensity when...

...Relaxing personality. Creates favorable relationship with...

...Great deductive power. Insatiable appetite for...

...Unquenchable quest for knowledge in...

...Became a moving force in ability to...

...Created perfect foundation for/to...

...Innovative ideas and close personal supervision of subordinates led to...

...A motivating force in achieving significant improvement in...

...Enjoys excitement of devising new ways to...

...Combined innate sense of leadership and keen foresight instrumental to...

...Use of sound and prudent judgment was instrumental in/to...

...Strong spirit of inquiry and drive led to...

...Awareness of people's strengths and capabilities led to...

...Possesses requisite competence and aptitude to...

...Possesses overwhelming capacity to/for...
...Possesses overabundance of energy and...
...Succeeded in reaching new heights in...

...Through diligent effort and patience became proficient in…
...Has decisive advantage over others in ability to...
...Strong spirit and character.  Not easily swayed to...

...Personal initiative and dedication directly responsible for...
...Demonstrated creative intelligence and wisdom by...
...Personal liaison efforts particularly effective in...

...Possesses concise knowledge and understanding of every facet of...
...One of the most accomplished expert/specialists in...
...Contributions both substantial and significant in...

...Successfully faced extremely complex...
...Carefully planned, organized, and executed successful...
...Personal example has been a positive influence on...

...Personal concern and initiative directly responsible for...
...Especially strong and effective in executing demanding duties of...
...Using foresight and exceptional planning ability, put together a
        complicated and comprehensive...

...Enthusiasm and dedication instrumental in promoting many innovative
        and progressive programs in...
...Flexibility and initiative responsible for upgrade in/of...
...Despite severe limitations of personnel resources, successfully...

...Carefully monitored diverse component demands on/of...
...Stimulated improved harmony and attitudes on/toward...
...Industrious manner and positive attitude resulted in...

...Successfully overcame potentially serious impediment to...
...Most impressive performer in...
...Places proper and heavy emphasis on...

...Developed superb plan of action and milestones for/in...
...Earned individual distinction by/for...
...Superb academic credentials.  A prime candidate for...

...Rendered outstanding support and service to...
...Responded positively and correctly to...
...Technical skill and farsightedness led to early identification and correction of...

...Superb common sense and professional knowledge led to...
...Played leading and aggressive role in establishing...
...Voluntarily contributed many off-duty hours to ensure timely and correct completion of...

...Proved more than equal to the task of...
...Implemented necessary management techniques and concepts to...
...Met goals across a diverse spectrum by...

...Won wide acclaim for promptness in responding to...
...Demonstrates untiring dedication to duty by...
...Has advanced knowledge and skill in…

...Already a quality performer, has not vet reached full potential in/for...
...Takes maximum advantage of opportunities to...
...Has style and finesse.  Others always willing to join in...

...A major contributing factor in the success of...
...As testimony to leadership skills, successfully...
...Technical knowledge and curiosity led to...

...Does not necessarily stay in beaten path of others when...
...Applies correct mental approach to...
...Enjoys unparalleled success.  Recently emerged as...

...Personal vision and courage led to...
...Possesses a wealth of information in/on...
...Superiors have complete confidence in abilities to...

...Despite ever increasing difficulty, accomplished/completed...
...Good mental capacity.  Quick to grasp significance of...
...Gives subordinates enthusiasm and...

...A person on the move who can adjust readily to changes in...
...Rapidly established dynamic and motivating leader image by...
...Remarkable ability to work with people and effectively organize tasks and priorities enhanced...

...Personally molded cohesive and dedicated team that...

...Constant personal examples of loyalty and professionalism earned complete respect and admiration of/from...

...Personal initiative and managerial skills overcame...

...Direct personal involvement instrumental in/to...

...Unselfishly contributed time and talents to numerous special projects, including...

...Skillful employment of manpower enabled...

...Demonstrated clearly a superior ability to...

...Professional knowledge and zeal significantly improved...

...Established stability and integrity in...

The words in the following section are general usage words.

# GENERAL

## ADJECTIVES

ABLE
ACCOMMODATING
ADEQUATE

ABREAST
ACCURATE
AGREEABLE

ACCEPTABLE
ACKNOWLEDGED
AMBIGUOUS

BENEFICIAL
CAREFUL
COMPETENT

CAPABLE
CATEGORICAL
COMPLAISANT

CAREFREE
COMPATIBLE
CONGRUENT

CONSISTENT
CREDIBLE
DEPENDABLE

CONVENTIONAL
CURSORY
DEPENDENT

CORRECT
CUSTOMARY
DEVIATE

DOCILE
EASYGOING
ELEMENTAL

DRUDGING
ECCENTRIC
ELEMENTARY

DULL
EFFECTIVE
ENCOURAGING

EQUABLE
FAIR
FEASIBLE

EQUITABLE
FAITHFUL
FELICITOUS

FACTUAL
FAVORABLE
FLEXIBLE

FRAGMENTARY
GINGERLY
GUILELESS

FUNDAMENTAL
GOOD
HARMLESS

FUZZY
GRADUAL
HEEDFUL

HELPFUL
IMPARTIAL
INCONSPICUOUS

HOPEFUL
IMPRESSIONABLE
INDEFINITE

HUMBLE
INCLINED
INDEPENDENT

INDIRECT
INFREQUENT
INVOLUNTARY

INDULGENT
INNOCENT
INVOLVED

INFORMAL
INTERMITTENT
IRONIC

ISOLATED
LEGITIMATE
LOW-KEY

JUST
LENIENT
LOW-PRESSURE

LABORIOUS
LIABLE
LOW-PROFILE

| | | |
|---|---|---|
| LUKEWARM | MARGINAL | MATTER-OF-COURSE |
| MATTER-OF-FACT | MEDIOCRE | MERE |
| METHODICAL | MILD | MODERATE |
| | | |
| MODEST | MORAL | NEAT |
| NEUTRAL | NONCHALANT | NO-NONSENSE |
| NORMAL | OBEDIENT | OBLIGING |
| | | |
| OBSERVANT | ODD | ONE-WAY |
| ORDERLY | ORDINARY | ORTHODOX |
| PARTIAL | PASSABLE | PASSIVE |
| | | |
| PATIENT | PECULIAR | PERFECTIBLE |
| PERFUNCTORY | PERTINENT | PLACID |
| PLIABLE | POTENTIAL | PRACTICAL |
| | | |
| PREFERENTIAL | PREOCCUPIED | PREMATURE |
| PRESENTABLE | PROPER | PROPITIOUS |
| PUNCTUAL | PURE | QUALIFIED |
| | | |
| QUESTIONABLE | READY | READY-MADE |
| REALISTIC | REASONABLE | REMEDIAL |
| RESPONSIVE | RUDIMENTARY | SATISFACTORY |
| | | |
| SCRUTABLE | SELF-MADE | SELF-SUFFICIENT |
| SEMISKILLED | SIMPLE | SLOW |
| SOPHISTICATED | SPARING | STABLE |
| | | |
| STODGY | SUBMISSIVE | SUFFICIENT |
| SUITABLE | SYSTEMATIC | TEDIOUS |
| TEMPTING | TOLERABLE | TOLERANT |
| | | |
| TRANQUIL | TRIVIAL | UNCOMMON |
| UNEXCEPTIONAL | UNFAMILIAR | USEFUL |
| VOLUNTARY | WATCHFUL | WELL-INTENTIONED |
| | | |
| WILLING | WILLFUL | WORKABLE |
| WISHFUL | WOULD-BE | |

## NOUNS

| | | |
|---|---|---|
| ABILITY | AMBIGUITY | ATTRIBUTE |
| COMMITMENT | COMMONPLACE | COMPETENT |
| COMPLIANCE | COMPOSURE | CONCERN |

CONFORMANCE CONFORMITY CONGRUITY
CONJECTURE CREDENTIAL CREDIBILITY
DECORUM DEPENDENCE EFFORT

ENIGMA EQUALITY ETHIC
FELLOWSHIP FIDELITY FIGUREHEAD
FLIP-FLOP FOLLOWER FORMALIZE

FRAGMENT GOOD GUIDE
HEARSAY HUMILITY IMITATION
HEED IDEALIST INDIVIDUALIST

INDULGENCE INTROVERT KNACK
LABOR LEGITIMACY LENIENCY
LONER MEDIOCRITY MODERATION

MODESTY MORALIST MORALITY
ODDITY ORTHODOXY PARITY
PASSIVISM PASSIVITY PATIENCE

PLEASANTRY PROPENSITY PLATITUDE
REALIST RELIANCE RESERVE
RESISTANCE RETRIBUTION ROOKIE

RUDIMENT SATISFACTION SCAPEGOAT
SCRUPLE SENTIMENT SOLITUDE
STABILITY STAMINA SURVIVOR

STYLE TRANQUILLITY TREADMILL
TRIVIA YES-MAN

## VERBS

ABIDE ACCOMMODATE AGREE
APPEASE AVOW COMPLY
CONFORM COPE DABBLE

DEPEND DEVIATE DRUDGE
EMPLOY ENABLE ENJOY
EXONERATE FLUCTUATE GENERALIZE

GUIDE HOPE IMITATE
INCLINE INDOCTRINATE INTERCEDE

| | | |
|---|---|---|
| INTERPRET | INTERROGATE | INTROVERT |
| LABOR | MORALIZE | OBEY |
| OBLIGE | ORIENTATE | OSCILLATE |
| PACIFY | PERFORM | PURPOSE |
| PROPITIATE | PURPORT | QUELL |
| REGRET | REPUTE | RESERVE |
| STABILIZE | SUCCEED | SURVIVE |
| TOLERATE | UNDERSTAND | WANDER |

## FIXED - LASTING

## ADJECTIVES

| | | |
|---|---|---|
| ADAMANT | CERTAIN | COHERENT |
| COHESIVE | DIFFICULT | DURABLE |
| ENDURABLE | FIRM | FORMIDABLE |
| HABITUAL | HARD-AND-FAST | HARD-SET |
| HARD-SHELL | IMMOBILE | IMMOVABLE |
| IMPENETRABLE | IMPERVIOUS | IMPONDERABLE |
| INCONTESTABLE | | INCONTROVERTIBLE |
| INCURABLE | INDEFECTIBLE | INDESTRUCTIBLE |
| INDISPENSABLE | INDISPUTABLE | INESCAPABLE |
| INEVITABLE | INEXORABLE | INFLEXIBLE |
| INGRAINED | INIMITABLE | INSUPERABLE |
| INSURMOUNTABLE | INTRANSIGENT | INVARIABLE |
| INVINCIBLE | IRREFUTABLE | IRREPRESSIBLE |
| LASTING | LIMITLESS | LITERAL |
| LONG-LIVED | | PREPONDERANT |
| RENITENT | RESISTANT | RIGID |
| SOLID | STAUNCH | STEADFAST |
| STEADY | UNBENDING | UNCOMPROMISING |
| UNDAUNTED | UNDENIABLE | UNRELENTING |

# NOUNS

ADHERENCE       CERTAINTY       COHESION
DIFFICULTY      ENDURANCE       PERSISTENCE
RESISTANT

# VERBS

ADHERE          COHERE          ENDLESS
ENDURE          INDURATE        INGRAIN
INUNDATE        PERDURE         PERVADE

RESIST          RIGIDIFY        SOLIDIFY
WITHSTAND

# MORE OR LESS

ABUNDANT (A)        CEILING (N)         COLOSSAL (A)
ENORMOUS (A)        EXCESSIVE (A)       FINITE (A)
EXORBITANCE (N)     EXORBITANT (A)      EXTRAVAGANT (A)

FULL-SCALE (A)      GIGANTIC (A)        GOOD DEAL (N)
GOODLY (A)          GREAT (A)           HUGE (A)
IMMEASURABLE (A)    IMMENSE (A)         IMMENSITY (N)

INCALCULABLE (A)    INFINITE (A)        INNUMERABLE (A)
INNUMEROUS (A)      LARGE (A)           LEAST (A)
LESS (A)            LITTLE (A)          MAMMOTH (A)

MAXIMIZE (V)        MAXIMUM (N)         MEAGER (A)
MINIMIZE (V)        MINIMUM (N)         MINISH (V)
MINOR (A)           MINUSCULE (N)       MINUTE (A)

MONUMENTAL (A)      MULTITUDE (N)       MYRIAD (N)
NEGLIGIBLE (A)      NOMINAL (A)         NAUGHT (N)
PALTRY (A)          PAUCITY (N)         SLACKEN (V)

SLACKER (N)         SMALL (A)           TENUOUS (A)
TREMENDOUS (A)      VAST (A)            WANE (A)

Legend:  (A) Adjective (N) Noun (V) Verb

# UNFAVORABLE APPRAISALS

The structure, content, and format used to document UNFAVORABLE Reports are no different from the FAVORABLE. Refer to the FAVORABLE Section for guidance.

The UNFAVORABLE words and PHRASES/BULLETS used in this section of the book are more than sufficient to draft UNFAVORABLE Reports. As can be seen from the examples on the following pages, describing poor or unfavorable performance is mostly a matter of listing what an individual fails to do, or does not do properly or correctly.

**Almost all of the material used in the FAVORABLE Section of this book can be used for UNFAVORABLE comments simply by changing the key FAVORABLE ADJECTIVES, NOUNS, or VERBS to the UNFAVORABLE equivalent.**

## UNFAVORABLE

(Name) performance, behavior, adaptability, and attitude took a downward turn at the start of this reporting period and continues to decline. UA ( ) times, and disobeyed direct orders of a commissioned officer and other superiors. (Name) is intelligent and clever and regardless of the offense or circumstance he has a ready made excuse. His recollection of recent conversations with various superiors routinely turn out to be in complete disagreement with those superiors. Constant vigilance is required to keep him at his work site and gainfully employed. A detriment to the morale and good order. Frequent counseling has been fruitless. (Name) is unreliable, untrustworthy, displays no initiative, and is a burden to this organization.

(Name) performance is substandard across the board. He has been reprimanded by the Commanding Officer ... times for violation of UCMJ Articles ... Routinely questioning motives of superiors, he asks for an undue amount of justification when assigned tasks. His frequent display of immaturity, bad judgment, and use of half-truths highlight his inability to adjust to a military lifestyle. He gets a haircut only when directed by superiors and routinely fails personnel inspections. Counseling has been required on numerous occasions for lateness, an attitude problem, and a habit of straying from assigned work area. His lack of enthusiasm, constant complaining, and unwillingness to do his share of work have had a detrimental affect on morale.

(Name) overall performance is below standard. He requires close and constant supervision to complete tasks because he is unable to keep his mind on the job at hand. Tardiness and an inability to pass personnel, and room inspections also detract from his performance. He has not demonstrated any ability to perform duties independent of supervision and he possesses no leadership qualities. Frequent counseling in all substandard performance areas has not resulted in any significant, lasting improvement. He is immature in behavior and lacks the mental acuity to think through everyday common logic situations. He is unable to work harmoniously with others and does not promote good morale.

(Name) is a competent performer with average technical skills. His effort and attention to detail during the early part of this reporting period was high. However, his performance, across the board, declined during the middle of this period because of personal problems. He had difficulty reporting on time for duty, concentrating on his work, and presenting an acceptable military appearance. Initial supervisory counseling sessions failed to show any positive results. Additional later counseling did improve his performance. More recently his attitude, behavior, and appearance have improved significantly, and have returned to the same high level displayed early in this reporting period.

(Name) is a below average performer. He works diligently to arrive at a satisfactory conclusion of an assigned task, usually getting the necessary response from subordinates. Improvements in his leadership skills are needed. He needs to be more demanding and geared to accept only maximum effort and quality performance. Generally a good worker, he sometimes becomes complacent and requires a reminder to present a more professional attitude and appearance.

# PERSONALITY

**The following list of words express, define, state, or describe UNFAVORABLE personality characteristics, traits, performance, or results.**

# ADJECTIVES

ABERRANT
ABSENTMINDED
AMBIVALENT

ABHORRENT
ADOLESCENT
ANTAGONISTIC

ABRASIVE
ALOOF
ANTISOCIAL

APATHETIC
ASTRAY
BERSERK

APPALLING
BASHFUL
BLAND

ARROGANT
BELLIGERENT
BLUNT

BOISTEROUS
CALLOUS
COCKY

BRASH
CARELESS
COLD

BRASSY
COCKSURE
COLORLESS

COMPLACENT
CORRUPT
CRUSTY

CONDESCENDING
CRASS
CURT

CONTEMPTIBLE
CRUDE
CYNICAL

DECEPTIVE
DERELICT
DEVIANT

DEFIANT
DESPAIRING
DEVIOUS

DEPRESSED
DESPONDENT
DIE-HARD

DIFFIDENT
DISDAINFUL
DISREPUTABLE

DISAGREEABLE
DISINCLINED
DISSATISFIED

DISCOURTEOUS
DISLOYAL
DRABBER

ENERVATE
FACETIOUS
FATUOUS

EGOCENTRIC
FAITHLESS
FAULTFINDING

EXANIMATE
FASTIDIOUS
FECKLESS

FICKLE
FLAPPABLE
FOPPISH

FINICKY
FOOLHARDY
FORGETFUL

FLACCID
FOOLISH
FRACTIOUS

FRUSTRATED
GALLING
GRUDGING

FURIOUS
GAUCHE
HALF-BAKED

FUSSY
GARRULOUS
HALF-COCKED

HALFHEARTED
HARDHANDED
HARD-NOSED

HAPLESS
HARDHEADED
HEARTLESS

HAPPY-GO-LUCKY
HARD-HEARTED
HEAVY-HANDED

HEEDLESS
HOSTILE
HYPERCRITICAL

HIGH-STRUNG
HUMORLESS
ILLEGIBLE

HIGH-TONED
HURTFUL
ILL-HUMORED

ILL-MANNERED
IMMODERATE
IMPERSONAL

ILL-NATURED
IMMORAL
IMPERTINENT

IMMATURE
IMPATIENT
IMPETUOUS

IMPIOUS
IMPUDENT
INARTICULATE

IMPOLITE
INANE
INATTENTIVE

IMPRUDENT
INAPT
INCOGITANT

INCOHERENT
INCONGRUOUS
INDIFFERENT

INCOMPETENT
INCONSIDERATE
INDIGNANT

INCONCEIVABLE
INDECISIVE
INDISCREET

INDOLENT
INEXPERT
INFURIATE

INELOQUENT
INEXPLICIT
INHARMONIOUS

INEPT
INFIRM
INHOSPITABLE

INHUMANE
INSENSIBLE
INSIPID

INIMICAL
INSENSITIVE
INSOLENT

INJUDICIOUS
INSINCERE
INSUBORDINATE

INSURGENT
IRATE
IRRESOLUTE

INVECTIVE
IRKSOME
IRRESPONSIBLE

INVIDIOUS
IRRATIONAL
IRRESPONSIVE

IRRITABLE
LACKADAISICAL
LAX

JEALOUS
LACKLUSTER
LETHARGIC

KINDLESS
LACONIC
LIFELESS

LIGHT-HEADED
LOFTY
LOW-SPIRITED

LOATH
LOQUACIOUS
MALADJUSTED

LOATHSOME
LOW-MINDED
MALEVOLENT

MALICIOUS
MERCILESS
MOODY

MANNERLESS
MISCHIEVOUS
NAIVE

MEEK
MISTAKEN
NEGLECTFUL

NERVELESS
OFFENSIVE
OVERBEARING

OBNOXIOUS
OPPRESSIVE
OVERCONFIDENT

OBSTINATE
OUTSPOKEN
PARANOID

PEEVISH
PERTINACIOUS
PITILESS

PERMISSIVE
PESSIMISTIC
POMPOUS

PERT
PETULANT
PORTENTOUS

PREJUDICIAL
QUARRELSOME
RELUCTANT

PRUDISH
REASONLESS
REMISS

PRYING
REBELLIOUS
REMORSEFUL

REMORSELESS
REPUGNANT
RHETORICAL

REPREHENSIBLE
REPULSIVE
RUDE

REPROBATE
RESENTFUL
RUTHLESS

SARCASTIC
SELF-CENTERED
SELF-IMPORTANT

SAUCY
SELF-CONSCIOUS
SELFISH

SCORNFUL
SELF-DEFEATING
SELF-OPINIONATED

SELF-RIGHTEOUS
SHAMEFUL
SHIFTLESS

SELF-SERVING
SHAMELESS
SHIFTY

SHALLOW
SHARP-TONGUED
SHORTSIGHTED

SHORT-SPOKEN
SLOVENLY
SNIDE

SHORT-TEMPERED
SMALL-MINDED
SNUFFY

SHY
SMUG
SOFTHEADED

SORROW
SUBTLE
SURLY

SPIRITLESS
SULLEN
TACTLESS

SPITEFUL
SUPERCILIOUS
TEMPERAMENTAL

TEPID
TIMID
TURBULENT

THANKLESS
TIMOROUS
UNACCOMPLISHED

THOUGHTLESS
TROUBLESOME
UNADVISED

UNAPT
UNDECIDED
UNFEELING

UNCHARITABLE
UNDERHANDED
UNFIT

UNCOMFORTABLE
UNFAIR
UNFRIENDLY

UNGRACIOUS
UNMERCIFUL
UNPRINCIPLED

UNINTERESTING
UNPLEASANT
UNPROFESSIONAL

UNMANNERLY
UNPOPULAR
UNREALISTIC

UNREASONABLE
UNSEASONED
UNSOCIABLE

UNRULY
UNSKILLED
UNSTABLE

UNSCRUPULOUS
UNSKILLFUL
UNSUITABLE

UNTIDY
VAIN
VIOLENT

UNTRUTHFUL
VERBOSE
WANTON

UNWILLING
VINDICTIVE
WEAKHEARTED

WEAK-MINDED WILL-LESS WITLESS
WORDY WRETCH WRETCHED
WROTH WRY

# PERSONALITY

## NOUNS

ABERRANT ABUSE ALTERCATION
ANTAGONIST APATHY ARROGANCE
AUDACITY BELLIGERENCE BERSERK

CHAOS CHARADE COMPLACENCY
CONDESCENDENCE CONFLICT CONTEMPT
CORRUPTION COVER-UP DECEPTION

DEFIANCE DEGRADATION DERELICTION
DESPONDENCY DISAGREEMENT DISCONTENT
DISFAVOR DISDAIN DISGUST

DISILLUSION DISLOYALTY DISMAY
DISREPUTE DISRESPECT DISSENSION
DISSENT DISSENTER DURESS

EGOISM EGOTISM ENMITY
FAKE FALSITY FATIGUE
FAULTFINDING FAVORITISM FEUD

FLEDGLING FLUSTER FOIBLE
FOLLY FOOLISHNESS FOOT-DRAGGING
FOUL-UP FRACAS FRAUD

FRUSTRATION FUROR FURY
GALL GAMESMANSHIP GARRULITY
GRIEVANCE GRIMACE GRUDGE

GUILE GUISE HALF-TRUTH
HATRED HOSTILITY ILLITERACY
ILLOGIC IMPATIENCE IMPERTINENCE

IMPROPRIETY IMPRUDENCE IMPUDENCE
INABILITY INACCURACY INAPTITUDE
INCAPACITY INCERTITUDE INCOMPATIBILITY

| | | |
|---|---|---|
| INCOMPETENCE | INDECISION | INDIFFERENCE |
| INDIGNATION | INDIGNITY | INDISCIPLINE |
| INDISCRETION | INEPTITUDE | INEQUALITY |
| | | |
| INEQUITY | INEXPERIENCE | INGRATITUDE |
| INHARMONY | INIQUITY | INJUSTICE |
| INSOLENCE | INSTABILITY | INSULT |
| | | |
| INTOLERANCE | IRE | JEALOUSY |
| KLUTZ | KNOW-IT-ALL | LAXITY |
| LETHARGY | LOATHING | MALEVOLENCE |
| | | |
| MALICE | NONCONFORMIST | |
| MENACE | MISGIVING | MISUNDERSTANDING |
| NEGLIGENCE | OBSESSION | OUTBURST |
| | | |
| OUTRAGE | PANIC | PARTISAN |
| PEDANT | PERTINACITY | PESSIMISM |
| POMPOSITY | PREJUDICE | PRUDE |
| | | |
| QUITTER | RAGE | RAMPAGE |
| REBUFF | REFUSAL | RELUCTANCE |
| REMORSE | REPRESSION | REPRIMAND |
| | | |
| REPROACH | REPUGNANCE | REPULSION |
| RESENTMENT | RHETORIC | RHETORICIAN |
| RIDICULE | RIVALRY | SARCASM |
| | | |
| SCOFF | SCORN | SELF-CONCEIT |
| SELF-DOUBT | SELF-INDULGENCE | |
| SELF-INTEREST | SHAM | SKIRMISH |
| | | |
| SOLVENT | SPITE | STUPOR |
| STYMIE | TEDIUM | TEMERITY |
| TROUBLEMAKER | TRUANT | TURMOIL |
| | | |
| UNREASON | UNTRUTH | WEAKNESS |
| WILE | WRONGDOER | WRONGDOING |

# PERSONALITY

## VERBS

ABASE
ANTAGONIZE
BALK

ABUSE
APPALL
BELITTLE

ACCOST
BAFFLE
BERATE

BETRAY
CENSURE
CONDEMN

BIAS
CHASTISE
CONFUSE

BLUNDER
COERCE
CONSPIRE

CRITICIZE
DELUDE
DEPRESS

DAUNT
DEMEAN
DESPAIR

DEGRADE
DEMORALIZE
DESPOND

DISACCORD
DISDAIN
DISMAY

DISAGREE
DISGRUNTLE
DISPUTE

DISCORD
DISGUST
DISREGARD

DISRESPECT
EMBITTER
EQUIVOCATE

DISSATISFY
ENERVATE
FALSIFY

DISSENT
ENRAGE
FINAGLE

FLAUNT
FORFEIT
FRUSTRATE

FLOUT
FORGET
FUMBLE

FORESTALL
FRET
GAB

GRIEVE
HARASS
IGNORE

GRIPE
HECKLE
IMPERSONALIZE

GROUSE
HUMILIATE
IMPUGN

INDULGE
INHIBIT
INTERRUPT

INFLAME
INSULT
INTIMIDATE

INFRINGE
INTERFERE
INTRUDE

IRK
LOATHE
MEDDLE

JABBER
LOOK DOWN
MISAPPLY

KNUCKLE UNDER
MALINGER
MISAPPROPRIATE

MISBECOME
MISCONDUCT
MISGUIDED

MISBEHAVE
MISCONSTRUE
MISINTERPRET

MISCALCULATE
MISFIT
MISJUDGE

| | | |
|---|---|---|
| MISLEAD | MISMANAGE | MISUNDERSTAND |
| MISUSE | MUDDLE | MUMBLE |
| OFFEND | OPPOSE | OPPRESS |
| | | |
| OSTRACIZE | OVEREXTEND | OVERREACT |
| OVERSIMPLIFY | PALTER | PAMPER |
| PARE | PATRONIZE | PERSECUTE |
| | | |
| PERTURB | PLOD | PROCRASTINATE |
| PRY | REFRAIN | RELAPSE |
| RELENT | RENOUNCE | REPREHEND |
| | | |
| REPRESS | REPROACH | REPROBATE |
| REPUDIATE | REPULSE | RESENT |
| SCORN | SHIRK | SPURN |
| | | |
| SQUABBLE | STUPEFY | STYMIED |
| SUCCUMB | SUFFER | UNDERMINE |
| UNNERVE | WANGLE | |

# UNFAVORABLE

## OF OR WITHIN THE MIND

The following list of words express, define, state, or describe
**UNFAVORABLE** individual intellect, intelligence, knowledge, wisdom,
or reasoning.

## ADJECTIVES

| | | |
|---|---|---|
| ABSURD | CRASS | DENSE |
| DULL | FEEBLEMINDED | FOOLISH |
| HALF-SCHOLAR | IGNORANT | ILLITERATE |
| | | |
| ILLOGICAL | INANE | INCONSEQUENT |
| INEPT | INSENSIBLE | INSIGNIFICANT |
| IRRATIONAL | MEANINGLESS | MINDLESS |
| | | |
| NESCIENT | OBTUSE | ONE-TRACK-MIND |
| ORDINARY | RIDICULOUS | SENILE |
| SENSELESS | SHALLOW | SHORTSIGHTED |
| | | |
| SIMPLE | SIMPLE-MINDED | SPECULATIVE |
| STUPID | SUPERFICIAL | THICK |
| TRIFLING | UNACQUAINTED | UNAWARE |
| | | |
| UNCONVERSANT | UNDISCERNING | UNDISTINGUISHED |
| UNERUDITE | UNFAMILIAR | UNIMAGINATIVE |
| UNINFORMATIVE | UNINFORMED | UNINTELLIGENT |
| | | |
| UNKNOWING | UNKNOWN | UNLEARNED |
| UNLETTERED | UNPERCEPTIVE | UNREASONING |
| UNREFINED | UNSCHOLARLY | UNTAUGHT |
| | | |
| UNTUTORED | UNVERSED | UNWISE |
| VACUOUS | | |

The following list of words express, define, state, or describe **UNFAVORABLE** individual intellect, intelligence, knowledge, wisdom, or reasoning.

## NOUNS

| | | |
|---|---|---|
| DULLNESS | IGNORANCE | INCAPACITY |
| INCOMPREHENSION | INEPTITUDE | INSENSIBILITY |
| INTELLECTUAL WEAKNESS | | IRRATIONALITY |

| | | |
|---|---|---|
| MENTAL DEFICIENCY | | MENTAL HANDICAP |
| MENTAL VOID | | MENTAL WEAKNESS |
| SENILE | SENILITY | SHALLOWNESS |

| | | |
|---|---|---|
| SHORTSIGHTEDNESS | | STUPIDITY |
| SUPERFICIALITY | UNKNOWING | UNPERCEPTIVENESS |
| UNWITTINGNESS | | |

## NEGATIVE - SHORTCOMING

The following list of words express. define, state, or describe **UNFAVORABLE** characteristics, traits, performance, or results not solely individual or personal.

## ADJECTIVES

| | | |
|---|---|---|
| ABNORMAL | ABRUPT | ADVERSE |
| AMISS | ASKEW | AWRY |
| CONFLICTING | COSTIVE | CUMBERSOME |

| | | |
|---|---|---|
| DEFECTIVE | DEFICIENT | DESPERATE |
| DISAPPOINTING | DISPASSIONATE | DISRUPTIVE |
| DETRIMENTAL | DUBIOUS | EFFETE |

| | | |
|---|---|---|
| EFFORTLESS | ELUSIVE | EQUIVOCAL |
| EROSIVE | ERRANT | ERRATIC |
| EVASIVE | ERRONEOUS | FACILE |

| | | |
|---|---|---|
| FALSE | FARCICAL | FARFETCHED |
| FLAGRANT | FLIMSY | FORBIDDING |
| FORMLESS | FRAGILE | FRAIL |

FRAUDULENT FRIVOLOUS FRUITLESS
FUTILE GLARING GLOOMY
GLUM GOOD-FOR-NOTHING GRAVE

GRIEVOUS GRIM GROSS
HAPHAZARD HARD PUT HARSH
HELPLESS HERKY-JERKY HIT-OR-MISS

HOPELESS HORRENDOUS HUMDRUM
HUMILIATING IDLE ILL-ADVISED
ILLAUDIBLE ILLEGAL ILL-FATED

ILL-GOTTEN ILLICIT IMAGINATIVE
IMAGINARY IMPERFECT IMPOSSIBLE
IMPOTENT IMPRACTICABLE IMPRACTICAL

IMPRECISE IMPROBABLE IMPROPER
INACCURATE INACTIVE INADEQUATE
INADVISABLE INAPPROPRIATE INCAPABLE

INCOMPARABLE INCOMPATIBLE INCOMPLETE
INCOMPREHENSIBLE INCONSEQUENTIAL
INCONSIDERABLE INCONSISTENT INCONVENIENT

INCORRECT INCORRIGIBLE INDEFENSIBLE
INDEFINABLE INDISCERNIBLE INDISTINCT
INDISTINCTIVE INEFFECTIVE INEFFECTUAL

INEFFICIENT INELIGIBLE INEQUITABLE
INERT INEXACT INEXCUSABLE
INEXPEDIENT INEXPLICABLE INFERIOR

INOPPORTUNE INORDINATE INSECURE
INSIDIOUS INSIGNIFICANT INSOLVABLE
INSUBSTANTIAL INSUFFERABLE INSUFFICIENT

INSUPPORTABLE INTOLERABLE INTOLERANT
INTRACTABLE INTRUSIVE INVALID
IRREDEEMABLE IRREFORMABLE IRREGULAR

IRRELATIVE IRRELEVANT LAST
LAST-DITCH LIMITED LOST
LOW-GRADE LOW-LEVEL LUDICROUS

MALADROIT
MISERABLE
NONPRODUCTIVE

NEGLIGENT
MUNDANE
NULL

MEANINGLESS
NEGATIVE
OBSCURE

OBSOLETE
OUT-OF-DATE
PATHETIC

OUTCAST
OUTRAGEOUS
PECCANT

OUTLANDISH
OVERDUE
PEJORATIVE

PELL-MELL
PLAUSIBLE
PREPOSTEROUS

PENITENT
POLEMIC
PROBLEM

PETTY
PRECARIOUS
PRODIGAL

PURPOSELESS
RIGOROUS
RUSTY

REDUNDANT
ROUGH
SCANT

RESISTLESS
RUN-DOWN
SCANTY

SHABBY
SKEPTICISM
SMALL-SCALE

SHAKY
SLIPSHOD
SOMBER

SKEPTICAL
SLOPPY
SORROWFUL

SPARSE
SPURIOUS
SUBSTANDARD

SPORADIC
STAGNANT
SUPERFICIAL

SPOTTY
SUBNORMAL
SUPERFLUOUS

THRIFTLESS
TRITE
UNFAVORABLE

TIRESOME
UNCERTAIN
UNFORTUNATE

TRICKY
UNEASY
UNLAWFUL

UNORGANIZED
UNTRUE
VALUELESS

UNSETTLED
UNWORTHY
WANTING

UNSUCCESSFUL
USELESS
WASHED-UP

WASTED
WEARIFUL
WHIMSICAL

WASTEFUL
WEARISOME
WISHY-WASHY

WEAK
WEARY
WORSE

WORST
WRONGFUL

WORTHLESS

WRONG

# NEGATIVE - SHORTCOMING

## NOUNS

ADVERSITY
CONFUSION
DEMISE

BLEMISH
DEFECT
DEPENDENCY

CHAGRIN
DEMERIT
DETRIMENT

DEVIATE
DISASTER
DISORDER

DISADVANTAGE
DISCORD
DISPARITY

DISAPPOINTMENT
DISCREDIT
DISSATISFACTION

EBB
ERROR
FAILURE

EGOIST
EXCUSE
FATUITY

ENCUMBRANCE
EYESORE
FAULT

FIASCO
FLUTTER
FUTILITY

FIZZLE
FORFEIT
GLITCH

FLAW
FRICTION
HAPHAZARD

HAPPENSTANCE
HINDRANCE
IMPERFECTION

HARDSHIP
IMBALANCE
IMPOSSIBILITY

HARM
IMPARITY
INACTION

INADEQUACY
INCONSONANCE
INEFFICIENCY

INATTENTION
INCONVENIENCE
INEXPEDIENCY

INCONSISTENCY
INEFFICACY
INFRACTION

INSIGNIFICANCE
INVALIDITY
LAG

INTERFERENCE
IRREGULARITY
LAPSE

INTRUSION
LACK
LEVITY

LIABILITY
MISFORTUNE
NONSENSE

LOSER
MISHAP
NUISANCE

MEANDER
MIX-UP
OPPOSITION

OVERSIGHT
PITFALL
REGRESS

PARODY
PROBLEM
REGRESSION

PELL-MELL
QUIBBLE
RESTRAINT

RIGOR
SHORTFALL
TRAVESTY

SHODDY
SLOPWORK
UNCERTAINTY

SHORTCOMING
TENSION
WASTE

# NEGATIVE - SHORTCOMING

## VERBS

| | | |
|---|---|---|
| COLLAPSE | CONCEAL | CONCEDE |
| CONDESCEND | CRIMP | DEBASE |
| DENOUNCE | DEPRIVE | DESTROY |
| | | |
| DETERIORATE | DILUTE | DIMINISH |
| DISAPPOINT | DISRUPT | DISTORT |
| DODGE | DWINDLE | EBB |
| | | |
| ELUDE | ENCUMBER | ERODE |
| ESCHEW | EXACERBATE | EXAGGERATE |
| EXTENUATE | FADE | FAIL |
| | | |
| FAKE | FALTER | FLOP |
| FLOUNDER | FLUNK | FOIL |
| FOUNDER | GLOOM | HAMPER |
| | | |
| HARM | HINDER | IMMOBILIZE |
| IMPAIR | IMPEDE | INCAPACITATE |
| IRRITATE | LACK | LAG |
| | | |
| LAPSE | LAVISH | LESSEN |
| LIMP | LOWER | MAR |
| MISTAKE | NEGATE | NEGLECT |
| | | |
| OBSTRUCT | OUST | PALL |
| QUIT | REBUT | REFUSE |
| REJECT | RELINQUISH | REPUGN |
| | | |
| RESTRAIN | RETARD | ROUSE |
| SQUANDER | STAGNATE | SUPPRESS |
| SWAY | THWART | TRANSGRESS |
| | | |
| VEX | VIOLATE | VITIATE |
| WEAKEN | WEAR OUT | WILT |
| WORK OVER | WORSEN | |

# UNFAVORABLE BULLETS/PHRASES

...Inexcusable behavior
...Distasteful behavior
...Not fit

...Of little value
...Not manageable
...Illogical performance and actions

...Produces inaccurate. faulty work
...Abrupt manner
...Lacking in knowledge

...Dispassionate leader
...Erratic work habits
...Erodes morale and team spirit

...Inferior workmanship
...Lacks physical vigor
...Indecisive and evasive

...Causes depression and gloom
...Lacks charisma
...Ambiguous and evasive in manner

...Stubborn and obstinate
...Crude, coarse personality
...Operates in a vacuum

...Poor planner, great hindsight
...Vague, ambiguous self-expression
...Evasive and indirect manner

...Disagreeable personality
...Emotionally immature
...Antisocial behavior

...Abrupt, blunt manner
...Deviant behavior
...Overly talkative

...Inconsiderate and uncaring
...Dull, uninspiring leader
...Inappropriate actions

...Indolent, sluggish personality
...Not a potent, effective leader
...Slow to act

...Abnormal behavior
...Causes disorder and unrest
...Has defeatist attitude

...Weak, ineffective leader
...Shows little or no effort
...Weak, inadequate leader

...Not well organized mentally
...Flagrant violation of orders
...Disagreeable personality

...Non-productive worker
...Overly bold and assertive
...Attracts trouble

...Aberrant behavior
...Unstable personality
...Impersonal leader

...Inferior performer
...Careless work habits
...Professionally stagnant

...Adolescent behavior
...Arrogant, overbearing manner
...Crude, tactless manner

...Drab, dull personality
...Fails to observe regulations
...Spiritless, lifeless leader

...Careless in manner and action
...Unprincipled behavior
...Unfriendly disposition

...Careless, untidy appearance
...Indiscreet and thoughtless action
...Lax in performance & behavior

...Accepts orders reluctantly
...Abusive in language and action
...Undisciplined and unruly

...Vain, self-centered personality
...Reluctant, unwilling performer
...Tends to be troublesome

...Bad in manner and disposition
...Short-tempered and arrogant
...Prone to indecisiveness

...Weak, vacillating leadership
...Prankish, childish mannerism
...Impolite and unmannerly actions

...Creates resentment & disharmony
...Impolite, insulting manner
...Insincere, careless manager

...Aggressive, challenging attitude
...Disrespectful to superiors
...Devious and cunning personality

...Cold, indifferent attitude
...Corrupt, immoral character
...Argumentative toward others

...Boisterous and rude personality
...Unsound management practices
...Misrepresents the facts

...Ineffectual leadership skills
...Interferes with progress
...Easily excitable and troublesome

...Unable to master job
...Overbearing and oppressive
...Acts on impulse, not plan

...Indecisive leader
...Benevolent behavior
...Ill-humored personality

...Obstinate and impudent
...Fault-finding to excess
...Misuses position

...Disorderly conduct
...Temperamental behavior
...Maladjusted personality

...Undignified manner
...Provokes arguments
...A problem person

...Careless appearance
...Unpredictable behavior
...Failed to improve

...Loses control
...Totally unconcerned
...Lack of desire

...Completely helpless
...Impedes progress
...Low self-esteem

...Lack of confidence
...Ignores reality
...Threat to morale

...Mentally malnourished
...Shirks responsibility
...Pressures subordinates

...Emotionally immature
...Leadership vacuum
...Mistaken judgment

...Improper behavior and conduct
...Indifferent towards others
...Seriously endangers morale

...Difficult to reason with
...Uncaring in reason or sympathy
...Impervious to counseling

...Subject to daily failure
...Ignores advice of superiors
...Inflexible, rigid taskmaster

...Practices deceit and trickery
...Doubtful, confusing leadership
...Undesirable personality traits

...Corruptive, dishonest nature
...Irritates and annoys others
...Faulty, defective workmanship

...Mundane, methodical leadership
...Concerned with own self-interest
...Discourages team unity

...Contemptible and arrogant
...Unjustly exploits others
...Suppresses subordinate initiative

...Avoids work and responsibility
...Circumvents chain of command
...Hot tempered, easily angered

...Becomes emotionally violent
...Without mercy or compassion
...Lacks proper mental discipline

...Becomes easily frustrated
...Has innate aversion to work
...Not dependable or reliable

...Unpredictable work habits
...Mild learning disability
...Persistently poor performance

...A complainer
...Bad judgment
...Carefree attitude

...Incapable and inept
...Distant and impersonal
...Plots and schemes

...Abrasive personality
...Throws weight around
...Wasted opportunities

...Slow and methodical
...Fabricates the truth
...Incites arguments

...Insensitive leadership
...Degrading to others
...Short temper

...Deviates from standards
...Inhibits progress
...Shuns duty

...Unimpressive leader
...Meek and humble manner
...Incompetent manager

...Brash and immature
...Loses emotional control
...Meager productiveness

...Serious judgment error
...Blatant negligence
...Disruptive influence

...Abnormal behavior
...Imperceptible progress
...Argues to excess

...Mediocre abilities
...Common and ordinary
...Inflexible leader

...Complete disregard for authority
...Does no more than required
...Less than moderate success

...Arrogant and overbearing
...Finds excessive leisure time
...Quarrelsome, touchy nature

...Unable to control emotions
...Intentionally avoids work
...Deliberately refuses orders

...Lacks depth and substance
...Hostile, aggressive temperament
...Unwilling to obey orders

...Without sorrow or remorse
...Immaturity and bad judgment
...Behavior and attitude problems

...Unimpressive performance
...Prejudicial to good order
...Detrimental to team spirit

...Less than marginal performer
...Fails to monitor subordinates
...Openly disagrees with superiors

...Causes extra work for others
...Lackadaisical attitude
...Continuing discipline problem

...Reluctant to abide by rules
...Unable to stay abreast of job
...Interferes with progress

...Indecisive under pressure
...Obvious lack of motivation
...Disobedient and disrespectful

...Volatile, explosive disposition
...Fails to accomplish tasks
...Negative outlook and disposition

...Dull, trite personality
...Undermines morale
...Lack of initiative

...Negative attitude
...Openly discontent
...Unacceptable behavior

...Ignores direction
...Not job-aggressive
...Lack of pride in work

...Flouts authority
...Lags behind others
...Becomes easily excited

...Stirs up trouble
...Breaks down morale
...Irregular work habits

...Lacks persistence
...Acts on impulse
...Frequent complainer

...Constantly complains
...Not trustworthy
...Plagued by indecision

...Not reliable
...Unwilling to conform
...Creates problems

...Exercises bad judgment
...Weak personality
...Abrupt manner

...Apathetic leader
...Not an inspiring leader
...Lacks self-discipline

...Shirks responsibility
...Sloppy workmanship
...Asks undue questions

...Lax in carrying out duties
...Requires routine reminders
...Wears down subordinate spirit

...Uses questionable leadership
...Impersonal, detached leader
...Gets less than desired results

...Not receptive to counseling
...Irrational, erratic behavior
...Overly aggressive personality

...Verbally abuses subordinates
...Spreads ill-will and disharmony
...Careless attention to duty

...Non-forgiving leadership traits
...Lack of personal conviction
...Unable to perform routine tasks

...Abusive and offensive language
...Ingrained disrespectful nature
...Fails to achieve consistency

...Lacks knowledge and ability
...A burden to leadership
...Disobedient and belligerent

...Improper counseling techniques
...Spreads discontent and resentment
...Not firm with subordinates

...Tries hard, accomplishes little
...Frequently in discord with superiors
...Lacks consistency of performance

...Deficient in skill and knowledge
...Inflexible, unimaginative leadership
...Insolent, overbearing personality.

...Unwilling to listen to reason or fact.
...Instigates and provokes disharmony
...Mechanical, non-inventive leadership

...Lack of initiative
...Indecisive leader
...Slow, plodding worker

...Erodes good order
...Prone to argument
...Inconsistent worker

...Frequent bad judgment
...Marginal performer
...Exerts minimum effort

...No future potential
...Overly bold and brash
...Emotional difficulty

...Inattentive to detail
...Suppresses subordinate growth
...Gives misguided direction

...Manipulates others to own end
...Of little worth or value
...Lack of confidence in abilities

...Helpless without supervision
...Unable to deal with reality
...Needs continued reminders

...Interprets rules loosely
...Overbearing and intolerant
...Reluctant to accept direction

...Chronic financial problems
...Fails to respond to direction
...Low level of self-confidence.

...Lackluster, lackadaisical attitude
...Inclined to stray from the truth
...Uncertain, indecisive in action

...Is a complete disappointment.
...Not correct and precise in detail.
...Acts out of emotion, not reason.

...Failed to live up to expectations.
...Unmanageable off-duty activities.
...Becomes easily agitated and excited

...Habitually reports to work late.
...Insulting and abusive to others.

...Blames others for own shortcomings
...Oppressive in character and action.
...Insulting and arrogant personality.

...Blames shortcomings on others.
...Unpleasant appearance and personality.
...Aimless management. Lacks plan, order, and discipline.

...Unable to overcome minor problems.
...Unpredictable attention to duty and detail.
...Incapable manager and supervisor.

...Incapable of sustained satisfactory performance.
...Not a potent, effective supervisor.
...Incapable of handling practical matters.

...Makes decisions that are not sensible or prudent.
...Incompatible, disagreeing personality.
...Incompetent without direct, consistent supervision.

...Unfair and inequitable treatment of subordinates.
...Personal behavior is incompatible with good discipline.
...Disruptive to good order and discipline.

...Uncertain and doubtful in making decisions.
...Aimless, errant decision making facilities.
...Lacks personal sincerity and believability.

...Frequently makes false or untrue statements.
...Organization lacks order and cohesiveness.
...Self-indulgent, irresponsible leadership.

...Sometimes impatient with subordinates.
...Achieves less than moderately successful results.
...Can achieve good results only under ordinary conditions.

...Deliberately goes out of way to irritate others.
...Intentionally makes minor mistakes.
...Efforts frequently prove fruitless and unsuccessful.

...Shows little forethought or preparation of task at hand.
...Lacks good judgment and common sense.
...Does not demonstrate a sense of responsibility.

...Too submissive and mild mannered to be an effective leader.
...Subject to mood changes without warning.
...Too emotional.  Overreacts to minor situations.

...Criticizes and reprimands subordinates in public.
...Evades and shirks duty when possible.
...Becomes confused and frustrated when forced to choose one of various
        options.

...Careless.  Makes mistakes through lack of attention.
...Argumentative with irritating persistence.
...Intentional disregard for following orders.

...Excessively lenient in handling subordinates.
...Policies are not uniform and consistent.
...Conveniently misunderstands or misinterprets orders.

...Superiors find it difficult to support independently made decisions.
...Excessively forceful toward subordinates.
...Fails to act according to professional standards.

...A bad leader and a worse follower.
...Plans lack breadth, originality, and substance.
...Lax and careless in performing professional duties.

...Off-duty conduct is disgraceful and unacceptable.
...Conduct is beyond the bounds of decency.
...Frequently breaks rules and disobeys orders.

...Overly strict and harsh leadership practices.
...Considers all jobs below personal dignity to accomplish.
...Apprehensive about accepting any new job or challenge.

...Does not abide by rules in an orderly fashion.
...Professional development lags behind contemporaries.
...Ignores direction and guidance of superiors.

...Wasteful and extravagant use of resources.
...Alters facts to suit own self-interest.
...Strays from work area if not closely watched.

...Unable to stay mentally involved with job, becomes preoccupied with personal matters.
...Deviates sharply from behavioral standards.
...Belligerent and hostile personality.

...Displays open contempt for authority.
...Devoid of hope for improvement.
...Has more than a mild dislike for work.

...Violates standards of behavior and conduct.
...Will violate any rule or regulation not to personal liking.
...Written products are not clear and coherent.

...Overly harsh and critical of minor mistakes by subordinates.
...Blunt and rude in speech and manner.
...Unable to choose correct courses of action.

...Thoughtless in considering feelings of others.
...Insensitive and callous leadership.
...Not responsive to guidance or direction.

...Destructive to good order and discipline.
...Unsophisticated behavior and attitude.
...Performance highlighted by neglect and negligence.

...Unpleasant, objectionable personality.
...Overly unreasonable. Unyielding to reason or rationale.
...Not a strong leader, too permissive and lenient.

...Lacks necessary personal traits to be a successful leader.
...Exaggerated self-opinion and self-importance.
...Acts without giving due consideration or thought.

...Personal problems demand excessive time and energy of others.
...Neglectful and forgetful work habits.
...Lacking in social grace and courtesy.

...Will not work unless prompted or prodded.
...Lacks orderly mental continuity.
...Careless of the feelings of others.

...Indiscreet personal affairs.
...Unable to restrain or control emotions.
...Stubbornly opposes corrective counseling.

...Refuses to yield or relent to change.
...Does not objectively evaluate evidence and conditions.
...Leadership too tolerant and permissive.

...Excessive minor infractions of discipline and regulations.
...Gross deviation from regulations.
...Becomes bogged down in petty, insignificant details.

...A slacker, shirks duty when possible.
...Administrative and disciplinary burden.
...Exhibits lack of desire to conform to standards.

...Persistent minor disciplinary infraction.
...Performance a deterrent to good order and discipline.
...A liability to the organization.

...Shows no desire for improvement.
...Frequently deviates from standards.
...Disrespectful attitude and behavior.

...Behavior goes beyond the bounds of good taste.
...Exhibits only short periods of success.
...Without personal restraint or calmness.

...Not straightforward and open in manner.
...Unable to distinguish right from wrong.
...Decisions are open to question.

...Expects success using guesswork and conjecture.
...Passive and submissive in nature.
...Unable to overcome personal problems and difficulties.

...Fails to maintain harmony and cohesiveness within work group.
...Fails to achieve minimum acceptable performance.
...Work marked by utter, complete failure.

...Has a personality clash with almost all co-workers.
...Makes careless, avoidable mistakes.
...Work frequently falls short of expectations and abilities.

...Failed to live up to expectations.
...Twists recollection of events to own ends.
...Actual performance falls well short of abilities.

...Counseled regarding incongruent interaction with others.
...Working relationship with subordinates does not reflect the necessary tact and maturity required.
...Very difficult for others to work with.

...Incapable of compassionate leadership.
...Neglects personal welfare of subordinates.
...Evasive when confronted with shortcomings.

...Helpless in meeting new situations without on-the-scene leadership.
...Hesitant and confused in unfamiliar surrounding.
...Suitable for routine, ordinary jobs.

...Excuses offered more frequently than productive performance.
...Tries very hard but achieves little.
...Has a deceptive and deceitful character.

...Mechanical, non-inventive or inspiring leadership.
...Exerts undue influence and pressure on subordinates.
...Works hard only when personally convenient.

...Turns simple tasks into complex problems.
...Disagreeing personality dims hopes and desires of others.
...Agitates others, creates ill-will and discontent.

...Routinely doubts and questions superiors.
...Unplanned, unforeseen problems hinder professional ability.
...Unforgiving leader.  Rubs a mistake in, not out.

...Superficial work doesn't hold up to close examination.
...Overly demanding and self-assertive.
...Overly concerned with self-image.

...Non-compassionate, harsh leader.
...Work suffers from plainness and simplicity.
...A prankster, not serious minded.

...Organization out of kilter and does not function properly.
...Cannot cope successfully with severe, trying situations.
...Discussions frequently turn into heated disputes.

...Gives in to pressure during crisis situations.
...Opposes improvement efforts of others.
...Inability to change or adapt to changing situations.

...Unable to stay abreast of events in fast-paced environment.
...Does not provide personal touch to leadership responsibilities.
...Not clear in thought or reasoning. Clouds or confuses issues.

...Cannot articulate in speech, incoherent in writing.
...Willful disobedience and open disrespect for authority.
...Can't make proper decisions under pressure.

...Dodges work and responsibility at almost every opportunity.
...Deviates from expected standards.
...Has strong tendency to stray from normal behavior.

...Not job-aggressive, waits for something to happen before taking action.
...Routinely displays unacceptable behavior and performance.
...Relies too heavily on others.

...Below average performer. May come around in due time.
...Not overly serious or concerned in doing tasks correctly.
...Functions well below level of performance capable and acceptable.

...Manipulates people to meet own ends.
...Not prudent in personal financial matters.
...Displays carefree and reckless abandon attitude.

...Prejudicial to good order and discipline.
...Substandard mission performance routinely displayed.
...Does not get things done in timely manner.

...Attempts to walk thin line between right and wrong.
...Needs continued reminders about personal hygiene, haircuts, and clean
        uniforms.
...Routinely fails personnel inspections.

...Good judgment sometimes impaired by short temper.
...Abrasive personality. Has difficulty getting along with others.
...Intractable unwillingness to conform to expected standards of behavior
        and conduct.

...Premature in judgment, does not always get all the facts before acting.
...Sometimes becomes absent minded or preoccupied with events not
        related to task at hand.
...Interprets rules loosely and usually to personal benefit.

...Weak leader, too easily influenced by subordinates.
...Becomes withdrawn and distraught when confronted on shortcoming.
...Prefers to forsake any personal help or assistance.

...Uses improper counseling techniques, often degrading and humiliating subordinates.
...Will stray or deviate from work standards if not closely watched.
...Sometimes overbearing and overly intolerant of mistakes.

...Not a strong personality. Overly apologetic and humble.
...Erodes good order and discipline.
...Abnormally high reluctance to accept direction and guidance.

...Argumentative. Opposes all views other than own.
...Not capable of continued good performance. Even best efforts frequently prove fruitless or unsuccessful.
...Not firm and resolute with subordinates.

...Abrasive personality and abrupt manner stirs discontent and resentment among others.
...Usually, but not always, in compliance with regulations.
...Treatment of subordinates less than desired and expected.

...Wears down spirit of subordinates.
...Inconsistent behavior, subject to sudden bursts of anger.
...Inattentive to routine work procedures, lacks persistence.

...Inconsistent. Arbitrarily enforces rules and standards.
...Believes job should be subordinate to personal interests.
...Poor leader. Unforeseen and unplanned problems routinely arise.

...Gives undue consideration and attention to personal likes and priorities at the expense of job performance.
...Accommodating to subordinate desires to a fault.
...Takes uncompromising stand in even minor matters.

...Speaks and acts on impulse, does not always think through situation.
...Overly challenging and aggressive personality. Has difficulty getting along with others.
...Blames others for own shortcomings.

...Displays no rational or orderly relationship in planning or assigning tasks.
...Condemns or shuns thoughts and ideas of others.
...Cannot be relied upon to take timely, correct action.

...Unconventional and unorthodox style of leadership produces less than desired results.
...Overconfident. Abnormally high self-opinion.
...Not receptive to constructive counseling.

...Views standing orders as a matter of personal convenience.
...Walks on thin edge between right and wrong.
...Displays irrational and erratic behavior.

...Harsh and coarse in leadership and language.
...Possesses ample knowledge and skill to perform routine tasks without constant supervision.
...Subordinates suffer from lack of own sense of direction and self-discipline.

...Abusive language and improper treatment are major flaws in leadership skills.
...Fails to abide by rules and regulations.
...Lacks quality and depth of character.

...Weak personality. Frequently concedes point of view without positive stand.
...Gets in verbal confrontation with others.
...Leadership and guidance lacks substance and purpose.

...Rigid thinking restricts ability to learn new courses of action.
...Unable to cope with difficult situations without assistance.
...Improper leadership takes its toll on organizational effectiveness.

...Plagued by lack of self-confidence and positive leadership.
...Defeatist attitude and lack of personal conviction proved to be a major disappointment.
...Possesses ingrained disregard for authority.

...Leadership style leaves uneasy feeling.
...Proposed plans and actions frequently riddled with paradox.
...Governs others by overly stern code of own ethics.

...Non-forgiving leader. Rubs in mistakes and doesn't forget.
...Asks for an undue amount of justification when assigned almost any task.
...Exerts only the minimum amount of initiative needed to complete assigned tasks.

...Fails to properly supervise subordinates. Assigns work but does not follow-up to ensure finished product.

...Has difficulty managing paperwork. Unable to ensure quality work completed in timely manner.

...Not steadfast in commitment, displays reversal of point of view or attitude.


...Leadership ability is questionable at best and routinely ends in confusion and no purpose of action by subordinates.

...Inattentive to detail, becomes easily distracted.

...Routinely questions motive of superiors.


...Reliability and effectiveness oscillates between extreme highs and lows, depending on daily mood and attitude.

...Superiors waste more hours counseling and documenting substandard performance than they receive productive work in return.

...Excels in jobs routine and repetitive in nature.


...Has difficulty understanding orders and correctly following direction.

...Reliable and competent in execution of technical duties, but when assigned other tasks there is noticeable decline in performance and increased supervision is required.

...Inconsistent supervisor. Plagued by indecisiveness.


...Exhibits neither desire nor ability to perform satisfactorily.

...Does not always consider gravity of situation at hand.

...Tries hard, but sometimes gets carried away with own enthusiasm and overlooks routine but necessary details.


...Slow and deliberate work pace.

...Weakens or breaks under pressure.

...Usually in compliance with rules and regulations.


...Becomes belligerent and disobedient when given direction by some superiors.

...Counseling required for sloppy workmanship, not paying attention to instruction, and not caring about a final product.

...Performance of duty totally unsatisfactory.


...Requires constant supervision and often leaves work area without permission.

...A less than positive attitude is reflected in consistent marginal performance.

...Does not seek, and reluctantly accepts, any responsibility.

...Performance marked by inconsistency and incompleteness.
...Sporadic in understanding and carrying out directives.
...Frequently displays immaturity and bad judgment.

...Inability to adjust to expected standards and half-truths highlight attitude and behavior problems.
...Not a self-starter, demonstrates little initiative and less desire for improvement.
...Adversely affects operations and morale of contemporaries.

...Received counseling on numerous occasions for lack of motivation and negative attitude
...Acceptance of orders depends upon issuing superior.
...Late for work on numerous occasions, fails to respond to counseling.

...Counseling on substandard performance results in only short- term improvement.
...Shoddy workmanship, takes not pride in work or job accomplishment.
...Performance, across the board, is unsatisfactory.

...Personal conduct is prejudicial to good order and discipline.
...Lateness for work places extra burden on co-workers and detracts from their otherwise high morale and team spirit.
...Performance is all valleys and no peaks.

...Impulsive, subject to actions without due thought or consideration.
...Considers counseling on off-duty activities an unwarranted intrusion into personal life.
...Unreliable performance persists despite counseling at various levels.

...Negative attitude is reflected almost daily by continued marginal performance.
...Conduct and performance have degenerated to unacceptable level.
...Flagrant violation of direction and guidance seriously detract from already low level of performance.

...Shows total lack of amenability to structured work environment.
...Displays open discontent toward superiors and job content.
...Inconsistent in accepting and reacting to supervision and direction.

...Performance well below that expected of peer group.
...Becomes involved in immediate task at hand and sometimes lets more broad-scope matters slip by without due attention.
...Less than marginal performer, requires almost constant supervision.

...Ignores explicit direction of superiors.
...Frequently voices displeasure at job assignments.
...Not aggressive in meeting established standards or goals.

...Performance migrates between acceptable and unsatisfactory.
...Habitually flouts authority, exhibits nonchalance, and engenders disrespect among peers.
...Fails to properly monitor and direct activity of assigned personnel.

...Continually commits minor offenses as if testing superiors.
...A below average performer who causes extra work for others.
...Unresponsive to normal and special counseling.

...Generally performs to full expectations.
...Disruptive to good order and discipline.
...Seriously lacking in initiative, requires almost constant supervision to accomplish assigned tasks.

...Openly voices disagreement with supervision and policy.
...Displays obvious lack of motivation by consistently placing higher priority on personal desires than on assigned duties.
...Flouts authority despite numerous attempts at counseling on formal and informal basis.

...Exhibits unsatisfactory performance in technical specialty.
...Lackadaisical attitude toward superiors and job.
...Becomes withdrawn and disdain when counseled on deficiencies.

...Leaves assigned place of work to take care of personal matters without advising or informing superiors.
...Has negative outlook and disposition regardless of subject matter.
...Complains openly when not assigned tasks to personal liking.

...Lack of motivation and frequent short absences cause supervisory and administrative burden.
...Continuing discipline problem evidenced in inability and unwillingness to comply with simplest direction and guidance.
...Despite extensive training, lacks requisite skill and knowledge required of assigned job.

...Unable to simultaneously monitor and control individual operations and functions of a diverse and dynamic environment.
...Inconsistent performance. Usually good worker, but at times requires close supervision. Works without any supervision when the mood strikes.

...Total lack of enthusiasm, constant complaining, and unwillingness to do personal share of work have detrimental impact on morale.

...Has great deal of difficulty following even the simplest of orders or direction.
...A marginal performer whose work must remain under constant supervision.
...Often requires reminders to commence job on schedule. Counseling results in only short-term improvement.

...Marginal performer, requires direct guidance and supervision in routine matters.
...Immature and undisciplined with no potential for continued, useful service.
...Reluctance to conform to standards and requirements maintained by continuous poor attitude and behavior.

...Early job-aggressiveness followed by steady and prolonged decline in performance and waning interest.
...Consistently failed to take positive, corrective action on shortcomings and deficiencies despite being given every opportunity.
...Performance of subordinates characterized by tension, dissension and half-effort.

...Leadership marred by indecisive and undisciplined practices.
...Inadequate performance brought about by inability to gain proficiency in functional skills.
...Has insufficient motivation to overcome personal deficiencies.

...Unable to take constructive criticism and private counseling.
...Ineptness in job accomplishment places undue burden on others.
...Will not acknowledge mistakes or failures. Always blames others.

...Does not exhibit a knack for making positive things happen like other supervisors.
...Performance below standard despite ability and well defined assignments.
...Attempts to correct deficiencies have been in vain.

...Inappropriate behavior and performance.
...Lacks mental depth and soundness.
...Unsophisticated reasoning and judgment.

...Fabricates the truth.
...Slow to learn and develop professionally.

The following pages contain bullets/phrases without an ending. This allows you, the drafter, to select an appropriate beginning and add whatever ending is desired.

...Habitually gets into trouble by...
...Not mentally capable to...
...Impairs morale by...

...Does not have the ability to...
...Below normal level of skill in...
...Lacks necessary ability to...

...Failed to achieve consistency in...
...Involved in unethical practice of...
...Under emotional strain when...

...Not qualified to be...
...Not worthy of...
...Lacking in ability to...

...Hinders and impedes progress by...
...Is of little or no use in/when...
...Unforgiving nature causes...

...Of little value in/when...
...Behavior not conducive to...
...Unable to grasp meaning of...

...Contemptuous disregard for...
...Slow to learn and develop as a/an...
...Enjoys a low reputation due to...

...Has open contempt for...
...Lacks mental aptitude to...
...Blatant disregard for...

...Will not maintain commitment to...
...Loses composure when/under...
...Becomes agitated and upset when...

...Openly defies and challenges...
...Lacks vigor or force to...
...Not mature enough to...

...Upsets normal operations by...
...A misfit, not suited for/to...
...Lacks the emotional stability to...

...Has not adjusted well to...
...Unable to refrain from...
...Bad habits include...

...Lax in complying and enforcing...
...Made crude attempt to...
...Lacks mental restraint to...

...Unsuitable and unfit for...
...Unsuitable for...
...Strongly opposed to...

...Incompetent in areas of...
...Careless and negligent in...
...Misguided efforts caused...

...Lacks inner discipline to...
...Of little use or value in...
...Has no idea of how to...

...A constant threat to morale by...
...Finds it most difficult to fit in with...
...Inexperienced in matters of...

...Not serious about...
...Has bad habit of...
...Not mentally equipped to...

...Displays marked indifference in...
...Usually drops behind others when...
...Fails to grasp essentials of...

...Has great difficulty in/with...
...Sometimes lax in...
...Stirs up trouble by...

...Helpless when confronted with...
...Does not totally comply with...
...Has chronic weakness of/in...

...Has distorted view of...
...Apathetic towards...
...Unable to fall in line with...

...Unable to deal with reality of...
...Has difficulty with...
...Planned badly for...

...Has not kept pace with...
...Ignores reality. Unable to...

...Unwilling to put forth necessary effort to...
...Does not give required importance to...
...Conduct not fit or becoming of a/an...

...Unable to maintain a stable balance of...
...Becomes hostile when approached about...
...Despite receiving sufficient counseling and supervision, continued to...

...Overall performance declined because of isolated incidence of...
...Lacks mental courage and conviction to...
...Did not exercise sound judgment by/when...

...Shows apathy and indifference to/toward...
...Disenchanted with present duties because...
...Rude and impolite, does not show proper respect to/for...

...Performance has deteriorated to point to...
...Becomes confused and puzzled when...
...Does not satisfy minimum requirements for/of...

...Does not possess the mental vigor and vitality to...
...Interferes with normal functioning of...
...Behavior has declined to point of...

...Has a strong moral weakness in...
...Suffers frequent minor setbacks because of...
...Failure to pay attention to detail caused...

...Has made insignificant progress in...
...Lags behind contemporaries in...
...Unable to take full advantage of...

...A major cause of disappointment because...
...Acts in haste without due regard of...
...Suffered total loss of integrity because of...

...Open distrust of subordinates causes...
...Lacks necessary wisdom and judgment to...
...Does not possess sufficient knowledge to...

...Made false statements concerning...
...Failed to act with promptness and dispatch in/when...
...Sometimes uses ethically dubious means to...

...Displayed improper judgment by/when...
...Refused to accept assistance to...
...Does not posses the necessary self-confidence to...

...Shows only artificial interest in...
...Deliberate lack of consideration for...
...Does not have the will or ability to...

...Excitable temper frequently cause of...
...Not an accomplished or skilled...
...Work characterized by complete absence of...

...Chronic personal and financial problems have lead to...
...Despite ample opportunity, failed to improve...
...Critically undermines morale by...

...Lacks knowledge or comprehension to...
...Impedes work and discipline by...
...Requires routine reminders to...

...Inconsistent and unimpressive performance led to...
...Attitude and performance not in tune with...
...Shows a marked unwillingness to...

...Has exaggerated ego problem which results in...
...Relinquishes control over subordinates when...
...Prone to substandard work because of...

...Becomes intensely excited and aroused by/when...
...Inconsistent work and irregular work habits caused by...
...Occasionally regresses to old habits of...

...Personal doubt and indecision sometimes hinders...
...Acts on spontaneous impulse, without due consideration of...
...Becomes easily distressed when/over...

...Deeply emotional, cannot control urge to...
...Sometimes uses excessive force or pressure to/in...
...Actions and deeds in sharp contrast with...

...Barely satisfactory in ability to...
...Compounds existing problems by...
...Carelessness and inattention to duty caused/led to...

...Belabors on nonessential matters to detriment of...
...Personal desires frequently at contrast with...
...Generally learned but totally inexperienced in...

...Relieved of duties for cause when...
...Suppresses subordinate growth potential by...
...Superiors began to lose trust in abilities when...

...Tries to do a good job, but is hindered by...
...Utterly helpless when it comes to...
...Tends to create a bad relationship with co-workers because...

...Lacks vigor and persistence required to...
...Management plans are without substance and marred by...
...Not reliable to work independently, needs a crutch to...

...Substandard behavior. Frequently engages in...
...Buckles under pressure. Loses control of/when...
...Becomes easily detached from job by...

...Unwillingness and inability to act decisively caused...
...Has difficulty dealing with others because...
...Produced minimal improvement despite...

...Exercised bad judgment and discretion in/by...
...Does not stay in strict compliance with...
...Does not support superior policies and objectives.

...Experienced isolated incidences of...
...Becomes degradation to morale by...
...Does not demonstrate potential for further useful...

...Failed to achieve consistency in...
...Suspended from regular duties for/because...
...Time after time proved a burden to...

...Positive aspects of performance outweighed by...
...Suffered loss of confidence in/by...
...Spends an inordinate amount of time on...

...Lacks requisite knowledge in/to...
...Has a noticeable imperfection in...
...Demonstrates a lack of interest and concern for...

...Not reasonable and rational in thought.  Unable to make sense of...
...Struggles to maintain correct balance of...
...Despite noble intentions, unable to...

...Personal desires and preferences frequently in discord with...
...Despite adequate time, failed to make satisfactory headway in...
...Not open minded.  Has predisposition toward...

...Has emotional difficulty in coping with...
...Exercised bad judgment and discretion by...
...Does not stay in strict compliance with...

# PERFORMANCE

# DICTIONARY

The following section contains 2000 of the most frequently used words in the English language to explain, state, define, or demonstrate individual performance or character. A brief definition/meaning is also provided.

## FOR EXPANDED USE, A DRAFTER CAN USE THE DEFINITION OF THE WORDS.

| WORD | CLASS | DEFINITION |
|------|-------|------------|
| **-A-** | | |
| Abase | Verb | Loss of esteem |
| Aberrant | Adj/Noun | Substandard behavior |
| Abet | Verb | Encourage |
| | | |
| Abhorrent | Adj | Disagreeable |
| Abide | Verb | Tolerate or accept |
| Ability | Noun | Skill, Competence |
| | | |
| Able | Adj | Capable. Have ability |
| Abnormal | Adj | Not normal |
| Abrasive | Adj | Irritating |
| | | |
| Abreast | Adj | At standard. Even |
| Abrupt | Adj | Cut short without warning |
| Absentminded | Adj | Drifting of the mind |
| | | |
| Absolute | Adj | Without doubt, fault |
| Abstract Thought | Noun | Theoretical thought process |
| Absurd | Adj | Obviously, clearly ridiculous |
| | | |
| Abundant | Adj | Plenty |
| Abuse | Noun | Be improper, misuse |
| Abuse | Verb | Improper, misuse |
| | | |
| Acceptable | Adj | Allowable. Passable. Adequate |
| Acclaim | Verb | Praise. Hold in high esteem |
| Acclaim | Noun | To praise |
| | | |
| Accolade | Noun | A praise or acclaim |
| Accommodate | Verb | Allow. Make room. Fit |
| Accommodating | Adj | Beneficial. Help. Assistance |
| | | |
| Accomplished | Adj | Skilled |
| Accost | Verb | Confront aggressively |
| Accurate | Adj | Correct |

| Ace | Adj | Top quality |
| Achieve | Verb | Accomplish. Reach |
| Achievement | Noun | Something achieved |
| | | |
| Achiever | Noun | One who achieves |
| Acme | Noun | The top, peak, highest point |
| Activation | Noun | Make or cause action |
| | | |
| Acuity | Noun | Keen. Acute |
| Acumen | Noun | Perceptive. Quickness |
| Acute | Adj | Keen or sharp |
| | | |
| Acuteness | Noun | Agile, keen mind |
| Adamant | Adj | Not moving or flexible |
| Adept | Adj/Noun | Expert. Skilled |
| | | |
| Adequate | Adj | Satisfactory |
| Adhere | Verb | Stick to. Abide by |
| Adherence | Noun | To stick to. Abide by |
| | | |
| Admirable | Adj | In high esteem. Acclaim |
| Admire | Verb | Hold in high esteem, acclaim |
| Adolescent | Adj | Not mature. Immature |
| | | |
| Adroit | Adj | Skillful |
| Adverse | Adj | Opposed or opposing |
| Adversity | Noun | Bad situation |
| | | |
| Advocate | Verb | To support, or back |
| Affable | Adj | Friendly. Gets along with others |
| Agree | Verb | In accord. Concur. Agreement |
| | | |
| Agreeable | Adj | Likable. Pleasant |
| Aggressive | Adj | Forceful, intense |
| Agile | Adj | Skillful and flexible |
| | | |
| Agile-minded | Adj | Mental dexterity, quickness |
| Agility | Noun | Being quick and agile |
| Agitate | Verb | Incite or fuel |
| | | |
| Agitator | Noun | Someone who incites or fuels |
| Agog | Adj | Excitement. Anticipation |
| Alacrity | Noun | Ready and willing |

| | | |
|---|---|---|
| Alert | Adj | Perceptive |
| All-around | Adj | Versatile. Multi-faceted |
| Altercation | Noun | Heated and aggressive argument |
| | | |
| Ambiguity | Noun | Not definite or precise. Obscure |
| Ambiguous | Adj | Not definite or precise. Obscure |
| Ambivalent | Adj | Indecisive. Not firm |
| | | |
| Amenity | Noun | Friendly |
| Amiable | Adj | Likable |
| Amicable | Adj | Likable. Harmonious |
| | | |
| Amity | Noun | Harmonious |
| Amiss | Adj | Awry. Wrong |
| Analyze | Verb | Study part by part, in detail |
| | | |
| Analytic | Adj | Skillful. Discernible |
| Analytical | Adj | Logical analysis |
| Animate | Verb | Show zest and action |
| | | |
| Animator | Noun | Active person. Puts into motion |
| Antagonist | Noun | One who agitates another |
| Antagonistic | Adj | Agitating |
| | | |
| Antagonize | Verb | To agitate, incite |
| Anticipate | Verb | Expect |
| Antisocial | Adj | Not social |
| | | |
| Anxious | Adj | Eager |
| Anxiousness | Noun | Anxious, apprehensive, eager |
| A1 | Adj | The best. Top. Number one |
| | | |
| Apathetic | Adj | Without interest |
| Apathy | Noun | Being without interest |
| Apex | Noun | The uppermost or highest point |
| | | |
| Aplomb | Noun | Under control |
| Appall | Verb | Dismay. Disagreeable |
| Appalling | Adj | Be in dismay. Disagreeable |
| | | |
| Appealing | Adj | Pleasing |
| Appease | Verb | To quell or quiet |
| Applaud | Verb | Show agreement, approval |

| | | |
|---|---|---|
| Apt | Adj | Quick to grasp, learn |
| Aptitude | Noun | Ability, gift |
| Aptness | Noun | Quick to grasp, learn |
| | | |
| Ardent | Adj | Strong. Passionate |
| Arduous | Adj | Hard. Strenuous. Difficult |
| Arouse | Verb | Excite to action |
| | | |
| Arrogance | Noun | Overbearing |
| Arrogant | Adj | Overbearing. Feeling egotistical |
| Artful | Adj | Of much skill, ability |
| | | |
| Articulate | Adj | Clear. Effective. Highly skilled |
| Artistic | Adj | Skillful thought, action |
| Artistic Imagination | Noun | Skillful, artful mental vision |
| | | |
| Arousal | Noun | Move, spark to action |
| Askew | Adj | Not normal. Awry. Slanted |
| Aspiration | Noun | High ambition |
| | | |
| Aspire | Verb | Attempt to reach |
| Assert | Verb | To compel or compelling |
| Assertive | Adj | Compel. Compelling |
| | | |
| Asset | Noun | Something owned of value |
| Astray | Adj | Move from correct, right |
| Astute | Adj | Mental alertness |
| | | |
| Attitude | Noun | Mental disposition |
| Attribute | Noun | Possessed trait, ability |
| Audacious | Adj | Bold, venturesome |
| | | |
| Audacity | Noun | Overly bold |
| Auspicious | Adj | Favorable. Successful |
| Autocratic | Adj | Self rule. Not democratic |
| | | |
| Aversion | Noun | Avoid |
| Avid | Adj | Extreme and intense |
| Avoid | Verb | Keep away from |
| | | |
| Avow | Verb | Acknowledge |
| Aware | Adj | To have knowledge. Know |
| Awareness | Noun | Be aware. Have knowledge |

| | | |
|---|---|---|
| Awe | Noun | Mixed feelings |
| Awry | Adj | Wrong. Not right, correct |

**-B-**

| | | |
|---|---|---|
| Baffle | Verb | Confuse. Mix up |
| Balk | Verb | Hesitate. Delay |
| Banner | Adj | Above others |
| Bashful | Adj | Introvert. Shy |
| Behavior | Noun | Conduct. Manner |
| Belittle | Verb | Make little. Small |
| Belligerence | Noun | Being aggressive. Hostile |
| Belligerent | Adj | Aggressive. Hostile |
| Beneficial | Adj | Of use, benefit |
| Benevolence | Noun | Kind disposition |
| Benevolent | Adj | Kind or charitable |
| Benign | Adj | Good-natured |
| Berate | Verb | Scold violently |
| Berserk | Noun/Adj | Violent, reckless action |
| Betray | Verb | To violate. Go against |
| Bias | Verb | Predetermined. Bent. Swayed |
| Big-hearted | Adj | Giving, caring |
| Bland | Adj | Dull, uninteresting |
| Blemish | Noun | To mar or scar |
| Blithe | Adj | Gay, cheerful |
| Blunder | Verb | To mistake or error |
| Blunt | Adj | Abrupt. Over candid |
| Boisterous | Adj | Openly noisy or rowdy |
| Bold | Adj | Forward. Without reservation |
| Bold Imagination | Noun | Daring, confident mental powers |
| Bolster | Verb | Support. Enforce. Back |
| Brainchild | Noun | Product of one's mental thought |
| Brainstorm | Noun | Fresh, new sudden idea |
| Brain Trust | Noun | Subject experts |
| Brash | Adj | Bold and harsh |

| | | |
|---|---|---|
| Brassy | Adj | Bold impudence. Brash |
| Brevity | Noun | Brief, to the point |
| Bright | Adj | Quick, keen mind |
| | | |
| Brilliance | Noun | Bright, keen intellect |
| Brilliant | Adj | Great. Bright |
| Brisk | Adj | Lively. Energetic |

## -C-

| | | |
|---|---|---|
| Calculating | Adj | Shrewd, cunning |
| Callous | Adj | Insensitive |
| Camaraderie | Noun | Loyal friendship |
| | | |
| Candid | Adj | Frank. Open |
| Capable | Adj | Possessing the ability |
| Capitalize | Verb | Use to advantage |
| | | |
| Carefree | Adj | Without care |
| Careful | Adj | Attention to detail |
| Careless | Adj | Without attention to detail |
| | | |
| Catalyst | Noun | Spark/stimulus for great change |
| Categorical | Adj | Without boundaries |
| Categorize | Verb | To classify |
| | | |
| Ceiling | Noun | Top. Upper most |
| Censure | Verb | Condemn. Criticize |
| Certain | Adj | Correct or true |
| | | |
| Certainty | Noun | True without doubt |
| Chagrin | Noun | Disappointment in mind |
| Challenging | Adj | Prompting or stirring action |
| | | |
| Champion | Verb | Lead or uphold |
| Chaos | Noun | Unorganized activity |
| Charade | Noun | Deceit. Hidden |
| | | |
| Charisma | Noun | Magnetic leadership |
| Charismatic | Adj | Magnetic leadership |
| Charm | Verb | Appealing. Personable |
| | | |
| Charmer | Noun | Someone with charm, appeal |
| Charming | Adj | Greatly appealing or personable |
| Chastise | Verb | Censure or punish |

| Cheerful | Adj | Happy. Gay |
| Circumvent | Verb | Go around |
| Clairvoyance | Noun | Extraordinary perceptive powers |
| | | |
| Clairvoyant | Adj | Extraordinarily perceptive |
| Clarity | Noun | Clear. Lucid |
| Clear-cut | Adj | Clear. Not ambiguous |
| | | |
| Clear-headed | Adj | Clear knowledge |
| Clear-sighted | Adj | Clear, understanding thought |
| Clear-witted | Adj | Clear, keen mental faculty |
| | | |
| Clever | Adj | Skillful wit |
| Cleverness | Noun | Quick, clever wit |
| Cocksure | Adj | Overconfident, sure |
| | | |
| Cocky | Adj | Too self-confident |
| Coerce | Verb | Compel through strength |
| Cogent | Adj | Convince through strength |
| | | |
| Cogitate | Verb | Deep meditation, thought |
| Cogitation | Noun | Of deep thought |
| Cognizance | Noun | Knowledge. Information |
| | | |
| Cohere | Verb | Hold together |
| Coherence | Noun | Consistency of mind, thought |
| Coherent | Adj | Holding or remaining together |
| | | |
| Cohesion | Noun | Hold together firmly |
| Cohesive | Adj | Held together firmly |
| Cohort | Noun | Associate. Companion |
| | | |
| Cold | Adj | Lacking in humanity |
| Collapse | Verb | Fall or fail |
| Colorless | Adj | Lacking in personality |
| | | |
| Colossal | Adj | Exceptionally large |
| Comfort | Noun | Caring aid |
| Commend | Verb | To merit commendation |
| | | |
| Commendation | Noun | Complimentary merit |
| Commitment | Noun | Obligation |
| Commonplace | Noun | Ordinary or routine |

| | | |
|---|---|---|
| Common sense | Noun | Judgment with or without logic |
| Compassion | Noun | Humane sympathy |
| Compassionate | Adj | Humane sympathy |
| | | |
| Compatible | Adj | Agreeable. Be, fit together |
| Compel | Verb | To make unavoidable |
| Compelling | Adj | Demanding |
| | | |
| Competent | Adj/Noun | Capable, able |
| Competitive | Adj | Challenging. Competition |
| Competitor | Noun | One who challenges |
| | | |
| Complacency | Noun | Satisfied to a fault |
| Complacent | Adj | Satisfied to a fault |
| Complaisant | Adj | Overly obliging |
| | | |
| Complexity | Noun | Difficult. Complex |
| Complex | Adj | Hard to integrate or answer |
| Compliance | Noun | Comply. In accord |
| | | |
| Complicate | Verb | Add difficulty |
| Complicated | Adj | Difficult, complex |
| Compliment | Noun | Give recognition |
| | | |
| Comply | Verb | Adhere or conform |
| Comportment | Noun | Personal bearing |
| Composed | Adj | Calm. Under control |
| | | |
| Composure | Noun | Calmness |
| Comprehend | Verb | Understand |
| Comprehensible | Adj | Understandable |
| | | |
| Comprehension | Noun | To grasp, understand, know |
| Comprehensive | Adj | Extensive or inclusive |
| Compulsive | Adj | Uncontrollable urge |
| | | |
| Conceal | Verb | Cover. Hide. Omit |
| Concede | Verb | Give in. Accept. Agree |
| Conceivable | Adj | Imaginable in thought |
| | | |
| Conceive | Verb | To think up |
| Concentrate | Verb | Direct, control thought process |
| Concentrating | Adj | Focusing one's mental powers |

| | | |
|---|---|---|
| Conception | Noun | Mentally conceiving |
| Conceptive | Adj | Ability to mentally conceive |
| Conceptual | Adj | Mental grasp, conception |
| | | |
| Conceptualize | Verb | Mentally conceive, formulate |
| Concern | Noun | Of interest |
| Concise | Adj | Brief and exact |
| | | |
| Condemn | Verb | Find at fault |
| Condescend | Verb | To degrade, descend lower |
| Condescendence | Noun | Act of degrading. Patronize |
| | | |
| Condescending | Adj | Degrading |
| Confidence | Noun | Assured belief |
| Conflict | Noun | At opposition |
| | | |
| Conflicting | Adj | In opposition |
| Conform | Verb | In compliance, agreement |
| Conformance | Noun | Acceptable compliance |
| | | |
| Conformity | Noun | Be in compliance |
| Confront | Verb | Openly challenge |
| Confuse | Verb | Not in order |
| | | |
| Confusion | Noun | Mixed up |
| Confute | Verb | Refute. False. Useless |
| Congenial | Adj | Genial. Friendly |
| | | |
| Congruent | Adj | Agreement. Harmony |
| Congruity | Noun | In agreement. Harmony |
| Congruous | Adj | Harmonious agreement |
| | | |
| Conjecture | Noun | Assumption. Something assumed |
| Conscious | Adj | Knowing self-awareness |
| Consciousness | Noun | Self-awareness |
| | | |
| Consistent | Adj | Steady and regular |
| Consonance | Noun | Harmonious. Agreement |
| Consonant | Adj | Harmony. In accord |
| | | |
| Conspire | Verb | Plot, plan, act together |
| Constructive Imagination | Noun | Positive mental creativity |
| Consummate | Adj | Complete. Perfect |

| Contagious | Adj | Infectious. Spread to others |
| Contemplate | Verb | Deep thought. Ponder |
| Contempt | Noun | Having ill-feelings |
| | | |
| Contemptible | Adj | Ill-feelings |
| Contribute | Verb | Give. Provide. Assist |
| Contribution | Noun | To give, provide |
| | | |
| Contrive | Verb | Formulate with deep thought |
| Controversy | Noun | Debate. Dispute |
| Conventional | Adj | Standard. Routine |
| | | |
| Conversant | Adj | Knowledgeable |
| Converse | Verb | Talk. Communicate |
| Convey | Verb | Get meaning across |
| | | |
| Convincing | Adj | To win agreement |
| Cope | Verb | Able to handle, deal with |
| Cordial | Adj | Friendly and sociable |
| | | |
| Correct | Adj | Without error |
| Corrupt | Adj | Not pure. Improper |
| Corruption | Noun | Not pure. Improper conduct/action |
| | | |
| Courage | Noun | Strength/will power to overcome |
| Courageous | Adj | Displaying courage, bravery |
| Courteous | Adj | Consideration |
| | | |
| Courtesy | Noun | Considerate behavior |
| Cover-up | Noun | Hide. Not disclose |
| Craftiness | Noun | Sly, devious cunning |
| | | |
| Crafty | Adj | Sly. Cunning |
| Crass | Adj | Without intelligent decency |
| Create | Verb | Conceive. Originate |
| | | |
| Creative | Adj | Create. Originate. Invent |
| Creative Ability | Noun | Intellectual creative power |
| Creative Imagination | Noun | Intellectual creativeness |
| | | |
| Creativeness | Noun | Creative intellect |
| Creative Power | Noun | Ability to originate, create |
| Creative Thought | Noun | Mental ability to create |

| Creativity | Noun | Able to create/originate/invent |
| Credential | Noun | Reputation or supportive fact |
| Credibility | Noun | Believable |
| | | |
| Credible | Adj | Believed |
| Crimp | Verb | Hinder. Impede. Slow down |
| Crisis | Noun | Extremely important |
| | | |
| Crisp | Adj | Terse. Clear |
| Critical | Adj | Extremely important |
| Criticize | Verb | Announce faults |
| | | |
| Crucial | Adj | Critical. Important |
| Crude | Adj | Rough. Crass. Unrefined |
| Crusty | Adj | Ill-mannered. Rough |
| | | |
| Cultivate | Verb | Nurture. Ignite. Spur on |
| Cultivated | Adj | Well refined, developed |
| Cultured | Adj | Refined, polished manner |
| | | |
| Cumbersome | Adj | Hard to manage or wield |
| Cunning | Adj | Sharp, sly skill |
| Curiosity | Noun | In interest. Inquisitive |
| | | |
| Curious | Adj | Keenly interested. Inquisitive |
| Cursory | Adj | Brief view or interest |
| Curt | Adj | Abrupt and offensive |
| | | |
| Customary | Adj | Routinely. Commonly. Usually |
| Cynical | Adj | Unbelieving with bad attitude |

**-D-**

| Dabble | Verb | Superficial involvement |
| Daunt | Verb | Unnerve. Discourage. Dismay |
| Dauntless | Adj | Unnerving. Intimidating |
| | | |
| Debase | Verb | To lessen or diminish |
| Deception | Noun | Mislead. Trick |
| Deceptive | Adj | Mislead. Trick |
| | | |
| Decisive | Adj | Without doubt or question |
| Decorum | Noun | Respectable behavior or dress |
| Deduction | Noun | Evaluate with logic |

| | | |
|---|---|---|
| Deductive Power | Adj | Evaluate by logical reasoning |
| Deductive Power | Noun | Ability to logically reason |
| Deep-Thinking | Adj | Deep, profound intellect |
| Defect | Noun | Error. Fault |
| Defective | Adj | Having error or fault |
| Defiance | Noun | Go against. Oppose |
| Defiant | Adj | Against. Oppose |
| Deficient | Adj | Shortcoming. Missing something |
| Degradation | Noun | Belittle. Lower. Degrade |
| Degrade | Verb | Lower. Belittle. Take away |
| Deliberation | Adj | Full, due consideration |
| Delude | Verb | Mislead. Trick. Deceive |
| Delve | Verb | Dig into. Research |
| Demean | Verb | Belittle. Lessen. Lower |
| Demeanor | Noun | Behavior |
| Demerit | Noun | Without merit, good |
| Demise | Noun | Loss. Decline. Failure |
| Demoralize | Verb | Great drop in morale |
| Demure | Adj | Shy. Modest |
| Denounce | Verb | Publicly criticize |
| Dense | Adj | Slow to pick up, comprehend |
| Depend | Verb | Rely on |
| Dependable | Adj | Reliable. Trustworthy |
| Dependence | Noun | Dependent or relied upon |
| Dependency | Noun | Something needing assistance |
| Dependent | Adj | Depend or rely on |
| Depress | Verb | Disheartened. Discourage |
| Depressed | Adj | Disheartened. Sad |
| Deprive | Verb | Do without |
| Derelict | Adj | Improper attention |
| Dereliction | Noun | Knowing improper attention |
| Despair | Verb | Lose hope. Give up |
| Despairing | Adj | Without hope. Despair |

| | | |
|---|---|---|
| Desperate | Adj | Without hope. Despair |
| Despond | Verb | Become without hope |
| Despondency | Noun | Being without hope |
| | | |
| Despondent | Adj | Great hopelessness |
| Destroy | Verb | Ruin. Tear down |
| Deter | Verb | To thwart or turn |
| | | |
| Deteriorate | Verb | Become less, lower |
| Determination | Noun | Firm resolve, conviction |
| Determined | Adj | Firmly committed |
| | | |
| Detriment | Noun | Ill-being. To damage |
| Detrimental | Adj | Damaging. Ill-being |
| Deviant | Adj | Change downward or for worse |
| | | |
| Deviate | Adj/Noun/Verb | Changing from the normal |
| Devious | Adj | Conniving, sly deviation |
| Devise | Verb | Originate. Invent |
| | | |
| Devoted | Adj | Loyal. Faithful |
| Dexterity | Noun | Mental or physical agility |
| Dexterous | Adj | Mental or physical agility |
| | | |
| Diction | Noun | Verbally clear, correct |
| Diehard | Noun | Decidedly against something |
| Die-hard | Adj | Positively against something |
| | | |
| Differentiate | Verb | Distinguish difference |
| Difficult | Adj | Hard. Demanding |
| Difficulty | Noun | Being hard, demanding |
| | | |
| Diffident | Adj | Self-confident |
| Dignity | Noun | High esteem. Praiseworthy |
| Dilute | Verb | Lessen. Reduce |
| | | |
| Diminish | Verb | To lessen or reduce |
| Diplomacy | Noun | Skillfully tactful |
| Diplomat | Noun | Someone skillfully tactful |
| | | |
| Diplomatic | Adj | Using tact with skill |
| Dire | Adj | Desperate. Distressful |
| Disaccord | Verb | Not in accord or agreement |

| | | |
|---|---|---|
| Disadvantage | Noun | Not to advantage |
| Disagree | Verb | Against. Opposed |
| Disagreeable | Adj | Being against or opposed |
| | | |
| Disagreement | Noun | At opposition. Against |
| Disappoint | Verb | Not to expectation, as expected |
| Disappointing | Adj | Not as expected |
| | | |
| Disappointment | Noun | To disappoint, not succeed |
| Disaster | Noun | Great disorder |
| Discern | Verb | Skillful understanding/judgment |
| | | |
| Discernible | Adj | Mentally recognize & separate |
| Discerning | Adj | Skillful understanding/judgment |
| Discipline | Noun | Self-control. Enforced control |
| | | |
| Discontent | Noun | Not content or pleased |
| Discord | Noun/Verb | Failure to get along |
| Discourse | Adj | Verbally communicating |
| | | |
| Discourteous | Adj | Not courteous. Not kind |
| Discredit | Noun | Without credit, belief |
| Discreet | Adj | Prudent judgment |
| | | |
| Discriminating | Adj | Recognize. Distinguish difference |
| Disdain | Noun/Verb | Low in regard. At distance |
| Disdainful | Adj | Showing low regard |
| | | |
| Disfavor | Noun | Not in favor, good standing |
| Disgruntle | Verb | Not happy, satisfied |
| Disgust | Verb | Sharp disapproval. Dislike |
| | | |
| Disgust | Noun | A sharp disapproval, dislike |
| Disillusion | Noun | Not content, satisfied |
| Disinclined | Adj | Not approving or agreeing |
| | | |
| Disloyal | Adj | Not loyal, trustworthy |
| Disloyalty | Noun | Without loyalty |
| Dismay | Noun/Verb | Disheartened. Disappointed |
| | | |
| Disorder | Noun | Not in order |
| Disparity | Noun | A difference, fault |
| Dispassionate | Adj | Without passion, personal feeling |

| | | |
|---|---|---|
| Dispute | Verb | Disagreement |
| Disregard | Verb | Without regard or attention |
| Disreputable | Adj | Bad reputation |
| | | |
| Disrepute | Noun | Low reputation |
| Disrespect | Noun/Verb | Without respect |
| Disrupt | Verb | Break up or apart |
| | | |
| Disruptive | Adj | Be out of order, routine |
| Dissatisfaction | Noun | Not satisfied, pleased |
| Dissatisfied | Adj | Not satisfied |
| | | |
| Dissatisfy | Verb | Not satisfying |
| Dissension | Noun | Not in agreement |
| Dissent | Noun/Verb | Not in agreement |
| | | |
| Dissenter | Noun | Someone who disagrees |
| Distinguished | Adj | With distinction. High esteem |
| Distort | Verb | Make cloudy, unclear, uncertain |
| | | |
| Diverse | Adj | Varied. Multi-faceted |
| Docile | Adj | Passive. Highly receptive |
| Dodge | Verb | To go around. Evade |
| | | |
| Dominant | Adj | Commanding or controlling |
| Dominate | Verb | To command or control over |
| Domineering | Adj | Prevail over, above |
| | | |
| Drabber | Adj | Dull. Not lively |
| Dramatic | Adj | Extreme effect |
| Drastic | Adj | Major effect. Extreme. Harsh |
| | | |
| Drive | Noun | Spur to action. Push. Urge |
| Drudge | Verb | Routine, recurring dull work |
| Drudging | Adj | Being routine and dull |
| | | |
| Dubious | Adj | Questionable. Doubtful |
| Dull | Adj | Not mentally quick, perceptive |
| Dullness | Noun | Not mentally quick, perceptive |
| | | |
| Durable | Adj | Long lasting without change |
| Duress | Noun | Under great pressure or strain |
| Dwindle | Verb | Continued decline |
| Dynamic | Adj | Powerful. Forceful |

## -E-

| | | |
|---|---|---|
| Eager | Adj | Ready. Zealous |
| Eager Beaver | Noun | Ready volunteer |
| Eagerness | Noun | Being ready, enthusiastic |
| | | |
| Earnest | Noun | Sincere. Serious |
| Easygoing | Adj | Carefree. Little effort |
| Ebb | Noun/Verb | To recede. Diminish |
| | | |
| Eccentric | Adj | Vary from norm, standard |
| Edit | Verb | Go over. Review |
| Editorialize | Verb | Communicate own opinion |
| | | |
| Educable | Adj | Able to learn |
| Educate | Verb | Teach |
| Educated | Adj | Advanced education |
| | | |
| Educator | Noun | A teacher |
| Effective | Adj | Obtain results. Satisfactory |
| Effervesce | Verb | Lively. Zestful |
| | | |
| Effervescent | Adj | Liveliness. Zest. Zeal |
| Effete | Adj | Old. Obsolete |
| Efficiency | Noun | Doing without needless waste |
| | | |
| Efficient | Adj | Without needless loss, waste |
| Effort | Noun | Attempt. Try |
| Effortless | Adj | Without effort, attempt |
| | | |
| Ego | Noun | Self-esteem |
| Egocentric | Adj | Concerned with one's self |
| Egoism | Noun | Overly interested in one's self |
| | | |
| Egoist | Noun | An ego person |
| Egotism | Noun | Overly self-centered |
| Elaborate | Adj | Go over in great detail |
| | | |
| Elated | Adj | Elevated, high in thought |
| Elegance | Noun | Cultured. Respectable |
| Elegant | Adj | Greatly cultured, respectable |
| | | |
| Elemental | Adj | Basic. Fundamental |
| Elementary | Adj | Basic elements |
| Elevated | Adj | Raised. Lifted |

| | | |
|---|---|---|
| Elicit | Verb | Bring forward or out |
| Eloquence | Noun | Persuasive, fluent communications |
| Elucidate | Verb | Make clear, lucid |
| | | |
| Elude | Verb | Avoid. Escape |
| Elusive | Adj | Avoid attention. Escape |
| Embitter | Verb | Bitter, harsh |
| | | |
| Embodiment | Noun | To encompass, embody something |
| Emerge | Verb | Come to view, focus |
| Embody | Verb | Encompass, incorporate, include |
| | | |
| Eminent | Adj | Be, stand above |
| Emotion | Noun | Mental condition or state |
| Emotional | Adj | Expressed emotion |
| | | |
| Empathetic | Adj | Humanely sensitive |
| Empathic | Adj | Exhibiting empathy |
| Empathize | Verb | Being humanely sensitive |
| | | |
| Empathy | Noun | Humanely sensitive |
| Emphasize | Verb | Point out with strong attention |
| Emphatic | Adj | Express actively and zealously |
| | | |
| Employ | Verb | Use. Occupy |
| Emulate | Verb | Imitate. Try to copy |
| Emulation | Noun | To imitate, copy, duplicate |
| | | |
| Enable | Verb | Make able, ready |
| Enchant | Verb | Charm. Entice |
| Enchantment | Noun | Charmed. Enticing |
| | | |
| Encourage | Verb | Prompt. Spur on |
| Encouragement | Noun | Prompting. Spurring |
| Encouraging | Adj | To encourage or prompt |
| | | |
| Encumber | Verb | Burden. Weigh down |
| Encumbrance | Noun | Being burdened |
| Endeavor | Noun/Verb | Try. Attempt |
| | | |
| Endless | Adj | Without end. Unending |
| Endurable | Adj | Able to last |
| Endurance | Noun | To last or hold up |

| Endure | Verb | To last, hold up |
| Energetic | Adj | Zeal, vim, vigor |
| Energize | Verb | Make energetic |
| | | |
| Energy | Noun | Having zeal, vim, and vigor |
| Enervate | Adj/Verb | Without vim, vigor, vitality |
| Enforce | Verb | Give force. To back |
| | | |
| Engaging | Adj | Attracting. Pleasant |
| Engender | Verb | Initiate. Foster. Spur |
| Engrossing | Adj | Engaging. Involving |
| | | |
| Enhance | Verb | Help. Promote. Add to |
| Enigma | Noun | Confusing, hard to understand |
| Enjoy | Verb | Like. Please |
| | | |
| Enjoyment | Noun | Being at joy. Pleasing |
| Enlighten | Verb | Bring to light. Inform |
| Enlightened | Adj | Brought to light. Informed |
| | | |
| Enlightenment | Noun | To enlighten |
| Enmity | Noun | Deep, bad feeling or will |
| Enormous | Adj | Great amount, size |
| | | |
| Enrage | Verb | Angry. Furious |
| Enrich | Verb | Add, contribute, or give to |
| Enterprise | Noun | Task or tasking. Project |
| | | |
| Enterprising | Adj | Energetic, vigorous, and ready |
| Entertain Ideas | Verb | Open to suggestion, thought |
| Enthuse | Verb | Inspire. Excite |
| | | |
| Enthusiasm | Noun | Inspiring. Exciting |
| Enthusiast | Noun | Someone with enthusiasm |
| Enthusiastic | Adj | Being enthused |
| | | |
| Entice | Verb | Skillfully tempt or excite |
| Entrust | Verb | To trust |
| Enunciate | Verb | Verbal dexterity and clarity |
| | | |
| Enviable | Adj | Having worthy qualities |
| Envious | Adj | Possessing worthy qualities |
| Envision | Verb | See, think within |

| | | |
|---|---|---|
| Epitome | Noun | Best. Ideal example |
| Epitomize | Verb | Idealize. Representative |
| Equable | Adj | Even. Consistent |
| | | |
| Equality | Noun | Equal. On par. Even |
| Equitable | Adj | Being even, consistent |
| Equivocal | Adj | Not definite, certain |
| | | |
| Equivocate | Verb | False. Vague |
| Eradicate | Verb | End. Finish off |
| Erode | Verb | Wear away. Tear down |
| | | |
| Erosive | Adj | Able to erode |
| Errant | Adj | Stray. Wander |
| Erratic | Adj | Not regular, consistent |
| | | |
| Erroneous | Adj | Error. Mistake |
| Error | Noun | Wrong. Incorrect. Not right/true |
| Erudite | Adj | Learned. Skilled |
| | | |
| Erudition | Noun | Highly learned, skilled |
| Erupt | Verb | Burst out, forward |
| Escalate | Verb | Heighten. Increase |
| | | |
| Eschew | Verb | Shun. Go around |
| Esprit de corps | Noun | Strong common spirit or bond |
| Essential | Adj | Mandatory part or ingredient |
| | | |
| Establish | Verb | Bring into being |
| Esteem | Noun | High regard. Honored |
| Ethic | Noun | Moral concepts or views |
| | | |
| Ethical | Adj | In accord, conformance |
| Etiquette | Noun | Social conduct |
| Euphoria | Noun | High in feeling |
| | | |
| Evasive | Adj | Evading. Elusive |
| Exacerbate | Verb | Increase in harshness, bitterness |
| Exact | Adj | Precise. Without error |
| | | |
| Exacting | Adj | Demanding. Correctness |
| Exaggerate | Verb | False or artificial largeness |
| Exalt | Verb | Favorable rise or raise |

| | | |
|---|---|---|
| Exanimate | Adj | Without spirit |
| Exceed | Verb | Go beyond. Surpass |
| Exceeding | Adj | Going beyond. Surpassing |
| | | |
| Excel | Verb | Surpass. Succeed |
| Excellence | Noun | High quality |
| Excellent | Adj | First rate. Top quality |
| | | |
| Exceptional | Adj | Very top quality |
| Excessive | Adj | More than needed, required |
| Excitable | Adj | Capable of arousing |
| | | |
| Excite | Verb | Arouse. Move to action |
| Excitement | Noun | Aroused. Moved to action |
| Exciter | Noun | One who excites |
| | | |
| Exciting | Adj | Arousing. Stimulating |
| Exclusive | Adj | Strictly limited |
| Excuse | Noun | Reason. Explanation |
| | | |
| Exemplary | Adj | Excellent. Finest quality |
| Exemplify | Verb | Embody. An example |
| Exhort | Verb | Incite. Urge |
| | | |
| Exonerate | Verb | Clear. Free |
| Exorbitance | Noun | Being exorbitant, in excess |
| Exorbitant | Adj | Too much. Excess |
| | | |
| Expand | Verb | Increase. Grow |
| Expectation | Noun | Anticipate. Look forward |
| Expedience | Noun | Speed-up |
| | | |
| Expediency | Noun | Speed-up. Expedient |
| Expedient | Adj | Easiest choice |
| Expedite | Verb | Proceed immediately |
| | | |
| Expeditious | Adj | To expedite, cause action |
| Experience | Noun | Learned earlier |
| Experienced | Adj | Knowledgeable. Skillful |
| | | |
| Expert | Adj | Most experienced or skilled |
| Expertise | Noun | Possessing experience or skill |
| Explicit | Adj | Not ambiguous. Exact |

| | | |
|---|---|---|
| Exploit | Verb | Make use of |
| Explore | Verb | Check into. Investigate |
| Explosive | Adj | Capable or erupting |
| | | |
| Expostulate | Verb | Consider. Evaluate |
| Expound | Verb | Explain. Clarify. Put forth |
| Extensive | Adj | To great extent |
| | | |
| Extenuate | Verb | Reduce. Lessen |
| Extra | Adj | More. Additional |
| Extraneous | Adj | Extra. More than enough |
| | | |
| Extraordinary | Adj | Extra to, or above ordinary |
| Extravagant | Adj | More than necessary, required |
| Extreme | Adj | Beyond reasonable |
| | | |
| Exuberance | Noun | Being exuberant, enthused |
| Exuberant | Adj | Enthused. Lively. Zealous |
| Exultant | Adj | Extreme joy, high thrill |
| Eyesore | Noun | Repulsive to see |

**-F-**

| | | |
|---|---|---|
| Fabricate | Verb | Make. Make up |
| Fabulous | Adj | Great almost beyond belief |
| Facetious | Adj | Unsuccessful wit |
| | | |
| Facile | Adj | Superficial. Without substance |
| Facilitate | Verb | Aid. Assist |
| Facility | Noun | Aptitude. Ability. Skill |
| | | |
| Factual | Adj | Truthful. Actual |
| Faculties | Noun | Possessed ability or capacity |
| Faculty | Noun | Possessed skill, ability |
| | | |
| Fade | Verb | Decrease, lessen with time |
| Fail | Verb | Without success or gain |
| Failure | Noun | Perform without success |
| | | |
| Fair | Adj | Without bias or prejudice |
| Fair-minded | Adj | Minded without bias or prejudice |
| Fair play | Noun | Equal and fair |

**144**

| | | |
|---|---|---|
| Fair-spoken | Adj | Light or soft spoken |
| Faith | Noun | Belief. Believe in |
| Faithful | Adj | True in faith |
| | | |
| Faithless | Adj | Without truth or faith |
| Fake | Noun/Verb | Impostor. Not true |
| False | Adj | Not true or correct |
| | | |
| Falsify | Verb | Make untrue or incorrect |
| Falsity | Noun | At or being false |
| Falter | Verb | Hesitate. Fall short |
| | | |
| Fantastic | Adj | Great. Almost beyond belief |
| Farcical | Adj | Ridiculous. Laughable |
| Farfetched | Adj | Far out. Hard to believe |
| | | |
| Far-reaching | Adj | Wide or long reaching |
| Farseeing | Adj | See far ahead |
| Farsighted | Adj | See or plan far ahead |
| | | |
| Fascinating | Adj | Enchanting. Engaging |
| Fascination | Noun | Being enchanted |
| Fastidious | Adj | Overly demanding |
| | | |
| Fatigue | Noun | Worn down or out |
| Fatuity | Noun | Extremely simple |
| Fatuous | Adj | Simple. Inane |
| | | |
| Fault | Noun | Error. Wrong. Fail |
| Faultfinding | Adj/Noun | Predetermined to find fault |
| Faultless | Adj | Without fault or wrong |
| | | |
| Faulty | Adj | Having fault, error |
| Favorable | Adj | Agreeable. Approving |
| Favoritism | Noun | Showing bias or favor |
| | | |
| Fearful | Adj | In fear from danger |
| Fearless | Adj | Without fear. Bold |
| Feasible | Adj | Allowable. Acceptable |
| | | |
| Feat | Noun | Good or great deed or act |
| Feckless | Adj | Without responsibility |
| Fecund | Adj | Fertile & productive intelligence |

| | | |
|---|---|---|
| Feeble | Adj | Weak. Frail |
| Feebleminded | Adj | Mentally lacking, deficient |
| Feeling | Adj | Emotion. Belief |
| | | |
| Feisty | Adj | Anxious. Exuberant |
| Felicitous | Adj | Talk with poise. Suitable |
| Felicity | Noun | Cheerful. Happy |
| | | |
| Fellowship | Noun | Camaraderie. Friendship |
| Fend | Verb | Defend. Do without assistance |
| Fertile | Adj | Reservoir of ability, thought |
| | | |
| Fertile Mind | Noun | Highly productive mind |
| Fervent | Adj | Feeling of friendly warmth |
| Fervor | Noun | Great passion, emotion |
| | | |
| Festive | Adj | Joyous. Happy. Active |
| Fetter | Noun | Restrain |
| Feud | Noun | Long-standing dislike, disagreement |
| | | |
| Feverish | Adj | At a hot pace |
| Fiasco | Noun | Utter failure |
| Fickle | Adj | Not consistent, constant, resolute |
| | | |
| Fiction | Noun | Not true or real |
| Fictitious | Adj | Being untrue or unreal |
| Fidelity | Noun | Faithful. In accord |
| | | |
| Fiduciary | Adj | State of high trust |
| Fierce | Adj | Intense, active hostility |
| Fiery | Adj | Hot, active emotion |
| | | |
| Figurehead | Noun | Not actual. In name only |
| Finagle | Verb | Deceit. False. Trick |
| Fine | Adj | Good. Excellent |
| | | |
| Finely | Adv | Extremely fine |
| Finesse | Noun | Mental skill, agility and ability |
| Fine-tune | Verb | Fine adjustment for best operation |
| | | |
| Finicky | Adj | Too exacting or petty |
| Finite | Adj | Limited. Not infinite |
| Firm | Adj | Resolute. Unmoving |

| | | |
|---|---|---|
| First | Noun | Top. Highest. Best |
| First class | Noun | Classed top, highest, or first |
| First-rate | Adj | First or top quality |
| | | |
| First-string | Adj | First-rate |
| Five-star | Adj | Best. Tops |
| Fizzle | Noun | Fade. Fail |
| | | |
| Flagged | Adj | Weak. Without zeal |
| Flagrant | Adj | Openly blatant, disagreeable |
| Flair | Noun | Special knack or skill. Ability |
| | | |
| Flappable | Adj | Not sure, confident |
| Flashy | Adj | Superficial. Words without deeds |
| Flaunt | Verb | Open defiance. Bold |
| | | |
| Flaw | Noun | Not correct or perfect |
| Fledgling | Noun | New. Not mature |
| Flexibility | Noun | Adaptability. Not rigid |
| | | |
| Flexible | Adj | Adaptable. Able to alter, change |
| Flimsy | Adj | Not firm, solid. Weak |
| Flip-flop | Noun | Not firm. Changes views, opinions |
| | | |
| Flop | Verb | Fail |
| Flounder | Verb | Hesitate. Lose way, direction |
| Flourish | Verb | Thrive. Excel |
| | | |
| Flout | Verb | Open defiance |
| Fluctuate | Verb | Move back and forth. Oscillate |
| Fluent | Adj | Skilled. Learned |
| | | |
| Fluid | Adj | Smooth flowing |
| Flunk | Verb | Fail. Flop |
| Fluster | Noun | Thwart. Discourage |
| | | |
| Flutter | Noun | Uncertain, non-directed motion |
| Focus | Noun | Center-in. Key in on |
| Foible | Noun | Fault. Error |
| | | |
| Foil | Verb | Stop. Prevent |
| Follower | Noun | One who follows. Not a leader |
| Folly | Noun | Foolish |

**147**

| | | |
|---|---|---|
| Foolhardy | Adj | Ill-advised |
| Foolish | Adj | Lack of proper judgment |
| Foolishness | Noun | Act of improper judgment |
| | | |
| Foolproof | Adj | Without chance of error, fault |
| Foot-dragging | Noun | Deliberate slowness |
| Foppish | Adj | Overly self-concerned, vain |
| | | |
| Forbidding | Adj | Refraining. Prohibiting |
| Force | Noun | Driving power, influence, strength |
| Forceful | Adj | Using force. Exerting pressure |
| | | |
| Forcible | Adj | Able to be forceful |
| Foremost | Adj | At the front, top |
| Foresee | Verb | See forward, ahead |
| | | |
| Foresight | Noun | See ahead. Plan ahead |
| Foresighted | Adj | Mentally see ahead, future |
| Foresightedness | Noun | Mentally see ahead, future |
| | | |
| Forestall | Verb | To stop or obstruct |
| Forfeit | Noun/Verb | Give up or away |
| Forget | Verb | Fail to remember |
| | | |
| Forgetful | Adj | Failing to remember |
| Forgive | Verb | To let pass. Excuse |
| Forgiveness | Noun | Letting pass. Excusing |
| | | |
| Forgiving | Adj | To forgive, overlook |
| Formality | Noun | Official procedure |
| Formalize | Verb | Make formal, official, complete |
| | | |
| Formative | Adj | Developing. Growing |
| Formidable | Adj | Very difficult, discouraging |
| Formless | Adj | Without form, order, or shape |
| | | |
| Formulate | Verb | Develop. Put together |
| Forte | Noun | Someone's best trait |
| Forthright | Adj | Direct. Frank. Open |
| | | |
| Fortify | Verb | To strengthen, build up |
| Fortitude | Noun | Mental strength and persistence |
| Fortuitous | Adj | By accident, chance |

| | | |
|---|---|---|
| Fortunate | Adj | Lucky. Favorable |
| Forum | Noun | Free discussion |
| Forward-looking | Adj | Look and plan ahead |
| | | |
| Foul-up | Noun | Botch. Bungle |
| Foundation | Noun | Base or founding frame |
| Founder | Verb | Fail. Fall. Decline |
| | | |
| Four-star | Adj | Top grade, quality |
| Fracas | Noun | Noisy confrontation |
| Fractious | Adj | Unruly. Difficult to control |
| | | |
| Fragile | Adj | Weak. Not strong. Frail |
| Fragment | Noun | A part or piece of something |
| Fragmentary | Adj | Not complete. In parts |
| | | |
| Frail | Adj | Weak. Not strong |
| Frank | Adj | Open, forward manner |
| Frantic | Adj | Fast, unorganized pace |
| | | |
| Fraud | Noun | Knowing deceit |
| Fraudulent | Adj | Being or doing deceit |
| Free-spoken | Adj | Too openly candid. Speak freely |
| | | |
| Freethinker | Noun | Unrestrained, independent thinking |
| Freewill | Adj | Spontaneous. Unrestrained |
| Frenzy | Noun | Unthinking, violent action |
| | | |
| Frequent | Adj | Often. At great frequency |
| Fresh | Adj | New energy, vigor |
| Fret | Verb | Worry. Concerned |
| | | |
| Friction | Noun | Disagree. Oppose |
| Friendly | Adj | Amicable. Kind disposition |
| Friendly | Noun | Someone friendly |
| | | |
| Frivolous | Adj | Without importance or value |
| Fruitful | Adj | Productive. Successful |
| Fruitless | Adj | Non-productive. Without gain |
| | | |
| Frustrate | Verb | Thwart. Ineffective |
| Frustrated | Adj | Being thwarted or ineffective |
| Frustration | Noun | Being frustrated |

| | | |
|---|---|---|
| Fulfill | Verb | Accomplish. Complete |
| Full-fledged | Adj | Fully completed |
| Full-scale | Adj | Maximum limit or scale |
| | | |
| Fumble | Verb | Blunder. Clumsy |
| Fundamental | Adj | Basic, central elements |
| Furious | Adj | Great, heated anger |
| | | |
| Furor | Noun | Furious. Angry |
| Fury | Noun | Anger. Rage |
| Fussy | Adj | Finicky. Overly particular |
| | | |
| Futile | Adj | Worthless. Ineffective |
| Futility | Noun | Being futile |
| Fuzzy | Adj | Unclear. Not defined. Blurred |

**-G-**

| | | |
|---|---|---|
| Gab | Verb | Talk too much or without substance |
| Gall | Noun | Boldness. Fortitude |
| Gallant | Adj | Bold. Energetic. Daring |
| | | |
| Galling | Adj | Annoying. Boldness |
| Gamesmanship | Noun | Improper advantage or tactics |
| Garrulity | Noun | Idle, insignificant talk |
| | | |
| Garrulous | Adj | Too much idle, insignificant talk |
| Gauche | Adj | Social unacceptance |
| Generalize | Verb | Vague. Broadly defined |
| | | |
| Generate | Verb | Start. Instill |
| Generous | Adj | Kind. Giving. Caring |
| Genial | Adj | Kind, sympathetic personality |
| | | |
| Genius | Noun | Innate superior intellect |
| Genteel | Adj | Polite. Poised. Polished |
| Gentle | Adj | Soft, kind |
| | | |
| Genuine | Adj | Actual. Real |
| Gesture | Noun | Express by body movement |
| Gift | Noun | Talent |
| | | |
| Gifted | Adj | Great natural intellect |
| Gigantic | Adj | Extremely large, big |
| Gimmick | Noun | Shrewd device or scheme |

| | | |
|---|---|---|
| Gingerly | Adj | Tenderly, tentative |
| Gist | Noun | Major thought or idea. Overview |
| Glad | Adj | Happy. Cheerful. Gay |
| | | |
| Glaring | Adj | Glowing. Gross. Obvious |
| Glitch | Noun | Problem. Trouble. Setback |
| Gloom | Verb | Dark, bleak in outlook |
| | | |
| Gloomy | Adj | Bleak, depressed outlook |
| Glorify | Verb | Make or add glory |
| Glorious | Adj | Having, or being, glory |
| | | |
| Glory | Noun | High in honor, esteem |
| Glum | Adj | Bleak. Gloomy |
| Good | Adj/Noun | Favorable. Positive |
| | | |
| Good | Noun | Something favorable, positive |
| Good deal | Noun | Great amount |
| Good faith | Noun | Earnest in faith |
| | | |
| Good-for-nothing | Adj | Worth nothing. Without value |
| Good-hearted | Adj | Kind at heart. Kind hearted |
| Good-humored | Adj | Positive, cheerful manner |
| | | |
| Goodly | Adj | Great amount |
| Good-natured | Adj | Pleasant, helpful manner |
| Goodwill | Noun | Caring and friendly |
| | | |
| Gracious | Adj | Poised and charming. Thoughtful |
| Gradual | Adj | Changing, shifting over time |
| Grandeur | Noun | Being grand or grandiose |
| | | |
| Grandiose | Adj | Overly impressive. Showy. Grandeur |
| Gratify | Verb | Pleasing. Satisfying |
| Gratifying | Adj | Being pleasing, satisfying |
| | | |
| Grave | Adj | Serious with harmful consequences |
| Gravity | Noun | Significant in importance |
| Great | Adj | Large. Significant. Remarkable |
| | | |
| Greathearted | Adj | Generous and caring |
| Gregarious | Adj | Sociable |
| Grievance | Noun | Gripe. Complaint |

**151**

| Grieve | Verb | Grief. Sorrow |
| Grievous | Adj | Grave, serious, painful |
| Grim | Adj | Dark. Dreary. Unpleasant |
| | | |
| Grimace | Noun | Disapprove by facial gesture |
| Grind out | Verb | To do methodically, mundane |
| Gripe | Verb | Complain. Object |
| | | |
| Grit | Noun | Strong resolute courage |
| Gross | Adj | Bad. Flagrant |
| Grouse | Verb | Fault-finding. Complain |
| | | |
| Grudge | Noun | Get back or even |
| Grudging | Adj | With reluctance |
| Grueling | Adj | Extremely strenuous or punishing |
| | | |
| Guide | Noun/Verb | Oversee, supervise. Point the way |
| Guile | Noun | Crafty, cagey |
| Guileless | Adj | Without guile |
| | | |
| Guise | Noun | False cover, front |
| Gumption | Noun | Common sense. Courage |
| Gung ho | Adj | Unbound enthusiasm |
| Gusto | Noun | Zeal, vigor, vim |

**-H-**

| Habitual | Adj | Recurring as by habit |
| Half-baked | Adj | Improper planning, forethought |
| Half-cocked | Adj | Improper planning, forethought |
| | | |
| Halfhearted | Adj | Without full support |
| Half-scholar | Adj | Not learned, knowing |
| Half-truth | Noun | Deliberate less than full truth |
| | | |
| Halo effect | Noun | Over grading based on few traits |
| Hamper | Verb | Interfere. Impede. Obstruct |
| Hands-on | Adj | Do physically. First hand |
| | | |
| Haphazard | Adj/Noun | Without plan. By chance |
| Hapless | Adj | Happen without luck |
| Happenstance | Noun | By chance. Haphazard |

| | | |
|---|---|---|
| Happy-go-lucky | Adj | Not properly concerned, caring |
| Harass | Verb | Continued bothering, troubling |
| Hard-and-fast | Adj | Firm. Fixed. Unyielding |
| | | |
| Hard-handed | Adj | Overly strict, firm |
| Hardheaded | Adj | Unrelenting. Firm. Stubborn |
| Hard-hearted | Adj | Without humane concern, sympathy |
| | | |
| Hard-nosed | Adj | Unrelenting. Firm. Stubborn |
| Hard put | Adj | With great difficulty |
| Hard-set | Adj | Unrelenting. Firm |
| | | |
| Hard-shell | Adj | Not giving or compromising |
| Hardship | Noun | Great difficulty. Suffering |
| Harm | Noun/Verb | Cause damage, danger, hurt |
| | | |
| Harmless | Adj | Without harm, damage, danger |
| Harmonious | Adj | Be in harmony |
| Harmony | Noun | Get along. No friction |
| | | |
| Harsh | Adj | Severe. Coarse. Rough |
| Hasten | Verb | Speed up. Quicken |
| Hasty | Adj | Hurried. Quick. Fast |
| | | |
| Hatred | Noun | To hate. Extreme dislike |
| Headlong | Adj | Without delay, hesitation |
| Headway | Noun | Gain. Progress |
| | | |
| Headwork | Noun | Mental work. Think. Ponder |
| Hearsay | Noun | Not sure, proven fact |
| Heartfelt | Adj | In sincere sympathy |
| | | |
| Heartless | Adj | Without heart, compassion |
| Hearty | Adj/Noun | Full. Complete. Sincere |
| Heavy-handed | Adj | Stern. Harsh. Overly demanding |
| | | |
| Heavyhearted | Adj | Deepest sympathy. Deep felt |
| Heckle | Verb | Antagonize. Annoy. Impede |
| Hectic | Adj | Frantic. Fast-paced |
| | | |
| Heed | Noun | To pay attention. Note |
| Heedful | Adj | To heed, take notice |
| Heedless | Adj | Without attention or heed |

| | | |
|---|---|---|
| Helpless | Adj | Without help, defense, assistance |
| Helpful | Adj | To assist, help. Cooperate |
| Heritage | Noun | Handed down over time |
| | | |
| Herky-jerky | Adj | Inconsistent. Fluctuating |
| Hero | Noun | Held in highest esteem, thought |
| Hidden | Adj | Not shown. Out of sight |
| | | |
| Hierarchy | Noun | Those higher in command, control |
| Higher education | Noun | Advanced or college education |
| Higher learning | Noun | Advanced or college learning |
| | | |
| High-flying | Adj | Exuberant. Excessive |
| High-minded | Adj | High ideals, principles |
| High-powered | Adj | Powerful. Mighty |
| | | |
| High-pressure | Adj | Great pressure. Tense. Demanding |
| High-spirited | Adj | Enthusiastic, energetic spirit |
| High-strung | Adj | Temperamental. Over bearing |
| | | |
| High-toned | Adj | Arrogant. Elevated principles |
| Hinder | Verb | Impede. Hamper. Harm |
| Hindrance | Noun | To hinder, harm, hurt |
| | | |
| Hindsight | Noun | Apply after-the-fact knowledge |
| Hit-or-miss | Adj | Be by chance. At random |
| Hone | Verb | To fine tune |
| | | |
| Honest | Adj | True. Truthful. No deceit |
| Honesty | Noun | Being honest |
| Honor | Noun | High moral standard |
| | | |
| Honorable | Adj | Having, deserving honor |
| Hope | Verb | Strong, positive desire |
| Hopeful | Adj | Having hope |
| | | |
| Hopeless | Adj | Without hope, chance, desire |
| Horrendous | Adj | Extremely bad, distasteful |
| Hospitable | Adj | Friendly. Caring |
| | | |
| Hostile | Adj | Not hospitable. Very unfriendly |
| Hostility | Noun | Aggressive, hostile conduct |
| Huge | Adj | Great many. Sizable |

| | | |
|---|---|---|
| Humane | Adj | Caring, concerned compassion |
| Humanitarian | Noun | Someone humane in thought, action |
| Humble | Adj | Submissive. Subordinate one's self |
| | | |
| Humdrum | Adj | Without vim, vigor. Dull |
| Humiliate | Verb | To belittle or shame another |
| Humiliating | Adj | Demeaning. To humiliate |
| | | |
| Humility | Noun | Being humble |
| Humor | Noun | Pleasing character |
| Humorless | Adj | Without humor |
| | | |
| Humorous | Adj | Having humor, wit, charm |
| Hurdle | Verb | Go over. Not impeded |
| Hurried | Adj | Rushed. Hastened |
| | | |
| Hurtful | Adj | Doing hurt, harm, damage |
| Hygiene | Noun | Personal health, sanitation |
| Hyper | Adj | Easily agitated, excited |
| Hypercritical | Adj | Over critical |

-I-

| | | |
|---|---|---|
| Idea | Noun | A thought from the mind |
| Ideal | Adj | Perfect. Exact. Precise |
| Ideal | Noun | Envisioned or sought goal |
| | | |
| Idealist | Noun | Placing ideals ahead of reality |
| Idealistic | Adj | Concerning ideals |
| Idealize | Adj | Be ideal, representative |
| | | |
| Idle | Adj | Not busy. Not doing |
| Ignite | Verb | Fire up. Start. Motivate |
| Ignorance | Noun | Having lack of knowledge |
| | | |
| Ignorant | Adj | Not knowledgeable |
| Ignore | Verb | Avoid |
| Ill-advised | Adj | Not properly advised |
| | | |
| Illaudable | Adj | Not laudable or praised |
| Illegal | Adj | Not legal or lawful |
| Illegible | Adj | Not legible, readable |

**155**

| | | |
|---|---|---|
| Ill-fated | Adj | Predetermined bad fate |
| Ill-gotten | Adj | Illegal or improperly gotten |
| Ill-humored | Adj | Without humor |
| | | |
| Illicit | Adj | Illegal |
| Illiteracy | Noun | Not literate. Not read or write |
| Illiterate | Adj | Not knowing, educated |
| | | |
| Ill-mannered | Adj | Bad manners. Crude |
| Ill-natured | Adj | Bad attitude or nature |
| Illogic | Noun | Being without logic |
| | | |
| Illogical | Adj | Not logical, reasonable |
| Illustrate | Verb | To show or make clear |
| Illustrious | Adj | Commendable actions |
| | | |
| Image | Verb | Visualize. See in mind |
| Imagine | Verb | Mental picture, image |
| Imaginable | Adj | Able to imagine or visualize |
| | | |
| Imaginary | Adj | Not real or fact |
| Imagination | Noun/Adj | Imagine, visualize in the mind |
| Imaginative | Adj | Unreal. Untrue |
| | | |
| Imbalance | Noun | Not proper balance |
| Imitate | Verb | Copy. Duplicate |
| Imitation | Noun | Not real, fact, true |
| | | |
| Immaculate | Adj | Without flaw. Pure |
| Immature | Adj | Not mature or completely developed |
| Immeasurable | Adj | Beyond measure |
| | | |
| Immediacy | Noun | Being immediate |
| Immense | Adj | Vast, huge. Large |
| Immensity | Noun | Being immense |
| | | |
| Immerge | Verb | Immerse. Throw into completely |
| Immerse | Verb | Become totally absorbed, involved |
| Immobile | Adj | Not mobile or movable. Fixed |
| | | |
| Immobilize | Verb | Make immobile or fixed |
| Immoderate | Adj | Not moderate. Excess. Excessive |
| Immoral | Adj | Not moral. Against moral values |

| | | |
|---|---|---|
| Immovable | Adj | Not movable. Fixed |
| Impair | Verb | Restrict, restrain, hinder |
| Imparity | Noun | Inequity. Uneven |
| | | |
| Impart | Verb | To pass along. Communicate |
| Impartial | Adj | Equal. Fair. No prejudice or bias |
| Impassioned | Adj | Great passion, feeling |
| | | |
| Impatience | Noun | Not patient. Anxious |
| Impatient | Adj | Not patient. Anxious |
| Impeccable | Adj | Without flaw or fault. Unblemished |
| | | |
| Impede | Verb | Interfere. Harm or slow |
| Impel | Verb | Push or force forward |
| Impenetrable | Adj | Unable to penetrate, enter |
| | | |
| Imperfect | Adj | Not perfect. Flawed. Error |
| Imperfection | Noun | Being not perfect. Flawed |
| Impersonal | Adj | Not personal. Not open, friendly |
| | | |
| Impersonalize | Verb | Make impersonal |
| Impertinence | Noun | Be impertinent |
| Impertinent | Adj | Not appropriate or relevant |
| | | |
| Impervious | Adj | Unable to penetrate, enter |
| Impetuous | Adj | Impulsive. Acting on emotion |
| Impetus | Noun | Motivating, or driving force |
| | | |
| Impious | Adj | Improper respect |
| Implicit | Adj | Exact, without question |
| Impolite | Adj | Not polite or socially acceptable |
| | | |
| Imponderable | Adj | Beyond question or evaluation |
| Importance | Noun | Being important |
| Important | Adj | Of considerable value |
| | | |
| Impose | Verb | Force or bring pressure to |
| Imposing | Adj | Impressively striking |
| Impossible | Adj | Not possible or capable |
| | | |
| Impossibility | Noun | To be impossible. Not capable |
| Impotent | Adj | Not potent. Unable |
| Impracticable | Adj | Not practicable, feasible |

| | | |
|---|---|---|
| Impractical | Adj | Not practical, prudent or sensible |
| Imprecise | Adj | Not precise, correct. Ambiguous |
| Impress | Verb | Influence. Leave mark. Impact |
| | | |
| Impressible | Adj | Able to impress |
| Impression | Noun | To influence or impact opinion |
| Impressionable | Adj | Easily impressed or influenced |
| | | |
| Improbable | Adj | Unlikely. Not probable |
| Impromptu | Adj | Without prior plan |
| Improper | Adj | Not proper or correct |
| | | |
| Impropriety | Noun | Being or doing improper |
| Improve | Verb | To make better |
| Improvement | Noun | Making or doing better |
| | | |
| Improvisation | Noun | To improvise |
| Improvise | Verb | To make do. Impromptu |
| Imprudence | Noun | Not prudent, wise |
| | | |
| Imprudent | Adj | Not wise or judicious |
| Impudence | Noun | Being impudent |
| Impudent | Adj | Contemptible. Bold. Not reserved |
| | | |
| Impugn | Verb | Aggressive, forceful attack |
| Impulsive | Adj | Act without thought |
| Impute | Verb | Accuse. Charge |
| | | |
| Inability | Noun | Not able, capable |
| Inaccuracy | Noun | Not accurate, correct |
| Inaccurate | Adj | Not accurate, correct |
| | | |
| Inaction | Noun | No action. Motionless |
| Inactive | Adj | Not active. Without movement |
| Inadequacy | Noun | Not adequate, sufficient |
| | | |
| Inadequate | Adj | Not adequate, sufficient |
| Inadvertence | Noun | By accident, chance. Not intended |
| Inadvertent | Adj | By accident, chance. Not intended |
| | | |
| Inadvisable | Adj | Not advised or recommended |
| Inane | Adj | Without substance or direction |
| Inappropriate | Adj | Not appropriate, acceptable |

**158**

| | | |
|---|---|---|
| Inapt | Adj | Not apt, suitable |
| Inaptitude | Noun | Lack of aptitude, ability |
| Inarticulate | Adj | Not clear, precise in expression |
| Inattention | Noun | Not giving proper attention |
| Inattentive | Adj | Not giving proper attention |
| Inborn | Adj | Born with. Natural |
| Inbred | Adj | Being in one's nature |
| Incalculable | Adj | Not able to calculate or determine |
| Incapable | Adj | Not capable, able |
| Incapacitate | Verb | Make not capable, able |
| Incapacity | Noun | Without capability or ability |
| Incentive | Noun | Something providing motive |
| Incertitude | Noun | Not certain, sure |
| Incisive | Adj | Most decisive, direct |
| Incite | Verb | Stimulate, move, urge |
| Incitement | Noun | Cause, arouse action, movement |
| Inclination | Noun | Personal character |
| Incline | Verb | Lean. Favor |
| Inclined | Adj | Leaning. Favoring |
| Incogitant | Adj | Without thought or consideration |
| Incoherent | Adj | Missing in coherence or presence |
| Incomparable | Adj | Not comparable |
| Incompatibility | Noun | Not able to get along, mix |
| Incompatible | Adj | Unable to get along, mix |
| Incompetence | Noun | Not having capability or capacity |
| Incompetent | Adj | Without capability or capacity |
| Incomplete | Adj | Not finished, complete |
| Incomprehensible | Adj | Not imaginable, believable |
| Incomprehension | Noun | Unable to understand, grasp |
| Inconceivable | Adj | Unable to convince, persuade |
| Inconclusive | Adj | Not conclusive, final, complete |
| Incongruous | Adj | Not in step, agreement |
| Inconsequent | Adj | Not planned, resulting from logic |

| | | |
|---|---|---|
| Inconsequential | Adj | Of little importance, matter |
| Inconsiderable | Adj | Of little value or worth |
| Inconsiderate | Adj | Not considerate of others |
| | | |
| Inconsistency | Noun | Being inconsistent |
| Inconsistent | Adj | Not constant, steady, same |
| Inconsonance | Noun | Not in agreement, accord |
| | | |
| Inconspicuous | Adj | Not visible, noticeable |
| Incontestable | Adj | Without doubt or question |
| Incontrovertible | Adj | Not changeable, questionable |
| | | |
| Inconvenience | Noun | Not convenient. Out of the way |
| Inconvenient | Adj | Out of the way |
| Incorrect | Adj | Not correct, accurate, true, right |
| | | |
| Incorrigible | Adj | Not manageable. Not changeable |
| Incredible | Adj | Almost beyond belief |
| Incurable | Adj | Not changeable, curable |
| | | |
| Indecision | Noun | Not decisive, resolute |
| Indecisive | Adj | Not decisive, final, complete |
| Indefectible | Adj | Without defect, fault, flaw |
| | | |
| Indefensible | Adj | Unable to defend, justify, excuse |
| Indefinable | Adj | Unable to define, clarify |
| Indefinite | Adj | Not definite or precise |
| | | |
| Independent | Adj | Along. Without assistance or aid |
| In-depth | Adj | Complete, comprehensive |
| Indestructible | Adj | Not able to destruct, destroy |
| | | |
| Indifference | Noun | Being indifferent |
| Indifferent | Adj | Not concerned, caring |
| Indignant | Adj | Showing indignation |
| | | |
| Indignation | Noun | Unjustified anger |
| Indignity | Noun | Without self-respect |
| Indirect | Adj | Not direct or straight |
| | | |
| Indiscernible | Adj | Not identifiable. Not clear |
| Indiscipline | Noun | Without discipline, control |
| Indiscreet | Adj | Not discreet. Too open |

| | | |
|---|---|---|
| Indiscretion | Noun | Not discreet, normal |
| Indiscriminate | Adj | Without logic, rhyme, reason |
| Indispensable | Adj | Not able to do/be without |
| Indisputable | Adj | Without question. Absolutely |
| Indistinct | Adj | Not clear, distinct |
| Indistinctive | Adj | Not distinct |
| Individualist | Noun | One going or standing along |
| Individuality | Noun | One's own character, self |
| Indoctrinate | Verb | Instruct, train in new areas |
| Indolent | Adj | Slow. Lazy |
| Induce | Verb | Indirect influence |
| Inducement | Noun | To induce, ignite |
| Indulge | Verb | Give in, submit |
| Indulgence | Noun | To indulge, submit |
| Indulgent | Adj | To indulge, submit |
| Indurate | Verb | Hard and fast. Unyielding |
| Industrious | Adj | Skillfully and productively active |
| Industry | Noun | Persistent pursuit |
| Ineffective | Adj | Not effective, or as expected |
| Ineffectual | Adj | Not effective, or as expected |
| Inefficacy | Noun | Without sufficient control, power |
| Inefficiency | Noun | Being inefficient |
| Inefficient | Adj | Not best use of resources |
| Ineligible | Adj | Not eligible, qualified |
| Ineloquent | Adj | Without eloquence |
| Inept | Adj | Not competent, fit |
| Ineptitude | Noun | Being inept |
| Inequality | Noun | Not equal, even |
| Inequitable | Adj | Not equitable, equal, even |
| Inequity | Noun | Not just, fair |
| Inerrant | Adj | Without error, fault, flaw |
| Inert | Adj | Not active. Slow |
| Inescapable | Adj | Unable to avoid, miss, omit |

| | | |
|---|---|---|
| Inevitable | Adj | No chance of avoiding |
| Inexact | Adj | Not exact, correct. Error |
| Inexcusable | Adj | Unable to excuse, overlook |
| | | |
| Inexhaustible | Adj | Unending. Without end |
| Inexorable | Adj | Unmoving. Relentless |
| Inexpedient | Adj | Not recommended, advisable |
| | | |
| Inexperience | Noun | Without experience, training |
| Inexpert | Adj | Not expert, trained, skilled |
| Inexplicable | Adj | Without explanation, reason |
| | | |
| Inexplicit | Adj | Not explicit, exact, correct |
| Inextinguishable | Adj | Unable to stop, end |
| Infallible | Adj | Not capable of mistake, error |
| | | |
| Infect | Verb | Communicate to, get into |
| Infectious | Adj | To infect by spreading |
| Inferior | Adj | Below standard, par |
| | | |
| Infinite | Adj | Without end. Unending |
| Infirm | Adj | Weak. Not strong or sound |
| Inflame | Verb | To agitate, excite |
| | | |
| Inflexible | Adj | Not movable, flexible. Rigid |
| Influence | Noun | Ability to control |
| Influential | Adj/Noun | To influence, control, power |
| | | |
| Informal | Adj | Not formal, official |
| Informative | Adj | Communicate information, knowledge |
| Informed | Adj | Knowing. Learned |
| | | |
| Infraction | Noun | Violation of rule, law |
| Infrastructure | Noun | Basic foundation or framework |
| Infrequent | Adj | Not frequent. Rare |
| | | |
| Infringe | Verb | Violate by entering, intruding |
| Infuriate | Verb | Make angry, mad |
| Infuse | Verb | Instill in someone, thing |
| | | |
| Ingenious | Adj | Original in something genius |
| Ingenuity | Noun | Genius in originating, devising |
| Ingenuous | Adj | Open. Not complex, complicated |

| | | |
|---|---|---|
| Ingrain | Verb | To instill, infuse. Put into |
| Ingrained | Adj | Deeply rooted within |
| Ingratitude | Noun | Not grateful in kind, return |
| | | |
| Inharmonious | Adj | Not getting along, fitting in |
| Inharmony | Noun | Not in harmony, accord, agreement |
| Inhibit | Verb | Mental restraint, reluctance |
| | | |
| Inhospitable | Adj | Not friendly |
| Inhumane | Adj | Not humane, caring |
| Inimical | Adj | Not friendly in nature, manner |
| | | |
| Inimitable | Adj | Not able to duplicate |
| Iniquity | Noun | Not just, fair. Biased |
| Initiate | Verb | To start, begin |
| | | |
| Initiative | Noun | Acting without guidance, direction |
| Injudicious | Adj | Not judicious or appropriate |
| Injustice | Noun | Without justice, fairness |
| | | |
| Innate | Adj | Possessed as natural, inner self |
| Innocent | Adj | Not wrong |
| Innovate | Verb | Originate new ways, means |
| | | |
| Innovation | Noun | Doing something new, better |
| Innovative | Adj | To innovate |
| Innuendo | Noun | Subtle hint. Infer indirectly |
| | | |
| Innumerable | Adj | Too many to number, count |
| Innumerous | Adj | Too many to number, count |
| Inopportune | Adj | Not opportune, convenient, timely |
| | | |
| Inordinate | Adj | Beyond expected limit |
| Inquisitive | Adj | Seek information. Ask questions |
| Insatiable | Adj | Unending appetite. Never satisfied |
| | | |
| Insecure | Adj | Not steady, secure |
| Insensibility | Noun | Not perceptive, aware, knowing |
| Insensible | Adj | Not sensible, reasonable |
| | | |
| Insensitive | Adj | Without feeling, caring |
| Insidious | Adj | Sly. Unsuspecting. Harmful |
| Insight | Noun | See into and through something |

| | | |
|---|---|---|
| Insightful | Adj | Mental understanding |
| Insignificance | Noun | Not significant or meaningful |
| Insignificant | Adj | Not significant or meaningful |
| | | |
| Insincere | Adj | Not sincere, honest, true |
| Insinuate | Verb | Subtle hint. Infer indirectly |
| Insipid | Adj | Dull and without interest |
| | | |
| Insolence | Noun | Being overbearing, contemptible |
| Insolent | Adj | Overbearing. Being in contempt |
| Insolvable | Adj | Without solution, answer |
| | | |
| Inspiration | Noun | Inspire others to do, move, act |
| Inspirational | Adj | Inspire. Influence |
| Inspire | Verb | Influence, prompt others to act |
| | | |
| Inspired | Adj | Possess inspirational traits |
| Inspiring | Adj | Affecting in, to inspire |
| Inspirit | Verb | Have spirit |
| | | |
| Instability | Noun | Not stable, sturdy, sound |
| Instantaneous | Adj | Without any delay |
| Instigate | Verb | To start, spur on or forward |
| | | |
| Instill | Verb | To place in or put in |
| Instinctive | Adj | Already known, within. Built in |
| Instrumental | Adj | A key or important ingredient |
| | | |
| Insubordinate | Adj | In violation of authority |
| Insubstantial | Adj | Not substantial, significant |
| Insufferable | Adj | Unable to tolerate |
| | | |
| Insufficient | Adj | Not sufficient enough |
| Insult | Verb | Openly offend |
| Insult | Noun | Open indignity |
| | | |
| Insuperable | Adj | Not able to overcome |
| Insupportable | Adj | Unable to support, defend |
| Insurgent | Adj | Opposed to authority |
| | | |
| Insurmountable | Adj | Not able to overcome |
| Intangible | Adj | Not tangible, touchable |
| Integral | Adj | Essential, necessary part |

| | | |
|---|---|---|
| Integrate | Verb | To bring together, combine |
| Integrative Power | Noun | Mental ability to sort, segregate |
| Integrity | Noun | In adherence. Abiding |
| | | |
| Intellect | Noun | Mental capacity, ability |
| Intellection | Noun | Power, reason of thought |
| Intellectual | Adj/Noun | Mental power. Intellect |
| | | |
| Intellectual Faculty | Noun | Mental, reasoning capability |
| Intellectual Grasp | Noun | Understand mentally |
| Intellectual Power | Noun | Mental ability |
| | | |
| Intellectual Weakness | Noun | Mentally lacking, deficient |
| Intelligence | Noun | Mental ability, capacity |
| Intelligent | Adj | High mental ability, capacity |
| | | |
| Intense | Adj | Extreme, extensive |
| Intercede | Verb | To come between |
| Interested | Adj | Curious, attentive, involved |
| | | |
| Interfere | Verb | Hinder, harm by entering |
| Interference | Noun | Interfere, obstruct, hinder |
| Interfuse | Verb | Fuse together. Bind |
| | | |
| Intermittent | Adj | Not regular, constant |
| Interpose | Verb | Place or put between |
| Interpret | Verb | Explain. Understand |
| | | |
| Interrogate | Verb | Question at length |
| Interrupt | Verb | To break, cease, interfere |
| Intestinal Fortitude | Noun | Internal courage |
| | | |
| Intimidate | Verb | Threaten |
| Intolerable | Adj | Not tolerable, cannot stand |
| Intolerance | Noun | Not tolerant, bearable |
| | | |
| Intolerant | Adj | Not tolerable, able to stand |
| Intractable | Adj | Hard to control, manage |
| Intransigent | Adj | Without giving, compromising |
| | | |
| Intrepid | Adj | Without fear. Bold |
| Intricate | Adj | Complex. Complicated |
| Intrigue | Verb | Mind-catching. Suspenseful |

| | | |
|---|---|---|
| Intrinsic | Adj | Inherent, within |
| Introvert | Verb | Inward. Not open, outward |
| Introvert | Noun | Someone not open, outward |
| | | |
| Intrude | Verb | Interfere |
| Intrusion | Noun | To intrude, interfere |
| Intrusive | Adj | Intruding, interfering |
| | | |
| Intuitive | Adj | Insight. Intuition |
| Inundate | Verb | Cover completely. Overwhelm |
| Invalid | Adj | Not valid, fact, true, good |
| | | |
| Invalidity | Noun | Not valid. Invalid |
| Invaluable | Adj | Value beyond calculation |
| Invariable | Adj | Not variable, changeable |
| | | |
| Invective | Adj | Verbal attack, abuse |
| Inveigle | Verb | Lure. Entice |
| Invent | Verb | To create, devise |
| | | |
| Invention | Noun | Invent. Create. Originate |
| Inventive | Adj | Able to invent, originate, create |
| Inventiveness | Noun | Ability to originate, invent |
| | | |
| Inventor | Noun | One who originates new ideas |
| Invidious | Adj | Not fair, pleasant. Offensive |
| Invigorate | Verb | Refreshing, lively |
| | | |
| Invincible | Adj | Not able to overcome |
| Involuntary | Adj | Not voluntary, by will, choice |
| Involved | Adj | Concerned. Into. Part of |
| | | |
| Irate | Adj | Angry |
| Ire | Noun | Openly angry |
| Irk | Verb | Annoy. Pester |
| | | |
| Irksome | Adj | To irk |
| Ironic | Adj | Say one thing, mean other in wit |
| Irradiate | Verb | Make clear by intellect |
| | | |
| Irradicable | Adj | Unable to end, get out |
| Irrational | Adj | Not rational, normal |
| Irrationality | Noun | Without reason, rationale |

| | | |
|---|---|---|
| Irredeemable | Adj | Not able to redeem, save |
| Irreformable | Adj | Not able to reform, change |
| Irrefutable | Adj | Unable to refute, disprove |
| | | |
| Irregular | Adj | Not regular, customary |
| Irregularity | Noun | Being irregular |
| Irrelative | Adj | Not relative, pertinent |
| | | |
| Irrelevant | Adj | Not relevant, pertinent |
| Irrepressible | Adj | Unable to hold, restrain |
| Irresolute | Adj | Not firm or sure |
| | | |
| Irresponsible | Adj | Not responsible |
| Irresponsive | Adj | Not responsible, timely |
| Irritable | Adj | Able to irritate, agitate |
| | | |
| Irritate | Verb | Spark resentment, hate |
| Isolated | Adj | Infrequent or once |

**-J-**

| | | |
|---|---|---|
| Jabber | Verb | Talk on without coherence |
| Jack-of-all-trades | Noun | Do many things well |
| Jealous | Adj | Envious suspicion |
| | | |
| Jest | Noun | Joke. Trick. Prank |
| Jester | Noun | One who jests. A joker |
| Jocose | Adj | Witty and humorous |
| | | |
| Jocular | Adj | Jolly, jesting |
| Jolly | Adj | Open. Friendly. Cheerful |
| Josh | Verb | Joke, tease in jest |
| | | |
| Journeyman | Noun | Experienced, knowledgeable |
| Jovial | Adj | Open, friendly natured |
| Joy | Noun | Happy, cheerful emotion |
| | | |
| Joyful | Adj | Having happy, cheerful emotion |
| Jubilant | Adj | Extreme joy, high thrill |
| Judgment | Noun | To compare, judge. decide |
| | | |
| Judicial | Adj | Prudent and careful |
| Judicious | Adj | Prudent, reasoned, wise |
| Juggle | Verb | Manipulate. Balance |
| Just | Adj | Reasonable. Fair. Right |

## -K-

| | | |
|---|---|---|
| Keen | Adj | Quick. Alert. Sharp |
| Keenness | Noun | A keen mental faculty |
| Keen-witted | Adj | Sharp, keen mental faculty |
| Keen-wittedness | Noun | Sharp, keen mental faculty |
| Keynote | Noun | A key or fundamental item |
| Kilter | Noun | On even keel. In order |
| Kind | Adj | Friendly, generous |
| Kindle | Verb | Ignite, start |
| Kindless | Adj | Not kind, friendly |
| Kindliness | Noun | Being kind, friendly |
| Kindly | Adj | Kind, friendly, sympathetic |
| Kingpin | Noun | Chief person in a group |
| Kindness | Noun | Showing or exhibiting kind deed |
| Kink | Noun | Unusual flaw or twist |
| Klutz | Noun | Someone awkward, clumsy |
| Knack | Noun | Unusual, ingenious ability |
| Know | Verb | Clear mental understanding |
| Know-how | Noun | Possessing knowledge |
| Knowing | Adj | Knowledge, knowledgeable |
| Know-it-all | Noun | Over confident of knowledge |
| Knowledge | Noun | Possessed wisdom, ability |
| Knowledgeable | Adj | Knowing. Learned |
| Knuckle down | Verb | Earnest effort |
| Knuckle under | Verb | Quit. Give in |
| Kudo | Noun | A "well done." Praise |

## -L-

| | | |
|---|---|---|
| Labor | Noun | Effort. Exertion. Work |
| Labor | Verb | To exert effort, work |
| Laborious | Adj | Hard work, labor |
| Lack | Verb | Deficient, missing, short |
| Lack | Noun | Being deficient, missing, short |
| Lackadaisical | Adj | Slow. Without zest, zeal |

| | | |
|---|---|---|
| Lackluster | Adj | Dull. Without life, energy |
| Laconic | Adj | Concise, offensive words |
| Lag | Noun/Verb | Behind. Slow |
| | | |
| Landmark | Noun | First of its kind |
| Lapse | Noun/Verb | Come overdue, behind. Mistake |
| Large | Adj | Big. Many |
| | | |
| Large-hearted | Adj | Warm. Caring. Sympathetic |
| Large-minded | Adj | Open-minded. Knowledgeable |
| Last | Adj | End. Bottom. Lowest |
| | | |
| Last-ditch | Adj | Final. Last |
| Lasting | Adj | Continuing on, enduring |
| Last minute | Noun | Final, ending move, action |
| | | |
| Latitude | Noun | Free to act, do, choose |
| Laudable | Adj | Commendable. Noteworthy |
| Laudatory | Adj | To commend. Commendable |
| | | |
| Launch | Verb | Go forth. Start |
| Laurel | Noun | In high standing, esteem honor |
| Lavish | Verb | More than necessary |
| | | |
| Lax | Adj | Not firm, resolute |
| Laxity | Noun | Being lax, not firm |
| Leading | Adj | Top. First |
| | | |
| Learn | Verb | Obtain knowledge |
| Learned | Adj | Knowledgeable. To learn |
| Learning | Noun | Gaining knowledge |
| | | |
| Least | Adj | Less. Lowest. Last |
| Legerity | Noun | Mental, physical agility |
| Legible | Adj | Understand writing |
| | | |
| Legitimacy | Noun | Legal. Lawful |
| Legitimate | Adj | Legal. Lawful |
| Leisure | Noun | Idleness. Lax |
| | | |
| Leniency | Noun | Not tough. Ease up. Easy |
| Lenient | Adj | Not tough. Ease up. Easy |
| Less | Adj | Lower. Below. Decrease |

**169**

| | | |
|---|---|---|
| Lessen | Verb | To be less. Decrease |
| Lethargic | Adj | Slow. Indifferent |
| Lethargy | Noun | Being slow, indifferent |
| | | |
| Lettered | Adj | Educated. Knowledgeable |
| Letter-perfect | Adj | Without error, flaw |
| Levelheaded | Adj | Reasonable in judgment |
| | | |
| Levelheadedness | Noun | Even in temperament & rationale |
| Levity | Noun | Not constant. Changing |
| Liability | Noun | A disadvantage. Non-asset |
| | | |
| Liable | Adj | Obligated. Responsible |
| Life blood | Noun | Crucial. Vital |
| Lifeless | Adj | Without life, vim, vigor |
| | | |
| Life-style | Noun | Way of life |
| Light-headed | Adj | Not serious, sound |
| Lighthearted | Adj | Carefree. Happy. Joyous |
| | | |
| Limelight | Noun | Center of attention |
| Limited | Adj | Restrained. Restricted |
| Limitless | Adj | Without limit. Continuous |
| | | |
| Limp | Verb | Not stout, strong, steady |
| Limpid | Adj | Pure. Clear. Not complex |
| Literacy | Noun | Being literate, educated |
| | | |
| Literal | Adj | Exact. Without error |
| Literally | Adv | In actuality. Actual |
| Literary | Adj | Literate. Well read |
| | | |
| Literate | Adj/Noun | Educated. Knowledgeable |
| Little | Adj | Small. Less than average |
| Liveliness | Noun | Active and energetic |
| | | |
| Lively | Adj | Energetic. Alert |
| Lively Imagination | Noun | Keen, active intellect |
| Loath | Adj | Not willing. Reluctant |
| | | |
| Loathe | Verb | Intense dislike. Hate |
| Loathing | Noun | An intense dislike |
| Loathsome | Adj | To be loath, detestable |

| | | |
|---|---|---|
| Lofty | Adj | High above. Overbearing |
| Logic | Noun | Reasoned deduction. Rational |
| Logical | Adj | Skilled logic, systematic |
| | | |
| Logical Thought | Noun | Rational, reasoning intellect |
| Loner | Noun | One avoiding others |
| Long-lived | Adj | Lasting. Enduring |
| | | |
| Long-range | Adj | Ahead in time. Future |
| Look down | Verb | Belittle |
| Loquacious | Adj | Excessive talking |
| | | |
| Loser | Noun | One unable to win, succeed |
| Lost | Adj | No longer possessed |
| Lower | Verb | Reduce. Make less |
| | | |
| Low-grade | Adj | Below average. Inferior |
| Low-key | Adj | Low profile |
| Low-level | Adj | Low value. Below average |
| | | |
| Low-minded | Adj | Low thoughts, behavior |
| Low-pressure | Adj | Little pressure, tension |
| Low-profile | Adj | Low visibility, attention |
| | | |
| Low-spirited | Adj | Dejected, depressed |
| Loyal | Adj | Faithful. Dedicated |
| Loyalty | Noun | Being loyal, dedicated |
| | | |
| Lucid | Adj | Clear knowledge |
| Lucidity | Noun | Clear understanding |
| Ludicrous | Adj | Foolish beyond belief |
| Lukewarm | Adj | Mediocre |

**-M-**

| | | |
|---|---|---|
| Maladjusted | Adj | Not adjusted to society |
| Maladroit | Adj | No grace or skill |
| Malevolence | Noun | Grudging, ill will |
| | | |
| Malevolent | Adj | Display grudging, ill will |
| Malice | Noun | Harmful intent |
| Malicious | Adj | Intending harm |
| | | |
| Malinger | Verb | Shirk responsibility |
| Mammoth | Adj | Massive. Very large |
| Manage | Verb | Control. Direct |

**171**

| | | |
|---|---|---|
| Management | Noun | Managing. Controlling |
| Manager | Noun | Someone who manages |
| Managerial | Adj | Management traits |
| | | |
| Manipulate | Verb | Control actions, movements |
| Manipulation | Noun | Intelligent use, control |
| Manner | Noun | Behavior |
| | | |
| Mannerism | Noun | Standard, expected behavior |
| Mannerless | Adj | Bad manners. Rude |
| Mannerly | Adj | Good manners. Polite |
| | | |
| Mar | Verb | Scar. Fault |
| Marginal | Adj | Barely. Minimum |
| Marvelous | Adj | Almost above belief |
| | | |
| Masterful | Adj | Most brilliant, skillful |
| Masterly | Adj | Display brilliance, skill |
| Mastermind | Noun | One who plans. Intelligent |
| | | |
| Mastery | Noun | Control over. Expert |
| Matter-of-course | Adj | Natural events, course |
| Matter-of-fact | Adj | Of, to the facts |
| | | |
| Mature | Adj | Developed. Grown full |
| Maturity | Noun | Being mature, developed |
| Maxim | Noun | A stated rule, fact |
| | | |
| Maximize | Verb | Do to the maximum |
| Maximum | Noun | Most possible |
| Meager | Adj | Small. Little |
| | | |
| Meander | Noun | Wander without cause |
| Meaningless | Adj | Without meaning, sense |
| Meddle | Verb | Pry uninvited |
| | | |
| Mediate | Verb | Intermediary. Go between |
| Mediation | Noun | Serving to mediate |
| Mediocre | Adj | Barely satisfactory |
| | | |
| Mediocrity | Noun | Being mediocre |
| Meditate | Verb | Mental pondering |
| Meek | Adj | Not strong. Weak |

| | | |
|---|---|---|
| Menace | Noun | A threat |
| Mental | Adj | The mind or intellect |
| Mental Alertness | Noun | Quick, alert intelligence |
| Mental Capacity | Noun | Intellectual limit |
| Mental Deficiency | Noun | Lacking proper intellect |
| Mental Faculty | Noun | Intellectual ability, capacity |
| Mental Handicap | Noun | Intellectually restrained/confined |
| Mentality | Noun | Mental power |
| Mental Process | Noun | Intellectual functioning |
| Mental Void | Noun | Without knowledge, intellect |
| Mental Weakness | Noun | Lack of intellectual perseverance |
| Mentor | Noun | A knowing teacher |
| Merciful | Adj | Having mercy, compassion |
| Merciless | Adj | Without mercy, compassion |
| Mercy | Noun | Compassionate. Forgiving |
| Mere | Adj | The minimum. Only |
| Merit | Noun | Worthy of praise |
| Merry | Adj | Cheerful and lively |
| Methodical | Adj | By orderly procession |
| Meticulous | Adj | Exacting in detail |
| Might | Noun | Power. Strength |
| Mild | Adj | Even tempered disposition |
| Mindful | Adj | Pay heed, attention |
| Mindless | Adj | Without knowledge, intelligence |
| Mingle | Verb | Mix |
| Minimize | Verb | Reduce. Decrease |
| Minimum | Noun | Least. Smallest |
| Minish | Verb | Diminish. Lower. Less |
| Minor | Adj | Less. Under |
| Minuscule | Noun | Extremely small |
| Minute | Adj | Extremely small |
| Misapply | Verb | Misuse. Misapplication |
| Misappropriate | Verb | Illegal use |

**173**

| | | |
|---|---|---|
| Misbecome | Verb | Not becoming, fit, proper |
| Misbehave | Verb | Wrong behavior |
| Miscalculate | Verb | Judge badly |
| | | |
| Mischievous | Adj | Minor tricks, pranks |
| Misconduct | Verb | Bad conduct |
| Misconstrue | Verb | Misunderstanding |
| | | |
| Miserable | Adj | Bad. Substandard |
| Misfit | Verb | Not fit, adjusted |
| Misfortune | Noun | Bad fortune, luck |
| | | |
| Misgiving | Noun | Doubt. Apprehension |
| Misguided | Verb | Led astray |
| Mishap | Noun | Unfortunate act |
| | | |
| Misinterpret | Verb | Misunderstand |
| Misjudge | Verb | Bad, wrong judgment |
| Mislead | Verb | Lead astray, wrong |
| | | |
| Mismanage | Verb | Manage badly |
| Mistake | Verb | Error |
| Mistaken | Adj | Be wrong, understand incorrectly |
| | | |
| Misunderstanding | Noun | Incorrect understanding |
| Misuse | Verb | Use incorrectly, wrongly |
| Mix-up | Noun | Foul-up. Blunder |
| | | |
| Moderate | Adj | Without excess. Reasonable |
| Moderation | Noun | Be moderate. Without excess |
| Modest | Adj | Not boastful, bragging |
| | | |
| Modesty | Noun | Being modest |
| Monumental | Adj | Great. Tremendous |
| Moody | Adj | Uneven temperament |
| | | |
| Moral | Adj | Discern right from wrong |
| Morale | Noun | Mental spirit |
| Moralist | Noun | Teach own morals |
| | | |
| Moralistic | Adj | Concerned with rights and wrongs |
| Morality | Noun | Right and wrong principles |
| Moralize | Verb | Explain right from wrong |

| | | |
|---|---|---|
| Motivate | Verb | Provide moving force |
| Motivation | Noun | Emotional drive to action |
| Motive | Noun | Reason. Driving force |
| | | |
| Muddle | Verb | Mix up or confuse |
| Multitude | Noun | Many. Large amount |
| Mumble | Verb | Speak indistinctly |
| | | |
| Mundane | Adj | Ordinary. |
| Myriad | Noun | Infinitely large. Many |
| Mystique | Noun | Magical intrigue |

**-N-**

| | | |
|---|---|---|
| Naive | Adj | Gullible. Simple |
| Neat | Adj | In order. Tidy |
| Negate | Verb | Go or work against |
| | | |
| Negative | Adj | No. Not positive |
| Neglect | Verb | Omit attention. Ignore |
| Neglectful | Adj | To neglect. Ignore |
| | | |
| Negligence | Noun | Showing neglect by intent |
| Negligent | Adj | Fail to attend to |
| Negligible | Adj | Not of much importance |
| | | |
| Nerveless | Adj | Without courage. Not bold |
| Nescient | Adj | Without adequate knowledge |
| Neutral | Adj | Not negative. Not positive |
| | | |
| Nice | Adj | Friendly. Cordial |
| Nicety | Noun | Being, doing nice |
| Nimble | Adj | Mental agility, quick |
| | | |
| Noble | Adj | High moral correctness |
| Nominal | Adj | Slight. Unimportant |
| Nonchalant | Adj | Not concerned, interested |
| | | |
| Nonconformist | Noun | Not comply to norm |
| No-nonsense | Adj | Serious |
| Nonproductive | Adj | Not fruitful, productive |
| | | |
| Nonsense | Noun | Not serious. Foolish |
| Normal | Adj | The norm, standard, average |
| Notable | Adj | Worthy of mention |

| | | |
|---|---|---|
| Nought | Noun | Nothing. None |
| Nourish | Verb | Foster. Feed |
| Novice | Noun | A beginner. New person |
| | | |
| Nuisance | Noun | Annoying |
| Null | Adj | No use or value |
| Nurture | Noun | Help grow, bring up |

**-O-**

| | | |
|---|---|---|
| Obedient | Adj | Obeying. Complying |
| Obey | Verb | Comply. Follow direction |
| Oblige | Verb | Commit or compel for favor |
| | | |
| Obliging | Adj | To favor. Give favor |
| Obnoxious | Adj | Crude. Rude |
| Obscure | Adj | Not clear. Hidden |
| | | |
| Observant | Adj | Watchful attention |
| Obsession | Noun | Uncontrollable desire |
| Obsolete | Adj | Out of date |
| | | |
| Obstacle | Noun | Something in way of objective |
| Obstinate | Adj | Overbearing. Stubborn |
| Obstruct | Verb | Hinder. Come between |
| | | |
| Obtuse | Adj | Mentally slow to comprehend |
| Odd | Adj | Out of the usual. Strange |
| Oddity | Noun | Being odd, strange |
| | | |
| Offend | Verb | Insult. Resent |
| Offensive | Adj | Disagreeable. Insulting |
| Omniscient | Adj | Limitless knowledge |
| | | |
| One-track-mind | Adj | Handle only one subject at a time |
| One-upmanship | Noun | Skill of getting one up |
| One-way | Adj | Single direction, action |
| | | |
| Open-eyed | Adj | Alert. Awake. Aware |
| Openhanded | Adj | Up front. Fair |
| Openhearted | Adj | Friendly, open personality |

| | | |
|---|---|---|
| Oppose | Verb | Against |
| Opposition | Noun | Resisting. Opposing |
| Oppress | Verb | Restrain by harsh methods |
| | | |
| Oppressive | Adj | Oppress with a force |
| Optimum | Noun | Ideal or best action |
| Oral | Adj | Speak. Speech |
| | | |
| Orator | Noun | Skilled speaker |
| Orchestrate | Verb | Lead. Control |
| Ordeal | Noun | Trying, hard situation |
| | | |
| Orderly | Adj | Tidy. In proper place |
| Ordinary | Adj | Routine. Normal. Common |
| Organize | Verb | Mesh together. Arrange |
| | | |
| Orientate | Verb | Adjust. Become familiar |
| Original | Adj | New. Fresh |
| Originality | Noun | New. Creative. Original |
| | | |
| Originate | Adj/Verb | Create. Bring into existence |
| Orthodox | Adj | Conventional. Normal |
| Orthodoxy | Noun | Be orthodox |
| | | |
| Oscillate | Verb | Move, go back and forth |
| Ostracize | Verb | Expel. Cast out |
| Oust | Verb | Cast out. Expel |
| | | |
| Outburst | Noun | Impulsive, offensive action |
| Outcast | Adj | Reject. Cast out |
| Outclass | Verb | Above in excellence |
| | | |
| Outdo | Verb | Do better. Excel |
| Outgoing | Adj | Open, friendly manner |
| Outlandish | Adj | Foolish. Odd |
| | | |
| Outlast | Verb | Last longer |
| Outlook | Noun | View of what is ahead |
| Outmatch | Verb | To do or be better |
| | | |
| Out-of-date | Adj | Obsolete. Old |
| Outrage | Noun | Violent anger |
| Outrageous | Adj | Extremely violent action |

| | | |
|---|---|---|
| Outshine | Verb | To outdo. Be superior |
| Outspoken | Adj | Too freely spoken, disagree |
| Outstanding | Adj | Above all others. Preeminent |
| | | |
| Outthink | Verb | Out wit. Out smart |
| Outwit | Verb | Outdo by sly, skill |
| Overbearing | Adj | Forceful. Arrogant |
| | | |
| Overcome | Verb | Prevail despite obstacles |
| Overconfident | Adj | More confident than justified |
| Overdue | Adj | Past due. Late |
| | | |
| Overextend | Verb | Extended beyond means |
| Overreact | Verb | React over requirement |
| Oversee | Verb | Watch over |
| | | |
| Overshadow | Verb | Outdo. Outshine |
| Oversight | Noun | To miss. In error |
| Oversimplify | Verb | To omit pertinent facts |
| | | |
| Overt | Adj | In the open. Not covered |
| Overwhelm | Verb | Overcome by force, weight |

## -P-

| | | |
|---|---|---|
| Pacify | Verb | To quiet, appease |
| Pall | Verb | Wear down. Boring |
| Palter | Verb | Squander without care, concern |
| | | |
| Paltry | Adj | Little. Petty. Without value |
| Pamper | Verb | Treat too easily. Give in |
| Panic | Noun | Fear and loss of calmness |
| | | |
| Paradox | Noun | Conflicting, true facts |
| Paragon | Noun | A model of excellence |
| Paramount | Adj | Primary or top importance |
| | | |
| Paranoid | Adj | Unreal beliefs, fears |
| Paraphrase | Noun | Quote in part. Rephrase |
| Pare | Verb | Cut down. Reduce |
| | | |
| Parity | Noun | Equal. Equality |
| Parlance | Noun | Language style |
| Parlous | Adj | Sly and risky |

| | | |
|---|---|---|
| Parody | Noun | Bad double, imitation |
| Partial | Adj | Inclined toward. Favoring |
| Partiality | Noun | Be biased, inclined |
| | | |
| Partisan | Noun | Extreme bias, preference |
| Passable | Adj | Just adequate |
| Passion | Noun | Strong seated emotion |
| | | |
| Passionate | Adj | Strong or heated emotion |
| Passive | Adj | Inactive. Neutral |
| Passivism | Noun | Inactive, neutral |
| | | |
| Passivity | Noun | Being inactive, neutral |
| Pathetic | Adj | Extremely sorrowful |
| Pathfinder | Noun | One who leads the way |
| | | |
| Patience | Noun | Being reserved. Able to wait |
| Patient | Adj | Wait calmly |
| Patriot | Noun | One loyal to country |
| | | |
| Patriotism | Noun | Feeling loyal to country |
| Patronize | Verb | Go along, lowering one's self |
| Paucity | Noun | Lack of. Little. Small |
| | | |
| Peccant | Adj | Go against rule |
| Peculiar | Adj | Unique. Odd |
| Peculiarity | Noun | Being unique, odd |
| | | |
| Pedant | Noun | One lacking in judgment |
| Peer | Noun | One of same rank, equal |
| Peerless | Adj | Without peer, equal |
| | | |
| Peevish | Adj | Immature. Bad humored |
| Pejorative | Adj | Become negative, worse |
| Pell-mell | Adj/Noun | Confusing. Unorganized |
| | | |
| Penetrate | Verb | To know, understand |
| Penetrating | Adj | Perceptive, discerning |
| Penetration | Noun | Sharp in mind |
| | | |
| Penitent | Adj | Admit wrong. Regret |
| Pensive | Adj | Deep, sad in thought |
| Pep | Noun | Full of zest, zeal & spirit |

**179**

| Perceive | Verb | To recognize, know, understand |
| Perception | Noun | To be, make aware. Understand |
| Perceptive | Adj | To penetrate, know |
| | | |
| Pendurable | Adj | Durable. Lasting |
| Perdure | Verb | Enduring. Lasting |
| Perfect | Adj | Without flaw. Exact |
| | | |
| Perfectible | Adj | Able to make perfect |
| Perfection | Noun | Being perfect. Without flaw |
| Perfectionism | Noun | Reaching for perfection |
| | | |
| Perform | Verb | To act or do. Accomplish |
| Performance | Noun | Performing. Accomplishing |
| Perfunctory | Adj | Casual. Indifferent |
| | | |
| Permissive | Adj | Overly allowable, lenient |
| Perpetual | Adj | Go on and on. Lasting |
| Perpetuate | Verb | Cause to go on, continue |
| | | |
| Perplex | Verb | Puzzle. Confuse |
| Perplexed | Adj | Being puzzled, confused |
| Perplexity | Noun | Being perplexed, confused |
| | | |
| Persecute | Verb | Inflict ill will, trouble |
| Perseverance | Noun | Enduring, lasting will |
| Persevere | Verb | To endure, continue on |
| | | |
| Persist | Verb | Continue on despite obstacles |
| Persistence | Noun | Being persistent, enduring |
| Persistent | Adj | Continue on despite obstacles |
| | | |
| Personable | Adj | Friendly personality |
| Personality | Noun | Expressed individual attitudes |
| Personification | Noun | Embodiment of thing, idea |
| | | |
| Personify | Verb | Serve as example |
| Perspicacious | Adj | Good perception, judgment |
| Perspicuous | Adj | Vivid, clear understanding |
| | | |
| Persuade | Verb | Convince |
| Persuasion | Noun | Ability to convince |
| Persuasive | Adj | Be able to convince, persuade |

| | | |
|---|---|---|
| Pert | Adj | Bold. Brash |
| Pertinacious | Adj | Stubborn. Persevere |
| Pertinacity | Noun | Being stubborn. |
| | | |
| Pertinent | Adj | Applicable. Relevant |
| Perturb | Verb | Upset. Alarm. Confuse |
| Pervade | Verb | Permeate. Penetrate. Prevail |
| | | |
| Pessimism | Noun | Always think, expect worst |
| Pessimistic | Adj | Expect worst. Not optimistic |
| Petty | Adj | Meaningless. Worth little |
| | | |
| Petulant | Adj | Insolent. Annoying |
| Pictured | Verb | Mental image, vision |
| Pillar | Noun | A mainstay |
| | | |
| Pinnacle | Noun | At highest point possible |
| Pitfall | Noun | Shortcoming. Trap |
| Pitiless | Adj | Without pity, compassion |
| | | |
| Pity | Noun | Sympathy. Sorrow |
| Placid | Adj | Under control. Calm |
| Platitude | Noun | Ordinary. Common. Trite |
| | | |
| Plaudit | Noun | Praise. Approval |
| Plausible | Adj | Questionable |
| Pleasant | Adj | Pleasing. Agreeable |
| | | |
| Pleasantry | Noun | Being pleasant |
| Pleasing | Adj | Agreeable. Pleasant |
| Pleasurable | Adj | Enjoyable. Gratifying |
| | | |
| Pleasure | Noun | Good feeling. Pleasing |
| Pliable | Adj | Able to adjust, influence |
| Plod | Verb | Steady, slow, mundane |
| | | |
| Poignant | Adj | Elicit compassion, emotion |
| Poise | Noun | Refined, dignified style |
| Polemic | Adj | Disrupt. Agitate. Incite |
| | | |
| Polish | Verb | Social grace, refinement |
| Polished | Adj | Having social poise, grace |
| Polite | Adj | Courteous and considerate |

| | | |
|---|---|---|
| Politic | Adj | Possessing prudent skill, wisdom |
| Polyglot | Adj | Conversant in language |
| Pomposity | Noun | Self-indulging or important |
| | | |
| Pompous | Adj | Conceived self importance |
| Ponder | Verb | Think. Go over. Consider |
| Ponderable | Adj | Thinking. Going over. Considering |
| | | |
| Popular | Adj | Widely accepted, liked |
| Portentous | Adj | Pretense of self importance |
| Positive | Adj | In affirm, favor |
| | | |
| Possessive | Adj | A desire to have, possess |
| Postulate | Verb | Speculate without proof |
| Postulator | Noun | Someone who postulates, assumes |
| | | |
| Potency | Noun | Ability, potential, capacity |
| Potent | Adj | Powerful |
| Potential | Adj | Ability. Capacity |
| | | |
| Power | Noun | Driving, moving force |
| Powerhouse | Noun | Mighty. Dynamic |
| Powerful | Adj | Mighty. Having great influence |
| | | |
| Power of Mind | Noun | Ability to know, think |
| Power of Reason | Noun | Ability to use ration, reason |
| Power of Thought | Noun | Ability to think and originate |
| | | |
| Practical | Adj | Sensible. Reasonable |
| Practical Knowledge | Noun | Realistic/useful mental capability |
| Practical Wisdom | Noun | Realistic, useful knowledge |
| | | |
| Pragmatic | Adj | Speculate. Conjecture |
| Praise | Verb | Hold in high esteem. Commend |
| Precarious | Adj | Vulnerable. At risk |
| | | |
| Precise | Adj | Exact |
| Precision | Noun | Being exact and finite |
| Predominant | Adj | Dominate without peer |
| | | |
| Predominate | Verb | Dominate over, above others |
| Preeminent | Adj | Be, exist above others |
| Preferential | Adj | Prefer, choose over another |

| | | |
|---|---|---|
| Prejudice | Noun | Judge before hand, facts |
| Prejudicial | Adj | Showing prejudice, favor |
| Premature | Adj | Before. Prior. Early |
| | | |
| Premium | Noun | Extra, added value |
| Preoccupied | Adj | Mentally occupied |
| Prepare | Verb | To get, make ready |
| | | |
| Preparedness | Noun | Being prepared |
| Preponderant | Adj | Over abundance |
| Preponderate | Verb | Dominant. Greater |
| | | |
| Preposterous | Adj | Ridiculous. Outrageous |
| Prepotency | Noun | Very potent, powerful |
| Presence | Noun | One's bearing, being |
| | | |
| Presence of mind | Adj | Mental clearness to act |
| Presentable | Adj | Acceptable to present |
| Prestige | Noun | Having renown, high stature |
| | | |
| Prestigious | Adj | High honor, esteem, acclaim |
| Prevail | Verb | To win out, be on top |
| Prevailing | Adj | Existing above or superior |
| | | |
| Prevalent | Adj | Dominant. Accepted |
| Pride | Noun | Esteem. Respect |
| Prime | Adj | Most important. First |
| | | |
| Privilege | Noun | Special favor, consideration |
| Privileged | Adj | Having special consideration |
| Problem | Noun | Something requiring a solution |
| | | |
| Problem | Adj | Hard to handle, deal with |
| Procrastinate | Verb | Put-off. Indecision |
| Prod | Verb | Push, stir to move |
| | | |
| Prodigal | Adj | Overly generous, extravagant |
| Prodigy | Noun | Someone held in awe, amazement |
| Produce | Verb | To originate, bring forth |
| | | |
| Productive Imagination | Noun | Creative results of the mind |
| Professional | Noun | One highly skilled |
| Professionalism | Noun | Exhibiting professional traits |

| | | |
|---|---|---|
| Proficiency | Noun | Highly skilled |
| Proficient | Adj | Skilled, productive |
| Profound | Adj | Sound, innate mental power |
| | | |
| Profound Knowledge | Noun | Broad intellectual depth |
| Progress | Noun | Improve. Advance. Forward |
| Progressive | Adj | Forward thinking |
| | | |
| Proliferate | Verb | Multiply, increase rapidly |
| Prolific | Adj | Produce great many |
| Prominence | Noun | Being prominent |
| | | |
| Prominent | Adj | Widely known or acknowledged |
| Promote | Verb | Foster. Further. Advance |
| Promoter | Noun | One who promotes or backs |
| | | |
| Prompt | Adj | Quick. Timely |
| Promptitude | Noun | Being prompt, quick |
| Propagate | Verb | Spread. Emit |
| | | |
| Propel | Verb | Push. Move |
| Propensity | Noun | Inclination |
| Proper | Adj | Correct. Right |
| | | |
| Propitiate | Verb | Appease. Please |
| Propitious | Adj | Favorable |
| Propone | Verb | Put forth. Propose |
| | | |
| Proponent | Noun | One who backs, promotes |
| Proposal | Noun | Submitting for view, review |
| Propriety | Noun | Proper and fit |
| | | |
| Prosper | Verb | Flourish. Thrive |
| Prosperity | Noun | To prosper, succeed |
| Prosperous | Adj | Succeed. Flourish |
| | | |
| Protégé | Noun | One trained by expert |
| Prototype | Noun | First of new breed, standard |
| Proud | Adj | Holding high esteem |
| | | |
| Provident | Adj | Prudent. Wise |
| Provocative | Adj | Agitate. Stimulate. Provoke |
| Provoke | Verb | Stir up. Agitate. Excite |

| | | |
|---|---|---|
| Provoking | Adj | To provoke |
| Prowess | Noun | Outstanding mental agility |
| Prude | Noun | One overbearing, crass |
| | | |
| Prudence | Noun | Being careful, tentative |
| Prudent | Adj | Careful. Tentative |
| Prudential | Adj | Showing prudence, judgment |
| | | |
| Prudish | Adj | Overly correct and proper |
| Pry | Verb | Unwanted inquiry, meddling |
| Prying | Adj | To pry |
| | | |
| Punctilious | Adj | Excessive about detail |
| Punctual | Adj | Timely. On time |
| Pundit | Noun | Self-proclaimed expert |
| | | |
| Pungent | Adj | Keen of mind |
| Pure | Adj | Without defect, impurity |
| Purge | Verb | Rid of unwanted parts |
| | | |
| Purport | Verb | Suppose. Profess |
| Purpose | Verb | Intend. Reason |
| Purposeful | Adj | Having purpose, meaning |
| | | |
| Purposeless | Adj | Without purpose, meaning |
| Puzzle | Verb | Perplex. Mix-up |

**-Q-**

| | | |
|---|---|---|
| Qualified | Adj | Capable. Able |
| Quality | Noun | A high state, degree |
| Quantify | Verb | Determine by quantity, amount |
| | | |
| Quell | Verb | To stop, silence, end |
| Query | Noun | Question |
| Quest | Noun | Venture. Seek. Pursue |
| | | |
| Questionable | Adj | Uncertain. Doubtful |
| Quibble | Noun | Petty item, concern |
| Quick | Adj | Prompt. Fast. Ready |
| | | |
| Quicken | Verb | To speed up, hasten |
| Quickness | Noun | Quick & perceptive mind |
| Quick-thinking | Noun/Adj | Quick in mental thought, action |

| | | |
|---|---|---|
| Quick Wit | Noun | Mentally quick & alert |
| Quick-witted | Adj | Mentally quick and alert |
| Quip | Noun | Witty remark |
| | | |
| Quirk | Noun | Unforeseen happening, twist |
| Quit | Verb | Stop. Cease |
| Quitter | Noun | One who quits too quickly |
| Quizzical | Adj | Unusually puzzling |

**-R-**

| | | |
|---|---|---|
| Radiance | Noun | Shine with brightness |
| Radiant | Adj | Beaming, as goodwill, joy |
| Radiant | Verb | Emit warmth, goodwill |
| | | |
| Rage | Noun | Violent anger |
| Rally | Verb | Renew, revive effort, action |
| Rampage | Noun | Violent action, behavior |
| | | |
| Rare | Adj | Unusual. Not ordinary, common |
| Rarity | Noun | Being rare, uncommon |
| Rational | Adj | Sound, logical reasoning |
| | | |
| Rationale | Noun | Rational reasoning |
| Rationalism | Noun | Use of reason |
| Rationality | Noun | Being rational. Able to reason |
| | | |
| Rationalize | Verb | Interpret actions, reasons |
| Rational Faculty | Noun | Reasoning, rational mind |
| Ready | Adj | Prepared. Capable |
| | | |
| Ready-made | Adj | Ordinary. Not original |
| Ready Wit | Noun | Mentally quick, alert, skillful |
| Realism | Noun | Being real vice idealistic |
| | | |
| Realist | Noun | Practical reality, not idealistic |
| Realistic | Adj | Of reality, practical |
| Reality | Noun | Being real, fact |
| | | |
| Realization | Noun | To realize |
| Reason | Noun | Rational thought |
| Reasonable | Adj | Within reason, justifiable |

| | | |
|---|---|---|
| Reasoning | Noun | Rational deduction |
| Reasoning Facility | Noun | Logical, reasonable mental ability |
| Reasonless | Adj | Without reason, logic |
| | | |
| Rebellious | Adj | Defiant. Opposing |
| Rebuff | Noun | Refute. Brisk refusal |
| Rebut | Verb | Formal refute, opposition |
| | | |
| Recall | Noun | Memory. Memory ability |
| Receptive | Adj | Able, willing to learn |
| Rectify | Verb | Fix. Correct |
| | | |
| Redress | Noun/Verb | To right a wrong |
| Redundant | Adj | In excess. Too much |
| Re-examine | Verb | Review again |
| | | |
| Reevaluate | Verb | To rethink, reconsider |
| Refine | Verb | To make better, more pure |
| Refined | Adj | Cultured. Learned |
| | | |
| Reform | Verb | Change for better. Correct |
| Refrain | Verb | To hold, keep back |
| Refreshing | Adj | New and invigorating |
| | | |
| Refusal | Noun | Not accepting |
| Refuse | Verb | Turn down |
| Refute | Verb | Prove wrong, false |
| | | |
| Regenerate | Adj | Renew. New vigor |
| Regress | Noun | Fall back. Lose ground |
| Regression | Noun | Regress. Move backward |
| | | |
| Regret | Verb | Remorse. Sorrow |
| Regretful | Adj | To regret, feel sorry |
| Rehabilitate | Verb | Renew. Put back |
| | | |
| Rehash | Verb | Go over again |
| Reject | Verb | Turn down |
| Rejuvenate | Verb | Give new, fresh life |
| | | |
| Relapse | Verb | Fall back, slip back, to before |
| Relent | Verb | To give in |
| Relentless | Adj | Not giving in, relenting |

| | | |
|---|---|---|
| Reliable | Adj | Dependable. Trustworthy |
| Reliance | Noun | Rely. Depend. Trust |
| Reliant | Adj | Trustworthy |
| | | |
| Relinquish | Verb | Give up |
| Reluctance | Noun | Being reluctant |
| Reluctant | Adj | Not fully willing |
| | | |
| Remarkable | Adj | Unusually good deed, feat |
| Remedial | Adj | To remedy, fix |
| Remedy | Noun | Fix. Correct |
| | | |
| Remiss | Adj | Negligent. At fault |
| Remorse | Noun | Self sense of guilt |
| Remorseful | Adj | Feeling remorse |
| | | |
| Remorseless | Adj | Without remorse, guilt |
| Renascent | Adj | Renewed stamina and vim |
| Renew | Verb | Make new, over |
| | | |
| Renitent | Adj | To resist, oppose |
| Renounce | Verb | Refuse. Rebut. Disown |
| Renovate | Verb | To fix up, renew, revive |
| | | |
| Renown | Noun | High reputation |
| Renowned | Adj | Having high renown, reputation |
| Renunciation | Noun | To forgo, give up |
| | | |
| Reorganize | Verb | Organize over, again |
| Repercussion | Noun | Reaction to action |
| Repertoire | Noun | Possessed special skills |
| | | |
| Reprehend | Verb | Offend. Criticize |
| Reprehensible | Adj | Very offensive, criticizing |
| Repress | Verb | Suppress. Hold down, back |
| | | |
| Repression | Noun | Being repressed |
| Reprimand | Noun | Official rebuke |
| Reproach | Verb | Blame for fault |
| | | |
| Reproach | Noun | To blame for fault |
| Reprobate | Verb | Condemn. Disapprove |
| Reprobate | Adj | Without moral principles |

| | | |
|---|---|---|
| Repudiate | Verb | Refuse. Deny |
| Repugn | Verb | Oppose |
| Repugnance | Noun | Utter dislike |
| | | |
| Repugnant | Adj | Not agreeable |
| Repulse | Verb | Repel. Reject |
| Repulsion | Noun | Repel. Dislike |
| | | |
| Repulsive | Adj | Repel. Dislike |
| Reputable | Adj | Good reputation |
| Reputation | Noun | Earned public character, stature |
| | | |
| Repute | Verb | Supposed. Assumed |
| Requisite | Adj | Requirement |
| Resent | Verb | Bad feeling. Dislike |
| | | |
| Resentful | Adj | To resent. Have bad feeling |
| Resentment | Noun | Bad, offensive feeling |
| Reserve | Verb | To hold back. Keep |
| | | |
| Reserve | Noun | Something held back |
| Reserved | Adj | Held back, restrained manner |
| Reservoir | Noun | Place used for storage |
| | | |
| Resilience | Noun | Ability to bounce back, recover |
| Resilient | Adj | Bounce back. Recover |
| Resist | Verb | Oppose. Go against |
| | | |
| Resistance | Noun | To resist, oppose |
| Resistant | Adj/Noun | To resist, oppose |
| Resistless | Adj | Without resistance, opposition |
| | | |
| Resolute | Adj | Firm. Determined |
| Resolution | Noun | Firm in resolve |
| Resolve | Noun/Verb | Firm determination. Decided |
| | | |
| Resounding | Adj | Complete. Unqualified |
| Resource | Noun | Possessed ability. Resourceful |
| Resourceful | Adj | Possessing resource, ability |
| | | |
| Respect | Noun/Verb | State of high esteem, regard |
| Respectable | Adj | Be held in high esteem, regard |
| Respectful | Adj | Being in respect |

| | | |
|---|---|---|
| Responsibility | Noun | Being held accountable |
| Responsible | Adj | Accountable |
| Responsive | Adj | Ability to respond, answer |
| | | |
| Restrain | Verb | Hold back |
| Restraint | Noun | Something that restrains |
| Resurge | Verb | Come or surge back |
| | | |
| Resurgent | Adj | Rise or surge back, again |
| Retard | Verb | Hinder. Slow down |
| Retentive | Adj | To retain, remember |
| | | |
| Retentivity | Noun | Capacity to retain, remember |
| Rethink | Verb | Think over again |
| Retribution | Noun | Due & just reward, punishment |
| | | |
| Revive | Verb | Bring back to life |
| Rhetoric | Noun | Double talk with skill over words |
| Rhetorical | Adj | Using rhetoric |
| | | |
| Rhetorician | Noun | One skilled in rhetoric |
| Rich Imagination | Noun | Unending mental originality |
| Ridicule | Noun | To belittle by joke |
| | | |
| Ridiculous | Adj | Foolish. Outlandish |
| Righteous | Adj | Be, act right, proper |
| Rigid | Adj | Stiff. Firm. Not flexible |
| | | |
| Rigidify | Verb | Be rigid |
| Rigor | Noun | Hard. Severe. Arduous |
| Rigorous | Adj | Hard. Strict. Severe |
| | | |
| Rival | Noun | Opponent. Competitor |
| Rivalry | Noun | Standing rival. Competition |
| Robust | Adj | Strong. Healthy. Hardy |
| | | |
| Rookie | Noun | A newcomer. Inexperienced |
| Rosy | Adj | Promising. Bright |
| Rough | Adj | Harsh. Not refined |
| | | |
| Rouse | Verb | Agitate. Stir up |
| Rude | Adj | Bad in manner |
| Rudiment | Noun | Not yet fully developed |

| | | |
|---|---|---|
| Rudimentary | Adj | New. Elementary |
| Run-down | Adj | Poor condition. Exhausted |
| Rusty | Adj | Not as capable/able as before |
| Ruthless | Adj | Without consideration, compassion |

**-S-**

| | | |
|---|---|---|
| Sacrifice | Noun | Give up or go without something |
| Sagacious | Adj | Great judgment, mental ability |
| Sage | Adj | Wise and judicious |
| | | |
| Sage | Noun | Someone wise and judicious |
| Salient | Adj | Main or major aspect |
| Sane | Adj | Rational mental faculty |
| | | |
| Sanity | Noun | In control of mental facilities |
| Sapid | Adj | Pleasant. Interesting |
| Sapient | Adj | Wise. Knowing |
| | | |
| Sarcasm | Noun | Remark in bad taste. Ridicule |
| Sarcastic | Adj | Displaying sarcasm |
| Satisfaction | Noun | Being satisfied, content |
| | | |
| Satisfactory | Adj | Good. Adequate |
| Saucy | Adj | Not in good taste |
| Savoir-faire | Noun | Verbal wit and tact |
| | | |
| Savvy | Verb | Know-how. Knowledge |
| Scant | Adj | Not sufficient, satisfactory |
| Scanty | Adj | Not sufficient. Meager |
| | | |
| Scapegoat | Noun | One taking blame for another |
| Scarce | Adj | Rare. Uncommon |
| Scheme | Noun | A plan, plot |
| | | |
| Scholar | Noun | Someone of knowledge |
| Scholarly | Adj | Having knowledge. Learned |
| Scoff | Noun | Contemptible |
| | | |
| Scorn | Noun/Verb | Ridicule. Contempt |
| Scornful | Adj | Displaying scorn |
| Scruple | Noun | Indecision of right and wrong |

**191**

| | | |
|---|---|---|
| Scrupulous | Adj | Proper, truthful, and careful |
| Scrutable | Adj | Questionable understanding |
| Scrutinize | Verb | Review closely, carefully |
| | | |
| Scrutiny | Noun | Close, careful attention |
| Seasoned Understanding | Noun | Knowledge acquired over time |
| Secluded | Adj | Hidden. Out of view |
| | | |
| Second-guess | Verb | Question after the fact |
| Self-assertion | Noun | Assert one's self. Be insistent |
| Self-assurance | Noun | Confident in one's self |
| | | |
| Self-centered | Adj | Overly concerned with one's self |
| Self-composed | Adj | Having composure. calmness |
| Self-conceit | Noun | Too high opinion of one's self |
| | | |
| Self-confidence | Noun | Confident in one's self |
| Self-conscious | Adj | Overly concerned about one's self |
| Self-control | Noun | Having control of one's self |
| | | |
| Self-defeating | Adj | Something that opposes itself |
| Self-determination | Noun | Providing one's own will |
| Self-discipline | Noun | Control of one's own actions |
| | | |
| Self-doubt | Noun | Not confident in one's self |
| Self-esteem | Noun | Pride in one's self |
| Self-examination | Noun | Study one's own actions |
| | | |
| Self-image | Noun | How someone views self |
| Self-important | Adj | Feeling overly important |
| Self-improvement | Noun | Individual effort to improve |
| | | |
| Self-indulgence | Noun | Indulge in own desires |
| Self-interest | Noun | Concerned with one's own interests |
| Selfish | Adj | Not share or concerned with others |
| | | |
| Selfless | Adj | Not selfish. Concerned for others |
| Self-made | Adj | Made or done by one's self |
| Self-opinionated | Adj | Conceited. Hold to own opinions |
| | | |
| Self-reliance | Noun | Rely on one's self |
| Self-respect | Noun | Respecting one's self, values |
| Self-restraint | Noun | Control over one's self |

| | | |
|---|---|---|
| Self-righteous | Adj | Showing self as morally better |
| Self-sacrifice | Noun | Sacrifice for others |
| Self-serving | Adj | Serve one's own interests |
| | | |
| Self-starter | Noun | Supply own initiative |
| Self-sufficient | Adj | Without outside help, assistance |
| Self-taught | Adj | Learning by one's self, efforts |
| | | |
| Self-will | Noun | Possessed will to do, go forth |
| Semiskilled | Adj | Partially skilled |
| Senile | Adj | Mental decline due to aging |
| | | |
| Senility | Noun | Mental decline due to aging |
| Senseless | Adj | Without proper sense, meaning |
| Sensibility | Noun | Mentally receptive, rational |
| | | |
| Sensible | Adj | Good sense of judgment |
| Sensitive | Adj | Compassion for others |
| Sensitivity | Noun | Being sensitive |
| | | |
| Sentiment | Noun | Opinion formed in part by emotion |
| Sentimental | Adj | Acting from feeling |
| Serious | Adj | Important. Critical |
| | | |
| Severe | Adj | Strict, stern |
| Severity | Noun | Being severe |
| Shabby | Adj | Not appealing, disgraceful |
| | | |
| Shaky | Adj | Not steady, firm, dependable |
| Shallow | Adj | Superficial. Without depth/meaning |
| Shallowness | Noun | Without depth, substance |
| | | |
| Sham | Noun | A deception |
| Shameful | Adj | Disgraceful |
| Shameless | Adj | Without shame. Not with modesty |
| | | |
| Sharp | Adj | Keen, clear |
| Sharpness | Noun | Mentally quick and keen |
| Sharp-tongued | Adj | Harsh spoken |
| | | |
| Sharp-witted | Adj | Quick, keen intelligence |
| Sharp Wittedness | Noun | Quick, keen mind or wit |
| Shiftless | Adj | Unsteady ability, character |

| Shifty | Adj | Unstable character |
| Shipshape | Adj | Neat and orderly |
| Shirk | Verb | Evade. Get around |
| | | |
| Shoddy | Noun | Bad quality. Inferior |
| Shortcoming | Noun | Fault. Not to expectation |
| Shortfall | Noun | Being, falling short |
| | | |
| Shortsighted | Adj | Not looking, thinking ahead |
| Shortsightedness | Noun | Not thinking, planning ahead |
| Short-spoken | Adj | Speak briefly, to the point |
| | | |
| Short-tempered | Adj | Lose temper easily |
| Shrewd | Adj | Clever. Cunning |
| Shrewdness | Noun | Keenly knowledgeable, clever |
| | | |
| Shy | Adj | Quiet, reserved |
| Significance | Noun | Of some importance |
| Significant | Adj | Of importance |
| | | |
| Silver-tongued | Adj | Convincing talker |
| Simple | Adj | Not complicated |
| Simple-minded | Adj | Mentally deficient, lacking |
| | | |
| Simplicity | Noun | Not complicated. Simple |
| Simplistic | Adj | Simplify difficult problem |
| Sincere | Adj | Honest. Straightforward |
| | | |
| Sincerity | Noun | Being sincere |
| Single-handed | Adj | Without assistance, help |
| Skeptical | Adj | Not convinced, sure |
| | | |
| Skepticism | Noun | Being skeptic |
| Skill | Noun | Proficiency |
| Skilled | Adj | Having skill |
| | | |
| Skillful | Adj | Having skill |
| Skirmish | Noun | Brief conflict |
| Slacken | Verb | Back-off. Do, become less |
| | | |
| Slacker | Noun | One who lets up, slows down |
| Slipshod | Adj | Careless |
| Sloppy | Adj | Careless. Bad quality |

| | | |
|---|---|---|
| Slopwork | Noun | Careless work |
| Sloven | Noun | One careless in manner, dress |
| Slovenly | Adj | Careless in manner, dress |
| Slow | Adj | Not quick |
| Sly | Adj | Skillfully clever or devious |
| Small | Adj | Little |
| Small-minded | Adj | Not open. Narrow |
| Small-scale | Adj | Not big. Limited in scale, scope |
| Smart | Adj | Intelligent. Sharp |
| Smartness | Noun | Intellectually sharp, capable |
| Smooth-spoken | Adj | Smooth, polished in speech |
| Smooth-tongued | Adj | Smooth, eloquent in speech |
| Smug | Adj | Complacent. Self-assured |
| Snappy | Adj | Lively. Active |
| Snide | Adj | Sly and cruel |
| Snuffy | Adj | Stuffy. Not agreeable |
| Sociable | Adj | Friendly. Gregarious |
| Social | Adj | Gregarious. Friendly |
| Socialize | Verb | Be social with others |
| Soft-headed | Adj | Not smart, wise |
| Softhearted | Adj | Kindly. Not firm, strict |
| Solace | Noun | To console, comfort. Kind |
| Solicitude | Noun | Care. Overly caring |
| Solid | Adj | Stout. Firm |
| Solidify | Verb | Make solid, firm |
| Solitary | Adj | Alone |
| Solitude | Noun | Being alone |
| Somber | Adj | Drab. Dull. Boring |
| Sophisticated | Adj | Wise, polished or advanced |
| Sorrow | Noun | Grief. Regret |
| Sorrowful | Adj | With, of sorrow |
| Soundness | Noun | Valid in thought, reasoning |
| Sound Understanding | Noun | Thorough thought or knowledge |

| | | |
|---|---|---|
| Sparing | Adj | Not in excess |
| Spark | Verb/Noun | Initiate. Stir. Stimulate |
| Sparkle | Verb | Actively clever and lively |
| | | |
| Sparse | Adj | Little. Thin. Shallow |
| Spartan | Noun | One with high discipline/bravery |
| Spearhead | Noun/Verb | Leading or moving force |
| | | |
| Specialist | Noun | Expert in a skill, field |
| Specialize | Verb | Develop special skill in area |
| Specialty | Noun | A particular field of endeavor |
| | | |
| Spectacle | Noun | Thing demanding visual attention |
| Speculate | Verb | Think of options. Ponder |
| Speculation | Noun | To speculate, guess |
| | | |
| Speculative | Adj | Not sure, certain. Guess |
| Speedy | Adj | Quick. Prompt |
| Spirit | Noun/Verb | Enthusiasm. Drive. Cheer on |
| | | |
| Spirited | Adj | Active. Lively |
| Spiritless | Adj | Without spirit. Lifeless |
| Spite | Noun | Of ill will |
| | | |
| Spiteful | Adj | Vindictive. Hateful |
| Splendid | Adj | High worth, value. Great |
| Spontaneous | Adj | On impulse |
| | | |
| Sporadic | Adj | Not regular, consistent |
| Spotless | Adj | Without flaw or fault |
| Spotty | Adj | Not consistent, regular |
| | | |
| Spurious | Adj | False. Not real, true |
| Spurn | Verb | Contempt. Reject |
| Spurt | Verb | Short burst of activity |
| | | |
| Squabble | Verb | Quarrel. Argument |
| Squander | Verb | Waste. Waste away |
| Stability | Noun | Stable. Firm |
| | | |
| Stabilize | Verb | Make stable |
| Stable | Adj | Unmoving. Fixed. Firm |
| Staggering | Adj | Too great, many to imagine |

| | | |
|---|---|---|
| Stagnant | Adj | Not moving. Inactive |
| Stagnate | Verb | Become stagnant |
| Stalwart | Adj/Noun | Strong. Unyielding. Firm |
| | | |
| Stamina | Noun | Endure for long periods |
| Standard-bearer | Noun | One carrying a standard |
| Standout | Noun | Something superior as to stand out |
| | | |
| Star | Noun | Someone who excels or shines |
| Staunch | Adj | Firm. Unrelenting |
| Steadfast | Adj | Firm. Resolute. Not wavering |
| | | |
| Steady | Adj | Fixed. Constant. Controlled |
| Stealth | Noun | Undercover. Secretive |
| Stealthy | Adj | To be stealth |
| | | |
| Stellar | Adj | Star, outstanding performance |
| Sterling | Adj | Of highest quality |
| Stimulant | Adj | To stimulate, increase activity |
| | | |
| Stimulate | Verb | Ignite, arouse, or spur action |
| Stimulator | Noun | One who excites increased activity |
| Stimulus | Noun | Something that excites action |
| | | |
| Stodgy | Adj | Mundane. Standard. Routine |
| Stoke | Verb | To fuel, stir up |
| Straight Thinking | Noun | Single direction of thought |
| | | |
| Strength | Noun | Strong. Powerful |
| Strengthen | Verb | Become more strong, powerful |
| Strenuous | Adj | Demanding great action, energy |
| | | |
| Strict | Adj | Firm. Solid. Exact |
| Stringent | Adj | Being strict |
| Strive | Verb | Try. Attempt |
| | | |
| Strong | Adj | Strength. Powerful |
| Strong-minded | Adj | Determination. Unrelenting will |
| Strong-willed | Adj | Determined. Headstrong |
| | | |
| Studious | Adj | Study. Pay attention. Watchful |
| Stupefy | Verb | To stun, numb, dull |
| Stupendous | Adj | Overpowering. Overwhelming |

| | | |
|---|---|---|
| Stupid | Adj | Not having normal intelligence |
| Stupidity | Noun | Being stupid, unknowing |
| Stupor | Noun | Mental dullness. Inattention |
| | | |
| Style | Noun | Fashion or manner of something |
| Stymie | Noun | To interfere, obstruct, get in way |
| Stymied | Verb | To stymie, interfere |
| | | |
| Suave | Adj | Sophisticated. Poised. Polished |
| Submissive | Adj | To submit, yield, give way |
| Subnormal | Adj | Below normal, average |
| | | |
| Substandard | Adj | Below standard, expectation |
| Substantial | Adj | Great amount. Much. Many |
| Subtle | Adj | Not direct or mentally sharp |
| | | |
| Succeed | Verb | Complete. Accomplish. Attain |
| Success | Noun | Complete correctly, favorably |
| Successful | Adj | Do with success |
| | | |
| Succinct | Adj | Brief, concise & correct in speech |
| Succumb | Verb | Submit, yield, give in |
| Suffer | Verb | Realize pain, unpleasantness |
| | | |
| Sufficient | Adj | Adequate. Enough |
| Suitable | Adj | Acceptable. To suit |
| Sullen | Adj | Quiet bitterness |
| | | |
| Superb | Adj | Top quality. Without equal. Grand |
| Supercilious | Adj | Contemptible. Arrogance |
| Superficial | Adj | On the surface only. Shallow |
| | | |
| Superficiality | Noun | Not meaningful, profound |
| Superfine | Adj | Super good, fine. Top quality |
| Superfluous | Adj | Excess. Not needed |
| | | |
| Superior | Adj | Better. Greater. Ace. Top |
| Superlative | Adj/Noun | Superior, better |
| Supporter | Noun | One who supports, backs, enforces |
| | | |
| Supportive | Adj | To support, back |
| Suppress | Verb | Hold down or back. Stop |
| Supremacy | Noun | Be supreme, superior, above |

| | | |
|---|---|---|
| Supreme | Adj | Best. Highest |
| Surly | Adj | Crass. Crusty. Rude |
| Surpass | Verb | Go past, beyond. Be superior |
| | | |
| Surpassing | Adj | To surpass, go beyond. Excelling |
| Survive | Verb | To continue, carry on |
| Survivor | Noun | One who comes through repetitively |
| | | |
| Sway | Verb | Waiver, give way. Change |
| Swift | Adj | Fast. Quick. Prompt |
| Swiftness | Noun | Fast. Quick |
| | | |
| Symbolize | Verb | To represent. Be a symbol/standard |
| Sympathetic | Adj | Understanding. Express sympathy |
| Sympathize | Verb | To share in sympathy |
| | | |
| Sympathy | Noun | Mutual feeling. Be understanding |
| Systematic | Adj | By system or methodical process |

## -T-

| | | |
|---|---|---|
| Tacit | Adj | Quiet. Silent. Without words |
| Taciturn | Adj | Tending to be quiet, not talkative |
| Tact | Noun | Diplomacy skill. Not offending |
| | | |
| Tactful | Adj | Using tact, diplomacy |
| Tactless | Adj | Having no tact. Not diplomatic |
| Talent | Noun | Ability. Skill. Power |
| | | |
| Talented | Adj | Possessing great abilities |
| Talkative | Adj | Talk too much, to extreme |
| Tangible | Adj | Being able to touch. Definitive |
| | | |
| Taskmaster | Noun | One who is demanding, exacting |
| Teach | Verb | Impart knowledge |
| Technique | Noun | A particular learned skill |
| | | |
| Tedious | Adj | Tiresome, grueling, boring |
| Tedium | Noun | Be tedious, tiresome |
| Temerity | Noun | Too bold, reckless |
| | | |
| Temperament | Noun | One's disposition or mood |
| Temperamental | Adj | Having excitable, erratic temper |
| Temperance | Noun | Restrained, reserved, even temper |

| | | |
|---|---|---|
| Temperate | Adj | Restrained. Even tempered |
| Tempting | Adj | Inclined to entice, provoke |
| Tenacious | Adj | Firm. Very cohesive. Together |
| Tenacity | Noun | Firm. Resolute. Cohesive |
| Tender | Adj | Considerate. Gentle |
| Tenderhearted | Adj | Sympathetic at heart |
| Tension | Noun | Strain. Stress |
| Tenuous | Adj | Thin. Tiny. Little |
| Tepid | Adj | Not friendly, feeling |
| Terrific | Adj | Great. Super. Outstanding |
| Terse | Adj | Eloquent, concise, to the point |
| Thankful | Adj | Gratitude. Grateful |
| Thankless | Adj | Without thanks, gratitude |
| Thick | Adj | Slow to comprehend, learn |
| Think | Verb | Conceive by mental action |
| Thinkable | Adj | Conceivable. Mentally possible |
| Thinker | Noun | One who think, plans |
| Thinking | Adj | Mental thought action |
| Think-up | Verb | Mentally originate, devise |
| Thought | Noun | Conceived mental act, process |
| Thoughtful | Adj | Showing care, consideration |
| Thoughtless | Adj | Without thought or consideration |
| Thrift | Noun | Careful use of resource |
| Thriftless | Adj | Without thrift |
| Thrifty | Adj | To be thrift. Not wasteful |
| Thrive | Verb | Prosper. Flourish. Grow |
| Thwart | Verb | To intervene, obstruct, spoil |
| Tidy | Adj | Neat. Orderly |
| Timid | Adj | Shy. Afraid |
| Timorous | Adj | Timid. Shy. Afraid |
| Tiresome | Adj | Boring. Restless. Being tired |
| Tolerable | Adj | To tolerate, allow, bear |
| Tolerant | Adj | To bear with, tolerate, allow |

| | | |
|---|---|---|
| Tolerate | Verb | Allow. Bear. Permit |
| Tough | Adj | Firm |
| Tough-minded | Adj | Tough, strong, firm of mind |
| | | |
| Tradition | Noun | Time honored custom |
| Traditional | Adj | Being in tradition |
| Traditionalism | Noun | Being in tradition, custom |
| | | |
| Traditionalist | Noun | One upholding tradition |
| Tranquil | Adj | At ease, calm |
| Tranquility | Noun | Be tranquil, calm, at ease |
| | | |
| Transform | Verb | Change to something else |
| Transgress | Verb | Go beyond established limit |
| Travesty | Noun | Bad imitation, replacement |
| | | |
| Treadmill | Noun | Boring. Repetitive. Monotonous |
| Tremendous | Adj | Great. Huge. Large |
| Trenchant | Adj | Clear cut. Keen |
| | | |
| Tricky | Adj | Deceitful. Clever |
| Trifling | Adj | Superficial. Shallow |
| Trite | Adj | No longer valid, fresh. Stale. Old |
| | | |
| Trivia | Noun | Unimportant in nature |
| Trivial | Adj | Of little value, worth |
| Troublemaker | Noun | One who routinely makes trouble |
| | | |
| Trouble-shooter | Noun | One who looks for trouble to fix |
| Troublesome | Adj | Making, causing trouble |
| Truant | Noun | One who fails to work, perform |
| | | |
| Trustful | Adj | To trust, believe |
| Trusting | Adj | To trust, believe |
| Trustworthy | Adj | Be able to trust. Reliable |
| | | |
| Truthful | Adj | Being at truth. Honest |
| Turbulent | Adj | Violent, disorderly |
| Turmoil | Noun | Confusion. Not stable |
| | | |
| Typical | Adj | Serving as example of kind, type |
| Typify | Verb | Be typical |

**-U-**

| | | |
|---|---|---|
| Ultimate | Adj | Conclusion. End |
| Unaccomplished | Adj | Not accomplished, skilled |
| Unacquainted | Adj | Not learned, taught, knowing |
| | | |
| Unadvised | Adj | Done without forethought. Hasty |
| Unapt | Adj | Not apt, likely, skilled, able |
| Unassuming | Adj | Not forward, aggressive |
| | | |
| Unaware | Adj | Not aware, knowing |
| Unbeatable | Adj | Unable to beat, conquer |
| Unbending | Adj | Firm. Resolute |
| | | |
| Unbiased | Adj | Not biased, prejudiced |
| Unbounded | Adj | Without bounds or limits |
| Uncanny | Adj | Unreal, unnatural act or feat |
| | | |
| Uncertain | Adj | Not certain, sure, positive |
| Uncertainty | Noun | Not certain, sure |
| Uncharitable | Adj | Without charity. Not forgiving |
| | | |
| Uncomfortable | Adj | Not comfortable, agreeable |
| Uncommon | Adj | Not common, ordinary. Rare |
| Uncompromising | Adj | Not giving, relenting. Fixed. Firm |
| | | |
| Unconventional | Adj | Not ordinary or standard |
| Unconversant | Adj | Lacking knowledge |
| Undaunted | Adj | Not failing, faltering |
| | | |
| Undecided | Adj | Unsure. Not decisive |
| Undeniable | Adj | Unable to deny. Without question |
| Underhanded | Adj | Not open, above board, honest |
| | | |
| Undermine | Verb | To weaken, wear away |
| Understand | Verb | To know, comprehend |
| Understanding | Noun | To understand |
| | | |
| Understudy | Noun | One who studies under another |
| Undiscerning | Adj | No good judgment/understanding |
| Undistinguished | Adj | Not looked up to, held in esteem |
| | | |
| Uneasy | Adj | Not comfortable. Anxious |
| Unequivocal | Adj | Clear. Plain |
| Unerring | Adj | Without error, fault |

| | | |
|---|---|---|
| Unerudite | Adj | Unlearned. Unskilled |
| Unexceptional | Adj | Plain. Common. Ordinary |
| Unfailing | Adj | Not fail. Reliable |
| | | |
| Unfair | Adj | Not fair, just, equitable |
| Unfamiliar | Adj | Not known, recognized |
| Unfavorable | Adj | Not favorable. Against. Adverse |
| | | |
| Unfeeling | Adj | Without feeling |
| Unfit | Adj | Not fit, able, capable |
| Unflappable | Adj | Composed. Calm |
| | | |
| Unfortunate | Adj | Bad luck |
| Unfriendly | Adj | Not friendly |
| Ungracious | Adj | Not polite, pleasant |
| | | |
| Unimaginative | Adj | No mental vision, inventiveness |
| Uninformative | Adj | Without knowledge, information |
| Uninformed | Adj | Not knowing, knowledgeable |
| | | |
| Uninhibited | Adj | Without mental reservation |
| Unintelligent | Adj | Lack of intelligence |
| Uninteresting | Adj | Dull. Boring |
| | | |
| Unique | Adj | Unusual. One of a kind. Rare |
| Uniqueness | Noun | Being unique |
| Unknowing | Adj/Noun | Not known. No knowledge |
| | | |
| Unknown | Adj | Not known, knowing |
| Unlawful | Adj | Not within the law. Not legal |
| Unlearned | Adj | Not learned, educated |
| | | |
| Unlettered | Adj | Uneducated |
| Unlimited | Adj | Without bounds or limits |
| Unmannerly | Adj | Bad manners. Rude |
| | | |
| Unmerciful | Adj | Without mercy, pity |
| Unmistakable | Adj | Without mistake, error, flaw |
| Unnerve | Verb | Lose nerve, confidence |
| | | |
| Unorganized | Adj | Not organized, in order |
| Unparalleled | Adj | Without peer, match, equal |
| Unperceptive | Adj | Not knowing, discerning |

| | | |
|---|---|---|
| Unperceptiveness | Noun | Not keen, penetrating, knowing |
| Unpleasant | Adj | Not pleasant, agreeable |
| Unpopular | Adj | Not popular, liked |
| | | |
| Unprincipled | Adj | Without moral values |
| Unprofessional | Adj | Not professional, proper, correct |
| Unquestionable | Adj | Without question |
| | | |
| Unrealistic | Adj | Not realistic, practical |
| Unreason | Noun | No reason, rationale |
| Unreasonable | Adj | Not reasonable, feasible, rational |
| | | |
| Unreasoning | Adj | Without rational reason |
| Unrefined | Adj | Lack of culture, social bearing |
| Unrelenting | Adj | Not relenting, yielding. Fixed |
| | | |
| Unrivaled | Adj | Without rival, match, equal |
| Unruly | Adj | Unable to control, manage |
| Unscholarly | Adj | Without knowledge, learning |
| | | |
| Unscrupulous | Adj | Without principles, morals |
| Unseasoned | Adj | Not mature, experienced |
| Unselfish | Adj | Giving. Caring. Generous |
| | | |
| Unsettled | Adj | Not settled, stable |
| Unskilled | Adj | Without skill, ability |
| Unskillful | Adj | Without skill, ability |
| | | |
| Unsociable | Adj | Not sociable, friendly |
| Unstable | Adj | Not stable, firm. Resolute |
| Unstoppable | Adj | Not able to stop, cease |
| | | |
| Unsuccessful | Adj | Without success |
| Unsuitable | Adj | Not appropriate, compatible |
| Untaught | Adj | Without learning, education |
| | | |
| Untidy | Adj | Not tidy, neat, orderly |
| Untrue | Adj | Not true. False |
| Untruth | Noun | Non-truth. False |
| | | |
| Untruthful | Adj | Be untrue, false |
| Untutored | Adj | Unlearned. Uneducated |
| Unversed | Adj | Not learned, knowledgeable |

| | | |
|---|---|---|
| Unwilling | Adj | Not willing. Reluctant |
| Unwise | Adj | Not wise, prudent |
| Unwittingness | Noun | Without wit. Dull |
| | | |
| Unworthy | Adj | Not worthy, deserving, fit |
| Unyielding | Adj | Not giving, yielding |
| Up-and-coming | Adj | New. Promising |
| | | |
| Upright | Adj | Just. Honest |
| Useful | Adj | Of use, benefit |
| Useless | Adj | Of no use, benefit |

## -V-

| | | |
|---|---|---|
| Vacuous | Adj | Without intelligence, thought |
| Vain | Adj | Empty. Futile |
| Valuable | Adj | Be important, meaningful, of value |
| | | |
| Valueless | Adj | Without value or worth |
| Vast | Adj | Great. Huge. Immense |
| Veracious | Adj | Truth. Honesty |
| | | |
| Veracity | Noun | Truthful. Honest |
| Verbalism | Noun | Word without form, meaning |
| Verbalist | Noun | Skilled orator, wordsmith |
| | | |
| Verbose | Adj | Too long, wordy |
| Versatile | Adj | Adaptable. Multi-dimensional |
| Versed | Adj | Experienced. Skilled |
| | | |
| Verve | Noun | Exuberant. Energetic |
| Vex | Verb | Troubling. Irritating |
| Vigilant | Adj | Watchful |
| | | |
| Vigor | Noun | Vim. Vitality. Strength |
| Vigorous | Adj | Lively. Sturdy. Full of energy |
| Vim | Noun | Vigor. Zest. Vitality |
| | | |
| Vindictive | Adj | Revengeful. Not forgiving |
| Violate | Verb | To break, penetrate in violation |
| Violent | Adj | Physical force, rage |
| | | |
| Virtue | Noun | Good moral value |
| Virtuous | Adj | Having virtue, high morals |
| Vision | Noun/Verb | Foresight. See to the future |

**205**

| | | |
|---|---|---|
| Visualization | Noun | Foresee by mental picture |
| Visualize | Verb | Mental picture or image |
| Vitality | Noun | Vim. Vigor. Energy |
| | | |
| Vitalization | Noun | Lively. Vim. Vigor |
| Vitiate | Verb | Go wrong, faulty, weak |
| Vivacious | Adj | Lively, with spirit, vigor |
| | | |
| Vivid | Adj | Clear in vision, picture, thought |
| Vivid Imagination | Noun | Active, lively mind |
| Vocabulary | Noun | Word capacity, ability |
| | | |
| Voluble | Adj | Talkative |
| Voluntary | Adj | Give freely. Free of will |

**-W-**

| | | |
|---|---|---|
| Wade | Verb | To plunge into |
| Wander | Verb | Stray about without reason |
| Wane | Verb | Become less. Diminish |
| | | |
| Wangle | Verb | Trick. Deceive |
| Wanting | Adj | Lacking. Deficient |
| Wanton | Adj | Without discipline, control |
| | | |
| Warm | Adj | Affectionate |
| Warmhearted | Adj | Affectionate. Caring. Giving |
| Washed-up | Adj | No longer of benefit, use |
| | | |
| Waste | Noun | Ruin. Spoil |
| Wasted | Adj | Ruined. Spoiled |
| Wasteful | Adj | To waste |
| | | |
| Watchful | Adj | Observant |
| Weak | Adj | Not strong, steady |
| Weaken | Verb | Make weak. Lose strength |
| | | |
| Weakhearted | Adj | Without conviction, courage |
| Weak-minded | Adj | Lack will power, judgment |
| Weakness | Noun | Being weak |
| | | |
| Weariful | Adj | Tired. Weary |
| Weariless | Adj | Does not weaken, tire |
| Wearisome | Adj | Being weary, tired |

| | | |
|---|---|---|
| Wear out | Verb | Use up. Expend. Exhaust |
| Weary | Adj | Drained of strength, energy |
| Weighty | Adj | Important. Meaningful |
| | | |
| Well-advised | Adj | Use wisdom, prudence |
| Well-bred | Adj | Well raised. Dignified. Sociable |
| Well-conditioned | Adj | Being well adjusted socially |
| | | |
| Well-defined | Adj | Clear, distinct |
| Well-disposed | Adj | Good disposition |
| Well-done | Adj | Done correctly, properly |
| | | |
| Well-founded | Adj | Based on solid reason |
| Well-groomed | Adj | Neat. Orderly. Tidy |
| Well-grounded | Adj | Well based knowledge |
| | | |
| Well-handed | Adj | Well managed, controlled |
| Well-informed | Adj | Possessing great knowledge |
| Well-intentioned | Adj | Intending, meaning well or good |
| | | |
| Well-known | Adj | Widely known |
| Well-meaning | Adj | Good meaning, intention |
| Well-off | Adj | In good condition |
| | | |
| Well-read | Adj | Well informed. Knowledgeable |
| Well-rounded | Adj | Well developed, educated |
| Well-spoken | Adj | Speak with skill |
| | | |
| Well-taken | Noun | To be well, happy, content |
| Well-timed | Adj | Timed to opportunity |
| Well-versed | Adj | Having expert knowledge |
| | | |
| Whimsical | Adj | Erratic, unpredictable |
| Whiz | Noun | A wizard, genius |
| Wholehearted | Adj | Sincere & complete support |
| | | |
| Wholesome | Adj | Healthy mind, morals, spirit |
| Wide-ranging | Adj | Wide in range, scope, context |
| Widely-read | Adj | Knowledgeable in many subjects |
| | | |
| Wile | Noun | Deceive. Trick |
| Willful | Adj | With one's own free will |
| Willing | Adj | With free will. Without reluctance |

| | | |
|---|---|---|
| Will-less | Adj | Without will |
| Wilt | Verb | Fade. Grow dim, weak |
| Wily | Adj | Skillful. Crafty |
| | | |
| Winner | Noun | One who wins, comes out on top |
| Wisdom | Noun | Knowledge. Wise |
| Wise | Adj | Wisdom. Knowledge. Experienced |
| | | |
| Wiseness | Noun | Of good judgment, wisdom |
| Wishful | Adj | Based on hope |
| Wishy-washy | Adj | Not firm, effective, steady |
| | | |
| Wit | Noun | Power of mind, reasoning |
| Wits | Noun | Possess keen mental faculties |
| Withstand | Verb | Hold up. Oppose |
| | | |
| Witless | Adj | Without wit |
| Witted | Adj | Having wit |
| Witticism | Noun | Sharp, penetrating joke |
| | | |
| Witty | Adj | Having ample wit |
| Wonderwork | Noun | Successful, skillful undertaking |
| Wondrous | Adj | Held in wonder, high esteem |
| | | |
| Wording | Noun | Convey in words |
| Wordplay | Noun | Skillful play at words |
| Wordsmith | Noun | One skillful at words |
| | | |
| Wordy | Adj | Too many words |
| Workable | Adj | Capable. Able |
| Workaholic | Noun | One filled with capacity for work |
| | | |
| Workhorse | Noun | One doing majority of the work |
| Workmanship | Noun | Quality of product |
| Work over | Verb | Redo. To do again, over |
| | | |
| Workup | Noun | Study. Preparation |
| Worldly-wise | Adj | Wise to the way of things |
| Worse | Adj | Less desirable or favorable |
| | | |
| Worsen | Verb | To do worse |
| Worst | Adj | Most faulty, bad |
| Worthful | Adj | Of value, worth |

| Worthless | Adj | Without worth, value |
| Worthwhile | Adj | Worth time, effort |
| Worthy | Adj | Having merit, value, worth |
| | | |
| Would-be | Adj | Having potential, ability |
| Wretch | Noun | One dissatisfied. Bad disposition |
| Wretched | Adj | Totally disagreeable personality |
| | | |
| Wrong | Adj | Erroneous. False. Amiss |
| Wrongdoer | Noun | One who does wrong |
| Wrongdoing | Noun | To do wrong |
| | | |
| Wrongful | Adj | Being wrong |
| Wroth | Adj | Irate. Angry |
| Wry | Adj | Grim humor |

## -Y-

| Yardstick | Noun | A standard, reference level |
| Yes-man | Noun | One always in agreement |
| Youthful | Adj | Young, fresh, refreshing |

## -Z-

| Zeal | Noun | Spirit. Vigor. Enthusiasm |
| Zealot | Noun | One with zeal |
| Zealotory | Noun | Overfilled with zeal |
| | | |
| Zealous | Adj | Having zeal |
| Zenith | Noun | Top. Uppermost point |
| Zest | Noun | Vigor. Enthusiasm |
| | | |
| Zestfulness | Noun | Stimulating. Invigorating. Active |
| Zesty | Adj | Have zest |
| Zip | Verb | Swift, speedy. Invigorating |

# SENTENCE SUBJECTS

The Sentence Subjects in this section are intended to give you hundreds of ideas with thousands of possible uses. Notice from the following example some of the ways in which the Sentence Subject can be changed into a variety of uses.

**These sentence subjects can also be used to form bullet phrase statements.**

Sentence Subject: ABOVE AND BEYOND
      Example: (Name) went above and beyond call of duty in/by...
      Example: Efforts to .... were above and beyond that normally
         expected of...
      Example: Despite risk of personal injury (name) went above and
         beyond that normally expected of...
      Example: (Name) efforts in field/area of..... were clearly above
         and beyond standards of .....

Sentence Subject: ABSOLUTE DEDICATION
      Example: (Name) absolute dedication to..... led to marked
         improvement in .....
      Example: (Name) absolute dedication exhibited during (period)
         directly responsible for vast increase in .....
      Example: Superior and successful performance in/as.....were a
         direct result of his/her absolute dedication to .....


**SUBJECT      EXAMPLE USE**

**Able to size up**
      Example: Able to size up any problem area and supply correct fix.
**Above and beyond**
      Example: Performance above and beyond call of duty
**Above board**
      Example: Honest and above board at all times.
**Absolute confidence**
      Example: Has absolute confidence in performance of...
**Absolute dedication**
      Example: Absolutely dedicated to improving standards of...
**Absolute faith in**
      Example: Others have absolute faith in his/her ability to...
**Absolutely committed to**
      Example: Deeply committed to absolute safety of...

**Absolutely essential**
   Example: (Name) was absolutely essential in meeting…
**Absorbed in**
   Example: Absolutely absorbed in every facet of…
**Abundance of**
   Example: Displaying an abundance of energy, he/she…
**Accelerated change**
   Example: Quick and accelerated change made possible by…
**Accepted challenge**
   Example: Accepted the demanding challenge of…
**Accepted responsibility**
   Example: Quickly accepted responsibility for … and implemented…
**Achieved greatness**
   Example: Achieved greatness in field of…
**Acquainted with success**
   Example: Acquaintance with success instrumental in…
**Across the board**
   Example: Across the board success resulted in…
**Acted in concert**
   Example: Others acted in concert to aid in…
**Acted prudently**
   Example: Acted prudently and decisively in achieving...
**Active role**
   Example: Played an active role in the completion of…
**Active support(er)**
   Example: (Name) active support in..... led to…
**Actively engaged in**
   Example: Actively engaged in efforts to stem tide of…
**Actively promoted**
   Example: Actively promoted new and innovative way to .....
      which led to vast improvements in .....
**Acutely aware**
   Example: (Name) is/was acutely aware of the necessity for/to.....
**Acutely sensitive** to
   Example: Performance to duty was exemplary while taking into
      account the acutely sensitive need to/for .....
**Adamant in stand**
   Example: Showing professional diligence, (name) was adamant in
      stand for/against .....
**Added extra dimension**
   Example: (Name) was able to add the extra dimension needed for
      the successful conclusion of .....
**Added value(s)**
   Example: (Name) added directly to the value of .....

**Address needs of**
> Example: (Name) never failed to address the needs of .....

**Addressed issue(s)**
> Example: Addressed the sensitive issue(s) of ..... without .....

**Admired character(istics)**
> Example: (Name) has many professional characteristics to be admired, not the least of which is .....

**Adopt a course**
> Example: Adopted a course of action that lead to real improvements in .....

**Advanced idea**
> Example: (Name) was able to advance the idea of ..... which led to dramatic improvements in .....

**Advanced state of**
> Example: Diligent work in area of ..... led to an advanced state of ..... and increased the overall readiness of .....

**Adversity**
> Example: Tackled and successfully completed all ..... despite adversity involved in/with .....

**Advocate for**
> Example: A firm advocate for increased.....

**Against all odds**
> Example: Completed the unenviable task of ... against all odds.

**Aggressive agenda**
> Example: (Name) executed an aggressive work agenda that included .....

**Ahead of times**
> Example: (Name) knowledge and expertise in the field of ..... is ahead of the times.

**Alert to possibilities**
> Example: Always alert to possibilities for improvement in .....

**Alive with**
> Example: His/Her (organization) personnel come alive with energy and excitement when .....

**All-out effort**
> Example: (Name) can always be counted on to give an all-out effort during times of .....

**Always eager to**
> Example (Name) is always eager and willing to volunteer to assume additional responsibility when/if .....

**Always gives 110 percent**
> Example: Regardless of the circumstances, (name) always gives 110 percent.

**Amassed abundance of**
    Example: (Name) amassed an abundance of talent that directly
        resulted in an marked increase/improvement in .....
**Amazing speed**
    Example: (Name) was able to complete the entire task in amazing
        speed, despite .....
**Ambitious campaign**
    Example: (Name) mounted an ambitious campaign in ..... that
        resulted in a significant improvement/increase in .....
**Ambitious initiatives/progress**
    Example: Brought into play a broad number of ambitious
        initiatives that led to .....
**Among the best**
    Example: His/Her (subject) are among the best I have ever seen.
**Analyzed various elements**
    Example: Correctly analyzed the various elements of ..... and then
        proceeded to construct and complete .....
**Appetite for**
    Example: (Name) has an insatiable appetite for knowledge in a
        field in which he/she is already considered an expert.
**Applaud efforts of**
    Example: I have to applaud the personal diligent and efforts to .....
**Appreciate uniqueness of'**
    Example: Appreciates the uniqueness of each individual's talent
        and skill and combined this into one of the most
        impressive .....
**Appreciates hard work**
    Example: (Name) fully appreciates the hard work and effort of
        others and rewards this contribution to total team effort by
**Architect of**
    Example: (Name) was the architect of the highly successful .....
**Around-the-clock**
    Example: (Name) is willing to work around-the-clock to fulfill
        mission requirements.
**Arouses**
    Example:(Name) arouses the spirit and energy of others by.....

**Articulate(d) new image**
    Example: Shortly after his/her arrival, he/she articulated a new
        image of the previously sagging .....
**Ascended to**
    Example: (Name) quickly ascended to the top of his/her field
        through hard work and persistent dedication.

**Aspire to excellence**
> Example: (Name) aspires to achieve excellence regardless of tasking difficulty or complexity.

**Assessment of situation**
> Example: Blessed with a rare ability to quickly make an assessment of any tactical/professional situation.

**At forefront**
> Example: (Name) is at the forefront in the field of .....

**At pinnacle**
> Example: (Name) is at the pinnacle of his/her profession.

**Atmosphere conducive to**
> Example: (Name) creates an atmosphere highly conducive to.....

**Attention to detail**
> Example: Displaying a meticulous attention to detail he/she was able to .....

**Attracts followers**
> Example: Natural leadership style attracts followers and allows him/her to accomplish more than .....

**Attuned to needs**
> Example: Ability to stay attuned to the needs of his/her personnel allows him/her to accomplish .....

**Awakened spirit(s) of**
> Example: Awakened the spirits of others with his/her unique leadership style that resulted in a highly successful .....

**Award-winning**
> Example: (Name) demonstrated his/her award-winning performance in the area/field of .....

**Backbone**
> Example: (Name) became the backbone in the organization by.....

**Ball of fire**
> Example: (Name) is a ball of fire when it comes to .....

**Bang up job**
> Example: (Name) did a bang up job on/as .....

**Bank on it**
> Example: When he/she sets out to do something, you can bank on it to be completed completely and on time.

**Barely missed a beat**
> Example: Despite being undermanned/under funded (etc.), he/she barely missed a beat completing the difficult job of .....

**Beacon of hope**
> Example: (Name) serves as a beacon of hope for others when .....

**Bear down**
> Example: (Name) can always be counted upon to bear down when it comes to .....

**Bear responsibility**
> Example: (Name) bears the heavy weight of responsibility for .....
> without skipping a beat.

**Bear the burden**
> Example: (Name) bears the burden of .....despite handicap of .....

**Beat all odds**
> Example: (Name) beat all odds with his/her completion of .....

**Became focal point**
> Example: (Name) became the focal point for the special project of
> ..... During this time he/she .....

**Became symbol for/to**
> Example: (Name) became a symbol to others with his/her ability
> to .....

**Beef up**
> Example: (Name) was able to beef up ..... area despite being .....

**Beehive of activity**
> Example: The (organization) became a beehive of activity in
> carrying out .....

**Began to take form/shape**
> Example: Showing great care and patience, the ..... began to take
> form and meet .....

**Behind the scene(s)**
> Example: Someone had to do the lack of credit, behind the scene
> work on .....(Name) volunteered to tackle this difficult task.

**Believability**
> Example: (Name) never has a believability problem when
> convincing others to .....

**Benchmark**
> Example: (Name's) work served as a benchmark for .....

**Bend over backwards**
> Example: He/She bends over backwards to maintain good order
> and discipline between/among .....

**Benefits from understanding**
> Example: Others benefit from his/her total understanding of .....

**Best foot forward**
> Example: (Name) is always ready and willing to help others,
> putting his/her best foot forward in an effort to .....

**Best interest of**
> Example: (Name) always puts best interest of (organization) first.

**Best tradition**
> Example: The performance of (name) was in the best tradition
> of.....

**Better prepared**
> Example: (Name) is always better prepared to meet the
> challenges of ..... than .....

**Beyond a doubt**
> Example: (Name) is beyond a doubt the best ..... in .....

**Blazed new trail**
> Example: (Name) blazed a new trail in the area/field of .....

**Blessed with**
> Example: Blessed with superior ..... ability/talent, name was able to complete .....

**Blistering pace**
> Example: (Name) set a blistering pace in/by .....

**Blue ribbon**
> Example: (Name) headed up/formed a blue ribbon panel that successfully .....

**Body of work**
> Example: (Name) complete body of work far exceeds .....

**Bold new/move**
> Example: In a bold move, (name) successfully integrated .....

**Boosted spirits**
> Example: (Name) always seems to find a way to boost the spirits of others when faced with .....

**Bottom line**
> Example: The bottom line is that (name) simply performs in a superior fashion, regardless of complexity of tasking.

**Bought into focus**
> Example: (Name) is an expert at bringing into focus the diverse elements inherent to/in .....

**Boyish excitement**
> Example: (Name) boyish excitement and zest for work was instrumental in gaining the support and loyalty of .....

**Brain trust**
> Example: (Name) is (organization) brain trust in area/field of .....

**Brainchild**
> Example: The successful completion of ..... was the brainchild of (name), to whom much of the credit is due.

**Brainstorm**
> Example: During a brainstorm session, (name) suggested the use of .....to ..... This proved immensely successful.

**Break new ground**
> Example: (Name) broke new ground in the area/field of .....when he/she .....

**Break through**
> Example: (Name) work in/as resulted in a major break through in...

**Breakneck speed**
> Example: (Name) completed all work associated with ..... with breakneck speed.

**Breakthrough**
    Example: A real breakthrough in ..... came when (name) suggested the use of ..... in .....

**Breath of fresh air**
    Example: (Name) arrival at (organization) was like a breath of fresh air. He/She brought with him/her a/an .....

**Breathed new life**
    Example: (Name) breathed new life into..... which was previously plagued with .....

**Bridged the gap**
    Example: (Name) was able to bridge the gap between .....

**Bright chapter/future**
    Example: (Name) has a bright future ahead of him/her as a .....
    Example: (Name) Brought a bright chapter to (organization) with his/her knowledge and enthusiasm in/on/of.....

**Brighten the day**
    Example: (Name) enthusiasm and zest for .....brightens the day in an otherwise .....

**Bring into focus**
    Example: (Name) penetrating work in/as ..... was able to bring into proper focus the major elements of .....

**Bring into line**
    Example: (Name) was able to bring into line all of the elements involved in/with .....

**Broad consensus**
    Example: (Name) was able to build a broad consensus that led directly to the improvement of .....

**Broad stroke**
    Example: With one broad stroke (name) was able to .....

**Broader understanding**
    Example: (Name) is possessed with a broader understanding of ..... than anyone else in the area/field of .....

**Brought about/out**
    Example: (Name) brought about a major change in ..... which directly led to a dramatic improvement in .....

**Brought to life**
    Example: (Name) brought to life a new chapter in (organization) in which efficiency and production took a decided upward turn, and .....

**Brought under control**
    Example: (Name) brought under control the runaway .....

**Build a fire under**
    Example: (Name) was able to bring life to .... by building a fire under the feet of .....

**Building blocks**
> Example: (Name) provided the essential building blocks that brought about the extraordinary improvement in .....

**Bulldog determination**
> Example: (Name) executed all tasks with bulldog determination.

**Burning desire**
> Example: (Name) displayed a burning desire to complete .....

**Burst of creativity**
> Example: With a burst of creativity, (name) successfully .....

**Bursting with**
> Example: Bursting with pride and determination, (name) was able to .....

**Business at hand**
> Example: (Name) ability to focus on the business at hand and eliminate distractions was instrumental in.....

**Business-like**
> Example: (Name) business-like professionalism approach to any task allows him/her to .....

**By the book**
> Example: A no nonsense who goes by the book person.

**Calculated risk/response**
> Example: The risk was calculated response to .....

**Call(ed) the signal(s)**
> Example: (Name) took the lead and called the signals in/on a very successful .....

**Called upon to**
> Example: (Name) was called upon to .... He/She responded with customary excellence in all aspects of .....

**Calm authority**
> Example: (Name) provided the calm presence and authority needed for the successful completion of .....

**Came of age**
> Example: (Name) came of age when he/she successfully orchestrated the complex task of .....

**Came prepared**
> Example: (Name) came fully prepared for the task of ..... He/She again demonstrated his/her unfailing ability to .....

**Came to aid of**
> Example: (Name) came to the aid of ....., and was instrumental in the successful completion of ..... despite .....

**Came to fruition**
> Example: His/Her work came to fruition with the completion of ..... This helped build up what had been .....

**Capitalized on**
> Example: (Name) capitalized on the strength of ..... This allowed him/her to organize a ..... second to none.

**Captured imagination of**
> Example: (Name) was able to capture the imagination of ... This in turn resulted in .....

**Captured the advantage**
> Example: (Name) was able to ..... by capturing the advantage through the use of .....

**Career defined by**
> Example: (Name) career can be defined by the frequent use of the word "outstanding."

**Carefully engineered**
> Example: (Name) carefully engineered the building/construction of ..... which in turn allowed him/her to .....

**Carefully planned**
> Example: (Name) carefully planned and brilliantly executed a program to/that .....

**Cares deeply**
> Example: (Name) cares deeply for the comfort and well being of others. This was fully demonstrated when he/she .....

**Carried forward**
> Example: (Name) carried forward on a program/project that had previously been put on hold due to ..... This resulted in ...

**Carry through**
> Example: Always carries through on difficult ..... to

**Carry(ied) the ball**
> Example: (Name) carried the ball for ..... who was out with .....

**Carry(ies) weight**
> Example: (Name) carries his/her weight and helps others at/in.....

**Cast a bond**
> Example: (Name) was able to cast a strong bond with .....

**Cast light upon**
> Example: (Name) research in ..... cast light upon .....

**Catalyst of/for**
> Example: (Name) acted as the catalyst for a new and improved way to .....

**Cemented relationships**
> Example: (Name) cemented relationship with ..... allowed him/her to .....

**Centerpiece**
> Example: (Name) became the centerpiece of activity when it became necessary to .....

**Certain curiosity**
> Example: (Name) has a certain curiosity about him/her that allows him/her to find new ways to .....

**Chain of events**
> Example: The chain of events that (name) started led to real improvement in (area)

**Chalk up success(es)**
> Example: (Name) chalked up another success with the implementation of .....

**Challenge of change**
> Example: (Name) enjoys the challenge of change and seems to do his/her best work when .....

**Challenges conventional ideas**
> Example: (Name) challenged the conventional ideas of ..... and then proceeded to revolutionize the .....

**Challenges(d) status quo**
> Example: (Name) seeks to challenge the status quo while searching for new and improved methods of/to .....

**Challenging opportunity(ies)**
> Example: (Name) thrives on challenging opportunities and difficult tasking.

**Challenging task(s)**
> Example: (Name) faces challenging tasks with a customary zeal rarely observed in .....

**Champion(s) cause(s)**
> Example: (Name) championed the cause of ..... This led to a marked upgrade/improvement in .....

**Championed efforts to**
> Example: (Name) was able to champion the efforts to ..... due to his/her .....

**Chance to carry on**
> Example: (Name) work on/in ..... gave others a chance to carry on with continued .....

**Changed face of**
> Example: (Name) changed the face of ..... with his/her major contribution as .....

**Changing climate of**
> Example: Amid a changing climate of ..... (name) was able to successfully overcome .....

**Changing times**
> Example: In today's changing times, (name) continues to produce top quality work by .....

**Characteristic enthusiasm**
> Example: (Name) characteristic enthusiasm always elicits the maximum effort of/from .....

**Characterized by**
  Example: (Name) performance is characterized by hard work, dedication, and .....

**Charged ahead**
  Example: (Name) charged ahead on .....without awaiting official orders or direction. This led to .....

**Charisma**
  Example: (Name) charisma quickly wins the willing support of .....

**Charismatic**
  Example: (Name) characteristic enthusiasm for any task has, and continues to, lead the way in .....

**Charted course**
  Example: (Name) charted a course for the future of ..... by his/her groundbreaking work in/as .....

**Choice of values**
  Example: (Name) choice of work and personal values far exceeds.....

**Clarity of purpose**
  Example: (Name) has a focus and clarity of purpose rarely seen in.....

**Class act**
  Example: (Name) is, without doubt, a class act. He/She became the first person to .....

**Classic example**
  Example: (Name) is a classic example of what one person can do with .....

**Clean and quick**
  Example: With one clean and quick stroke (name) successfully ....

**Clean slate**
  Example: (Name) maintained a clean slate during .....

**Clean sweep**
  Example: (Name) made a clean sweep of all .....

**Cleaned up problems**
  Example: (Name) cleaned up problems left by ..... and quickly rose to the top of .....

**Clear agenda**
  Example: (Name) proceeded ahead with a clear agenda on how to ..... Noted improvements were quickly noted in.....

**Clear picture**
  Example: (Name) came up with a clear picture of the problems associated with..... He/She proceeded to .....

**Clearly articulated**
  Example: (Name) was able to clearly articulate the workings of .... into .....

**Clever idea(s)**
>   Example: (Name) has come up with one clever idea after another
>   for the improvement of .....

**Climate of**
>   Example: In a climate of scarce resources and manpower, name
>   was able to .....

**Climbed to top**
>   Example: (Name) climbed to the top of ..... with his/her
>   persistence and dedication. This led to an improved .....

**Close cooperation**
>   Example: Working in close cooperation with ..... (name) was able
>   to achieve more than .....

**Close scrutiny**
>   Example: (Name) gave close scrutiny to the internal workings of
>   ..... then followed up with .....

**Close(d) ranks**
>   Example: (Name) closed ranks with other ..... This close-knit
>   working relationship proved highly successful in .....

**Coalition building**
>   Example: Behind the scenes coalition building afforded (name)
>   the opportunity to .....

**Cohesive group**
>   Example: (Name) formed a very cohesive group of ..... This
>   highly professional group succeeded in .....

**Cold analysis**
>   Example: (Name) took a cold analysis look at ..... and decided to
>   ..... This ultimately led to .....

**Collective influence**
>   Example: The collective and continued influence exerted by
>   (name) was the prime reason for .....

**Colorful style**
>   Example: (Name) colorful style of leadership allowed him/her to
>   continue the difficult task of ..... with (results)

**Come alive**
>   Example: (Name) organization came alive with a flurry of .....

**Come to grips with**
>   Example: (Name) came to grips with the problems in/of ..... and
>   took immediate and effective corrective action that led
>   to.....

**Comfort level**
>   Example: (Name) is in his/her comfort level when others are in
>   disarray. He/She has a unique ability to .....

**Commands attention**
>   Example: The work of (name) commands the attention of his/her
>   superiors. He/She simply accomplished more than .....

**Committed to**
Example: (Name) is fully committed to professional excellence. He/She was able to demonstrate this recently when he/she .....

**Common cause**
Example: (Name) always pulls together for the common cause of (organization). Putting ..... ahead of personal needs.

**Common effort**
Example: (Name) pulls together the common effort of others into a cohesive .....

**Competitive spirit/edge**
Example: (Name) has a competitive spirit. He/She is not satisfied with ..... performance. Instead, he/she looks forward to ...

**Complete success**
Example: (Name) tackled various difficult assignments with complete success. One example is .....

**Complete turnaround**
Example: (Name) was able to institute a complete turnaround in the ..... Where performance had previously been ..... it is now the front-running organization in .....

**Concept became reality**
Example: The concept of ..... became reality when (name) transformed ..... into .....

**Concrete benefits**
Example: Tangible, concrete benefits were derived by ..... when (Name) .....

**Concrete ideas**
Example: (Name) contributed concrete ideas in/for ..... This contribution was instrumental in/to .....

**Concrete support**
Example: (Name) gave his/her concrete support in the area of .....

**Confidence builder**
Example: (Name) is a real confidence builder. This was most recently demonstrated in/by .....

**Confidence restored**
Example: (Name) restored the confidence of his/her (organization). This was accomplished by .....

**Confronted challenge(s)**
Example: (Name) confronted the challenges of ..... head-on and without hesitation.

**Connects with others**
Example: (Name) connects with others with relative ease. This allows him/her to ..... with highly effective results.

**223**

**Conquered**
>Example: (Name) conquered the highly complex .....
>Example: (Name) conquered the almost insurmountable problem
>of .....

**Conscious effort**
>Example: In a conscious effort to ..... (name) ventured into the a
>previously little known .....

**Consistent pattern of**
>Example: (Name) has demonstrated a consistent pattern of .....
>This, without doubt led to .....

**Constructive attitude**
>Example: (Name) always maintains a constructive attitude toward
>..... None has been more .....

**Consummate**
>Example: (Name) is the consummate professional. He/She was
>the first person to .....

**Content of character**
>Example: The content of (Name) character was never more
>evident than when he/she .....

**Continued quest for**
>Example: (Name) continued quest for ..... led him/her to the
>outstanding .....

**Continued success**
>Example: (Name) continued to demonstrate the success that
>brought him/her to the forefront of .....
>Example: (Name) continued success in ..... serves as an excellent
>example of how .....

**Continued to adapt**
>Example: (Name) has continued to adapt to the changing
>environment of ..... with relative ease.

**Continued to advance**
>Example: (Name) has continued to advance the cause of .....

**Continuous improvement**
>Example: (Name) continuous improvement in ..... has led to .....

**Contributed to success of**
>Example: (Name) directly contributed to the success of ..... This
>was accomplished through the continued display of .....

**Controlled response**
>Example: (Name) controlled response to ..... in a situation where
>..... proved highly successful in .....

**Conventional barrier(s)**
>Example: (Name) overcame the conventional barriers of .....

**Conventional wisdom**
>Example: Despite conventional wisdom, (name) was able to
>implement and direct a plan that .....

**Conveys style**
  Example: (Name) has been very successful in the style of .....
  he/she conveys to .....
**Convinced others**
  Example: (Name) convinced others to ..... This led to a dramatic
  improvement in .....
**Cooperative spirit**
  Example: The cooperative spirit exhibited by (name) was
  instrumental in .....
**Cornerstone of**
  Example: (Name) was the cornerstone of success in the timely
  completion of ..... that saved (/hours/dollars).
**Countless hours/numbers**
  Example: (Name) dedicated countless hours working on .....
  This was so successful that .....
**Courage to face**
  Example: (Name) has the courage to face adversity. He/She fully
  demonstrated this when .....
**Courageous act(s)**
  Example: (Name) performance was a courageous act of .....
**Course of action**
  Example: (Name) steered a course of action that led to .....
  His/Her rich imagination in this action .....
**Coveted award**
  Example: (Name) earned the coveted award of ..... His/Her
  penetrating look at ..... led to .....
**Cream of the crop**
  Example: (Name) is the cream of the crop in ..... He/She is able
  to intellectually grasp all the elements of .....
**Cream rose to top**
  Example: Everyone was given an equal shot at ..... The cream
  rose to the top as (name) .....
**Created (new) process of**
  Example: (name) created the new process of .....This logical and
  comprehensive method led to .....
**Created atmosphere/climate**
  Example: (Name) created an atmosphere of unparalleled .....
**Creative approach to**
  Example: (Name) creative approach to ..... was both farsighted
  and comprehensive.
**Creative masterpiece**
  Example: (Name) creative masterpiece of ..... was the result of
  his/her fertile mind and professional .....

225

**Crisis situation**
> Example: (Name) performs with uncommon cool and ease in crisis situations, always .....

**Critical time/juncture**
> Example: At the critical juncture of ..... (name) came to the forefront with his/her recommendation that .....

**Critically acclaimed**
> Example: (Name) performance in/as ..... has been critically acclaimed by .....

**Crown jewel**
> Example: (Name) creativeness and understanding of ..... was the crown jewel in ..... It was a brilliant stroke of .....

**Crowning achievement(s)**
> Example: (Name) crowning achievement in .....was the result of his/her astute awareness of .....

**Crucial issue(s)**
> Example: Concerning the crucial issue of ..... (Name) aptitude at dealing with ..... was insightful and .....

**Crusader's zeal**
> Example: (Name) jumped into ..... with a Crusader's zeal. His/Her skillful and artistic response resulted in .....

**Crusader for**
> Example: (Name) has been a crusader for improvement in .....

**Crystal clear**
> Example: It became crystal clear that what was needed was ..... (Name) was quick to take the lead in .....

**Culmination of**
> Example: The culmination of... was a direct result of the bold action taken by (name).

**Cushion of safety**
> Example: While maintaining a cushion of safety, (name) was able to ..... by creating and applying .....

**Customary confidence**
> Example: (Name) customary confidence was a cornerstone in expanding virtually every aspect of .....

**Cut above**
> Example: (Name) performance is a cut above other ..... He/She energized a high-powered .....

**Cut teeth on**
> Example: (Name) handled the difficult and delicate job of ..... He/She cut his/her teeth on being able to .....

**Cutting edge**
> Example: (Name) is on the cutting edge of ..... No one in recent memory has .....

**Daily challenges of**
>Example: Despite the daily challenges of ..... (name) has been able to maintain .....

**Dazzling performance**
>Example: (Name) dazzling performance as .....led to the orderly and practical completion of ......

**Debt of gratitude**
>Example: Everyone at ..... owes a debt of gratitude for his/her resounding success in/as/at .....

**Deceptively simple**
>Example: Despite the difficulty involved, (name) made the job deceptively simple by .....

**Decisive action(s)/step**
>Example: (Name) took decisive action on the time-critical .....

**Dedicated efforts**
>Example: (Name) dedicated and matchless efforts culminated in the most successful .....

**Deep respect**
>Example:(Name) enjoys the deep respect of .....

**Defender of**
>Example: (Name) is a staunch defender of .....He/She considers no ..... too small or trivial that/to .....

**Defined character/essence**
>Example: The defined character of (name) can best be summed up as/by .....

**Definition of character**
>Example: A good definition of character is ..... (Name) has no equal when it comes to .....

**Degree of certainty**
>Example: Without any measurable degree of certainty, (name) managed to .....

**Delicate balance**
>Example: (Name) was able to ..... without disturbing the delicate balance of .....

**Delivered as expected**
>Example: Faced with the prospect of ..... (name) was nevertheless able to deliver as expected the .....

**Despite deep cuts**
>Example: (Name) was able to complete ..... despite deep cuts in .....He/She is unbeatable in this area.

**Develop full potential**
>Example: (Name) developed the full potential of ..... This resulted in the superlative .....

**Devoted resources to**
> Example: (Name) was able to devote scarce resources to the .....
> This allowed ..... to .....

**Devoted to**
> Example: (Name) is devoted to this profession. He/She has
> become a standout in/at .....

**Diehard**
> Example: Only (Name) diehard persistence saved the ...

**Difficult business of**
> Example: (Name) meticulous and unparalleled .....made the
> difficult business of ..... relatively easy.

**Difficult event/circumstances**
> Example: Even under the most difficult circumstances (name)
> manages to produce .....

**Diligent patience**
> Example: Diligent patience and persistence by (name) led the way
> when (organization) was faced with ..... He/She always came
> through with .....

**Directly influenced**
> Example: (Name) directly influenced ..... with his/her distinguished
> performance as/in .....

**Directly responsible for**
> Example: (Name) was directly responsible for the meritorious
> service of ..... during the time/period of .....

**Disciplined passion**
> Example: "(Name) tackled (assignment) with disciplined passion
> which resulted in unparalleled work/improvement in.....

**Discovered**
> Example: Always alert for ways to improve ..... (Name)
> discovered a new way to ..... This directly increased .....

**Distinct advantage**
> Example: (Name) has a distinct advantage over (peers) in the
> area of ..... because of his/her prowess in/as .....

**Distinctively different**
> Example: (Name) tried a new and distinctively different way to .....
> This top-notch idea turned out to be .....

**Distinguished**
> Example: (Name) distinguished himself/herself while serving as
> ..... This sterling performance carried over to .....

**Distinguished tradition**
> Example: In keeping with the long and distinguished tradition of
> (organization), Name outmatched .....

**Distinguishing characteristic(s)**
> Example: One distinguishing characteristic of (name) is his/her
> ability to ....

**Diverse background**
    Example: (Name) diverse background allowed him/her to venture into new areas of ..... with superb results.

**Diverse point(s) of view**
    Example: After reviewing many diverse points of view, (name) decided on a course of action that led to .....

**Do great things**
    Example: (Name) courageous nature allowed him/her to do great things in the area of ....., directly contributing to .....

**Dominant force**
    Example: (Name) is a dominant force in .....His/Her standout performance surpassed .....

**Dominated area of**
    Example: (Name), a proven expert in ....., dominated the area of ..... with his/her .....

**Dominated field**
    Example: (Name) dominated the field of ..... because of his/her ability to ..... and mastery of .....

**Down to the wire**
    Example: The ..... project went down to the wire on whether or not it would succeed. (Name) proved to the deciding factor in the ultimate success of .....

**Dramatic change/time**
    Example: In this dramatic time of change, (name) proved to be a journeyman ..... when he/she .....

**Dramatic swing in**
    Example: (Name) performance produced a dramatic change in ..... because of his/her ability to .....

**Dramatic turn of events**
    Example: A dramatic turn of events caught everyone by surprise. (Name) never missed a beat, his/her outstanding performance led to a dramatic .....

**Dramatically illustrated**
    Example: (Name) ability to be a trailblazer in the area/field of ..... was dramatically illustrated when he/she .....

**Draw the line**
    Example: (Name) was able to draw the line on ..... Immediate and marked improvement in .....quickly followed

**Dream come true**
    Example: (Name) performance in/as has been a dream come true for (organization). He/she is the personification of .....

**Drew heavily on/upon**
    Example: (Organization) drew heavily on (name) expertise in ..... This led the perfection of .....

**Driving force**

Example: (Name) proved to be a driving force in ..... by outclassing the entire field of .....

**Dynamic**

Example: (Name) was a dynamic force in ..... His/Her energy never skipped a beat and resulted in .....

**Eager anticipation**

Example: (Name) always looks in eager anticipation for the most challenging and the most difficult tasking.

**Eager to**

Example: (Name) has shown by ..... that he/she is eager to.....

**Ear marked for**

Example: (Name) should be ear marked for tasks involving ..... His/Her expertise in the field of ..... identifies him/her as the best ..... around.

**Earned place in**

Example: (Name) earned a place in the hearts of ..... because of his/her ability to .....

**Eclipsed previous record**

Example: (Name) eclipsed the previous record of ..... which had stood for ..... with the faultless execution of .....

**Electrified**

Example: (Name) electrified everyone with his/her remarkable ability to ..... Prior to this no one had .....

**Element of risk**

Example: Despite a high element of risk, (name) top-notch work on/as ..... led the way to an unprecedented level of .....

**Elevated to level of**

Example: (Name) was elevated to the level of .....by demonstrating an exceptional level of .....

**Eliminated all**

Example: (Name) sterling performance as ..... eliminated all waste sometimes associated with .....

**Eliminated need for**

Example: (Name) virtually eliminated the need for ..... using his/her superb level of .....

**Elite**

Example: (Name) is one of the elite members of .....because of his/her impeccable talent for .....

**Embarked upon**

Example: (Name) embarked upon the strenuous task of ..... which brought his/her supreme talents of ..... to the forefront of...

**Embodies unique**

Example: (Name) embodies the unique qualities of .....

**Embraced concept**
> Example: (Name) was quick to embrace the concept of .....and took the lead in action that eventually led to .....

**Embraced with enthusiasm**
> Example: The (organization) embraced with enthusiasm (name) proposed concept to .....

**Emerging**
> Example: (Name) is an emerging superstar in the field of .....

**Employing strategy of**
> Example: Employing the strategy of ..... (name) was able to achieve supreme results in/as .....

**Endless possibilities**
> Example: (Name) concept of ..... brings almost endless possibilities into play in the area of ..... which should prove to become the standard-bearer in .....

**Enduring place in**
> Example: (Name) earned an enduring place in the hearts of ..... for his/her exemplary ability to .....

**Energy devoted to**
> Example: (Name) devoted much energy to .....the difficult task of ..... and distinguished himself/herself by .....

**Engaged in**
> Example: Being well versed in all aspects of ....., (name) engaged in the more difficult task of ..... and proved more than equal to the task by .....

**Engineered path of future**
> Example: (Name) diligently engineered a path of the future by personally ....., culminating with the successful .....

**Enhanced image**
> Example: (Name) enhanced the image of ..... through his/her unselfish devotion to duty and .....

**Enjoys(ed) increase(d)**
> Example:(Name) enjoys the increased responsibilities as/of ..... and responded with this assignment by .....

**Enriched the lives**
> Example: (Name) has enriched the personal and professional lives of ..... by .....

**Enthusiasm ran high**
> Example: When the task of ..... arose, enthusiasm ran high throughout (organization) because of (name) belief and trust in .....

**Enthusiastic support**
> Example: (Name) gained the enthusiastic support of ..... when he/she .....

**Entirely new perspective**
> Example: (Name) brought an entirely new perspective to the table on the subject of ..... With the benefit of his/her expertise the (organization) was able to .....

**Entrenched position**
> Example: (Name) was able to pull people from their old-way entrenched positions of ..... and bring them forward to a point of .....

**Entrusted with**
> Example: (Name) was entrusted with the unenviable task of ..... He/She responded with customary excellence in completing .....

**Envisions the future**
> Example: (Name) vision of the future allowed him/her to bring excellent foresight and planning abilities that .....

**Epitome of**
> Example: (Name) is the epitome of a true professional. He/She always responds to ..... with unwavering .....

**Equal to challenge**
> Example: (Name) was equal to the challenge when faces with .....

**Equal to task**
> Example: (Name) was equal to the task of ..... with his/her positive mental attitude and outlook.

**Equitable distribution**
> Example: (Name) received more than an equitable distribution of the work load when/during ..... He/She responded without missing a beat

**Escalation of**
> Example: Despite an escalation of the workload in ....., (name) invigorated and impassioned others to .....

**Especially significant**
> Example: (Name) performance was especially significant during ..... when .....

**Essential element/trait(s)**
> Example: (Name) exhibits the traits most needed to ..... Without him/her the job of ..... would not have been .....

**Established foothold**
> Example: (Name) established a foothold in the mountain of work left to him/her by.....His/Her invigorating spirit resulted in .....

**Established legacy/stability**
> Example: (Name) was able to establish stability in the area of .... which had been plagued by .....

**Ever ready to**
Example: (Name) is ever ready to accept new challenges and proved up to the task when given the responsibility to .....

**Ever-expanding obligations**
Example: Faced with the ever expanding obligations of ..... (name) has managed to successfully .....

**Ever-present/growing**
Example: Facing an ever growing expansion of ..... (name) powerhouse performance overcame .....

**Every possible avenue**
Example: After evaluating every possible avenue of ..... (name) settled on ..... His/Her stimulus to others turned the tide on .....

**Every step of the way**
Example: Faced with stringent guidelines on ....., (name) was able to ..... every step of the way.

**Examined all aspects**
Example: (Name) examined all aspects of ..... and with swift and sustained action he/she transformed .....

**Example of**
Example: (Name) is a sterling example of ....., continually leading the way in actual performance and .....

**Exceeded expectations**
Example: (Name) accomplishes more in the morning than most people do all day, exceeding all expectations of .....

**Excellence grew**
Example: (Name) excellence grew in ..... with his/her standard-bearer performance.

**Exciting accomplishment(s)**
Example: (Name) many exciting accomplishments include his/her unparalleled performance in/as .....

**Exciting development**
Example: (Name) came up with an exciting development that ..... This has increased the .....

**Exciting possibilities**
Example: (Name) proposed many exciting possibilities that could lead to a dramatic improvement in ..... Some of these have already .....

**Exercise(d) best judgment**
Example: (Name) exercised the best judgment possible when he/she ..... At this critical juncture .....

**Exerted influence**
Example: (Name) exerted a positive influence on .....

**Expended great energy**
> Example: (Name) expended a great deal of energy in the
> completion of ..... This wide-ranging (task/project)
> became the best .....

**Experienced viewpoint**
> Example: The experienced viewpoint put forth by (name) resulted
> in a dramatic increase in .....

**Exploited**
> Example: (Name) exploited the weakness in/of ..... which proved
> extremely helpful in .....

**Exploits noteworthy**
> Example: Many of (name) noteworthy exploits in ..... are the result
> of a special talent he/she has for .....

**Explore new direction(s)**
> Example: (Name) wide and diverse background allowed him/her
> to explore new directions in .....

**Explore(d) new methods**
> Example: (Name) is not afraid to explore new methods of .....
> He/She never ceases to stay on top of the latest .....

**Extended range**
> Example: (Name) was able to extend the range of .....using
> his/her superior ..... talent.

**Extensive analysis**
> Example: (Name) completed an extensive analysis on ..... and
> found a way to increase efficiency by .....

**Extra motivation**
> Example: When extra motivation is needed, (name) is the person
> to see to .....

**Extraordinary challenge(s)**
> Example: Faced with the extraordinary challenge of ..... (Name)
> was able to ..... without missing a beat in the progress
> of .....

**Extreme measures**
> Example: Despite the extreme measures faced by (Name) as a
> result of ....., he/she proved equal to the task by .....

**Extremely delicate**
> Example: During the extremely delicate ..... (Name) brilliantly
> executed .....

**Exuberant**
> Example: (Name) exuberant personality was instrumental in .....

**Eye on future**
> Example: With an eye on the future, (name) transformed the
> workplace from ..... to ....

**Face challenge(s)**
Example: (Name) faced the new challenges of ..... with his/her customary .....

**Face up to**
Example: (Name) faced up to the mammoth undertaking by .....

**Face(d) issue(s) head on**
Example: (Name) faced the issue head on. His/Her first important task was to overcome .....

**Faced tall odds**
Example: The task/project faced tall odds at succeeding. However, (name), who thrives on new challenges, was able to .....

**Far and away**
Example: (Name) is far and away the best ..... in .....

**Far more reliable**
Example: (Name) developed a/an ..... that was far more reliable than .....

**Far-reaching**
Example: (Name) far-reaching work in ..... lead others to .....

**Farsighted**
Example: With (name) farsighted approach to ..... the (organization) was able to .....

**Fast-moving**
Example: (Name) enjoys a fast-moving work environment and is at his/her best when .....

**Faultless**
Example: (Name) faultless performance in/as ..... resulted in .....

**Fertile imagination**
Example: (Name) has an active mind and a fertile imagination.

**Feverish activity**
Example: The feverish activity brought about by ..... did not phase (name), for he/she was able to .....

**Few and far between**
Example: People like (name) are few and far between.

**Fierce determination**
Example: (Name) fierce determination and great ability to ..... led to .....

**Fill the bill**
Example: (Name) was able to fill the bill of/as ..... with great success.

**Final touch(es)**
Example: When (name) put the final touches on ....., he/she had developed a/an ..... that set an outstanding example.

**Fine detail**

Example: (Name) ability to pay close attention to the fine detail involved in ..... led to the high standards of performance of .....

**Finest**

Example: (Name) is the finest example .....

**Finest tradition**

Example: (Name) performance were in keeping with the finest tradition of .....

**Firm constructive element**

Example: One constant during the recent ..... was the firm constructive element of (name).

**Firm conviction**

Example: (Name) sets the finest example for others because of his/her firm conviction in/that .....

**Firm position/resolve**

Example: (Name) ability to hold on to his/her firm resolve was directly responsible for the marked improvement in .....

**First and foremost**

Example: First and foremost (name) is the most successful ..... in .....

**First ever**

Example: (Name) was the first person ever to .....

**First in long line of**

Example: (Name) success in/at ..... was the first in a long line of successes that culminated in .....

**First rank importance**

Example: What ranks of first importance in (name) is his/her ability to .....

**First stabilized, then reversed**

Example: (Name) first stabilized and then reversed the decline of .....

**First step(s)**

Example: (Name) all-important first steps in ..... proved invaluable in/for .....

**Firsthand experience**

Example: (Name) firsthand experience in/at ..... allowed him/her to successfully .....

**Flag bearer**

Example: (Name) became the flag bearer for ..... because of his/her ability to .....

**Flawless**

Example: The flawless execution of ..... by (name) set an outstanding example for .....

**Flawlessly executed**
> Example: (Name) flawlessly executed the critical duties of .....
> with uncommon perception and .....

**Flourish in face of**
> Example: (Name) flourishes in the face of ..... where others would
> flounder and fall.

**Flourishes in environment of**
> Example: (Name) flourishes in an environment of .....

**Focus attention on**
> Example: (Name) has the rare ability to be able to focus due
> attention on the important issues and .....

**Focus(es) on**
> Example: With his/her focus on ..... (name) was able to .....

**Focused and re-doubled efforts**
> Example: (Name) focused and re-doubled efforts to ..... despite
> being .....

**Followed footsteps**
> Example: (Name) followed the footsteps of the highly successful ..

**Foothold in**
> Example: (Name) gained a foothold in area of ..... by .....

**For good measure**
> Example: (Name) successfully completed ..... and then for good
> measure he/she .....

**For others to emulate**
> Example: (Name) performance is a model for others to emulate.

**Force in**
> Example: (Name) was a real force in ..... when he/she .....

**Forever changed**
> Example: (Name) performance in/as has forever changed .....

**Forged ahead**
> Example: (Name) forged ahead in ..... despite the inherent
> problems associated with.....

**Forged united effort**
> Example: (Name) and his/her people forged a united effort to .....

**Formed diverse**
> Example: (Name) formed a diverse group that was able to .....

**Formed the foundation**
> Example: (Name) formed the foundation of/for (area). This was a
> resounding success because of his/her .....

**Formidable**
> Example: (Name) was a formidable force in ..... with his/her
> masterful accomplishment of .....

**Formula for success**
> Example: (Name) found the formula for success in ..... He/She is
> recognized as the most .....

**Forward-looking**
> Example: (Name) is a forward-looking individual with a phenomenal record in/as .....

**Foster(s) sense of**
> Example: (Name) fosters a strong sense of pride among .....

**Fostered improved**
> Example: (Name) fostered an improved understanding of ..... with his/her stellar performance as .....

**Fought diligently**
> Example: (Name) fought diligently to .....with unequaled success.

**Fought long and hard**
> Example: Disregarding the obstacles involved, (name) fought long and hard to .....

**Found satisfaction**
> Example: (Name) found great satisfaction when he/she transformed .....

**Foundation built on**
> Example: (Name) leadership is built on a strong foundation based on .....

**Founder of**
> Example: (Name) was the founder of a/the highly successful .....

**Fragile situation**
> Example: When a fragile situation arose in ..... (name) diplomatic approach resulted in .....

**Frank assessment**
> Example: A frank assessment was made in the problem area of ..... (Name) was selected to ..... He/She contributed significantly to the immediate improvement of ....

**Frantic pace**
> Example: (Name) maintained a frantic pace in the on-time completion of .....

**Free of incident**
> Example: The (area) was completed free of incident due in large part to the effort(s) of (name).

**Free rein**
> Example: (Name) was given a free rein in making improvements in ..... He/She immediately responded by rejuvenating ....

**Free-spirited**
> Example: (Name) free-spirited personality made him/her ideally suited to tackle the problem of ..... His/Her high standards of excellence quickly came to the forefront when he/she .....

**Frequent contributor**
> Example: (Name) is a frequent contributor the excellent .....

**Fresh new**
Example: The fresh new ideas put forth by (name) quickly won the support of .....

**Fresh page in**
Example: (Name) arrival at (organization) was a fresh page in an otherwise .....

**Fresh start**
Example: (Name) was given a fresh start in/as ..... His/Her relentless drive and ..... were instrumental in .....

**From the onset**
Example: From the onset (name) proved to be .....

**Fruitful**
Example: (Name) has been a fruitful contributor to .....

**Fruits of labor**
Example: The fruits of (name) labor materialized as .....

**Fuel the imagination**
Example: (Name) is able to fuel the imagination of others and .....

**Full cooperation**
Example: (Name) enjoys the full and complete cooperation of ..... This has allowed him/her to .....

**Full court press**
Example: (Name) put a full court press on the problem of .....

**Full extent/measure**
Example: (Name) contributed full measure to .....

**Full force**
Example: (Name) put his/her full weight of force behind ..... resulting in consistently superior performance.

**Full of hope**
Example: (Name) is always full of hope and enthusiastic in the completion of .....

**Full of possibilities**
Example: (Name) innovative suggestions in the area of ..... are full of possibilities.

**Full range of**
Example: (Name) has a full range of skills in .....

**Full steam ahead**
Example: (Name) believes in full steam ahead, choosing to conquer instead of just tackling difficult tasks/projects.

**Full-grown**
Example: Tackled the full-grown and mature problem of .....

**Full-time job**
Example: Despite an already full-time job of/as ..... he/she tackled the .....

**Fully prepared to/for**
Example: (Name) is always fully prepared for any eventuality.

**Fundamental principal/values**
>Example: (Name) holds close to the fundamental values of .....

**Fundamentally sound**
>Example: (Name) always offers fundamentally sound suggestions and ideas in .....

**Furthered cause**
>Example: (Name) furthered the cause of ..... my personally .....

**Future-oriented**
>Example: A future oriented person. This was demonstrated recently when he/she .....

**Gain(ed) ground**
>Example: (Name) was able to gain ground where others had failed in the area/field of .....

**Gained admiration**
>Example: (Name) recently gained the admiration of ..... by his/her achievement/accomplishment on/in .....

**Gained favor**
>Example: (Name) gained the favor of ..... with his/her ability to .....

**Gained foothold**
>Example: (Name) gained a foothold in the correction of .....

**Gained notoriety**
>Example: (Name) gained notoriety for his/her recent work in .....

**Gave birth to**
>Example: (Name) gave birth to a new procedure in ..... This was so revolutionary that .....

**Gave rise to**
>Example: (Name's) work in ..... gave rise to ..... which in turn led to a vast improvement in .....

**General order of things**
>Example: (Name) changed the general order of the way things operated in/by ...... This led to vast improvements in .....

**Generous assistance**
>Example: (Name) provided generous assistance in the successful completion of ..... ahead of schedule, and saving (manhours/dollars, etc.)

**Generously gave**
>Example: (Name) gave generously of his/her normal off time to work in the time-sensitive .....

**Genuine act of/article**
>Example: (Name's) genuine act of .....resulted in vast improvements in .....

**Genuine desire**
>Example: (Name) displays(ed) a genuine desire to/for .....

**Get a fix on**
 Example: (Name) was able to get a fix on the nagging problem of
  ..... and then took immediate action to/that .....
**Get a grip on**
 Example: (Name) quickly got a grip on the problem(s) of .....
  through his/her experience in/as .....
**Get to heart of**
 Example: (Name) is able to get to the heart of any problem in
  short order and find an effective solution.
**Giant step forward**
 Example: (Organization) took a giant step forward when (Name)
  identified and corrected .....
**Give(n) blank check**
 Example: (Name) was given a blank check to fix ..... He/She
  responded with .....
**Glaring reality**
 Example: Faced with the glaring reality of ..... (Name) was able
  to .....
**Glimmer of hope**
 Example: Despite a glimmer initial of hope, (Name) successfully
  fought his/her way though .....
**Go along with**
 Example: (Name) is not content to go along with the crowd.
  Instead, he/she took the lead in .....
**Go extra mile**
 Example: (Name) always goes the extra mile to ensure that all
  projects are completed correctly and ahead of schedule.
**Go hand-in-hand**
 Example: (Name) knows experience and ..... go hand in hand.
  This allowed him/her to .....
**Go to bat for**
 Example: (Name) is always willing to go to bat for ..... This
  enhances his/her .....
**Go to limit(s)**
 Example: (Name) always goes to the limit to ..... He/She leaves
  no stone unturned in .....
**Golden opportunity**
 Example: (Name) was able to take full advantage of a/the golden
  opportunity to .....
**Good first step**
 Example: (Name) made a good first step toward ..... when
  he/she .....
**Good fortune/measure**
 Example: (Name) completed ..... ahead of schedule and then for
  good measure tackled the problem of .....

**241**

**Got jump on**
>  Example: (Name) got a jump on others by/when he/she .....

**Grace under fire**
>  Example: (Name) kept his/her composure and grace under fire when he/she .....

**Gracefully accepted**
>  Example: (Name) gracefully accepted .....

**Graduated to level**
>  Example: (Name) has graduated to a level above contemporaries. He/She is truly a level above .....

**Grand scale**
>  Example: (Name) was able to complete ... on a grand scale rarely seen in (organization)

**Grass roots**
>  Example: (Name) quickly gets to the grass roots of problem areas and .....

**Gratifying**
>  Example: It was a gratifying experience having (Name) working with ..... on .....

**Gravitate toward(s)**
>  Example: While others tend(ed) to gravitate toward(s) ..... (Name) was ultimately successful in/by .....

**Gravity of situation**
>  Example: (Name) immediately saw the gravity of the situation and took correct corrective action by .....

**Great chapter in history**
>  Example: (Name's) arrival was a great chapter in the history of (organization). He/She brought with him/her .....

**Grew in intensity**
>  Example: The problem of ..... grew in complexity and intensity. (Name), however, was able to .....

**Grew in sophistication**
>  Example: (Name) (organization) grew in size of scope and structure. This did not slow down his/her efforts to .....

**Grew in wisdom and stature**
>  Example: (Name) grew in wisdom and stature when he/she .....

**Groomed to/for**
>  Example: (Name) has been well groomed to take the helm of .....

**Ground breaking**
>  Example: (Name's) ground breaking work in/as ..... led to the ultimate development of .....

**Ground floor**
>  Example: Working from the ground floor up, (Name) quickly became the person to see when/if .....

**Ground-breaking**
    Example: (Name') ground breaking work in ..... led to vast
        improvements in .....
**Guide the way**
    Example: (Name) was able to guide the way for others in .....
**Guided change**
    Example: (Name) guided the change from ..... to ..... without a
        decrease in efficiency.
**Guiding hand**
    Example: (Name) was always available, giving a guiding hand to
        others while maintaining a steadying influence on .....
**Guiding light/vision**
    Example: (Name's) superlative effort in/as ..... served as a
        guiding light to/for .....
**Had free rein**
    Example: (Name) had a free rein in .....  His/Her trailblazing effort
        led to distinct improvements in .....
**Hallmark**
    Example: (Name's) work has become a hallmark of excellence.
**Hammer away**
    Example: Despite the hectic work schedule (Name) hammered
        away at ..... until .....
**Hand picked**
    Example: (Name) was hand picked to .....  This turned out to be
        an excellent choice as he/she .....
**Hand-in-hand**
    Example: (Name) worked hand-in-hand with .....    Their efforts
        led to standout improvements in .....
**Handled delicate issue(s)**
    Example: (Name) handled the delicate issue of ..... with the skill
        normally observed in .....
**Handled with respect**
    Example: (Name) handled with respect the subject of ..... while
        displaying a preeminent .....
**Hands full**
    Example: (Name) already had his/her hands full in (area) when
        he/she tackled the unenviable task of .....
**Hands-on person**
    Example: (Name) is a hands-on person.  He/She leaves nothing
        to chance.
**Hard-earned**
    Example: (Name) has a hard-earned reputation for .....

**Hard-pressed**

 Example: When others become hard-pressed to ....., they know they can always call on (Name) to give them a helping hand and a .....

**Hardy attitude**

 Example: (Name) has a hardy attitude for .....

**Harm's way**

 Example: (Name) is unafraid of going in harm's way. He/She will tackle and successfully complete any .....

**Harmonious relationship(s)**

 Example: (Name) established a harmonious relationship with ..... which led to laudatory improvements in/with .....

**Hats off to**

 Example: Hats off to (Name) for his/her faultless performance in/as ..... which led to a masterful .....

**Head(ed) off**

 Example: (Name) headed off a potential ..... with his/her quick action and unbeatable combination of .....

**Headed in right direction**

 Example: (Name) moved things off center and got the (organization) headed in the right direction.

**Healed wounds**

 Example: (Name) healed the wounds of ..... caused by ..... with his/her exceptional .....

**Heart and soul**

 Example: (Name) is the heart and soul of (organization) with is/her tireless efforts and exemplary .....

**Heavy burden**

 Example: (Name) was able to carry the heavy burden of ..... because of his/her unique .....

**Hectic schedule**

 Example: Despite an already hectic schedule, he/she successfully assumed the duties of ..... and performed them with the characteristic .... we have come to expect of (Name)

**Heightened activity**

 Example: In a period of heightened activity because of ..... (Name) was able to surpass .....

**Held firm**

 Example: (Name) held firm in his/her convictions despite heavy pressure from .....

**Helped build**

 Example: (Name) helped build ..... from the ground up. His/Her unequalled performance resulted in .....

**Helped inspire**
    Example: (Name) helped inspire confidence and dedication in an
        organization previously ham strung by .....
**Helped solidify**
    Example: (Name) helped solidify the gains made in ..... by .....
**Helping hand**
    Example: (Name) is always willing to give a helping and to .....
        and frequently works passed normal hours to ensure .....
**Herculean effort**
    Example: (Name) gave a Herculean effort in ..... despite having to
        deal with the additional hardship fo .....
**Hidden qualities**
    Example: (Name) has many hidden qualities that do not show up
        in his/her daily activities, including .....
**High gear**
    Example: (Name) turned his/her ..... in to high gear and
        completed ..... on time despite .....
**High hope(s)**
    Example: (Name) has high hopes and high goals and always
        follows through on .....
**High stress environment**
    Example: (Name) enjoys working in a high stress environment.
        Some of his/her best work comes when .....
**High/Low profile**
    Example: (Name's) ability to keep a low profile while/as/in ..... is
        especially noteworthy..
**Higher goal(s)**
    Example: (Name) has set and reached higher goals than .....  due
        to his/her exceptional ability to/as .....
**Highly developed**
    Example: (Name) has a highly developed .....
**Historic event**
    Example: (Name) became the first person ever to .....  This is
        considered a historic event because .....
**History of**
    Example: (Name's) performance in/as ..... is the best in the recent
        history of .....
**Hit the books**
    Example: (Name) works a full day at ..... and hits the books to
        study/learn ..... during off-work hours.
**Hit the mark**
    Example: (Name's) suggestion hit the mark on how to .....  This
        resulted in a savings of .....
**Honed to perfection**
    Example: (Name's) skills at ..... have been honed to perfection.

**Honest feedback**
> Example: (Name) can always be depended upon to give an honest and complete feedback on .....

**Hope for future**
> Example: (Name) brought new hope for the future of (organization) by his/her .....

**Host of problems**
> Example: Faced with a host of problems, (Name) nevertheless succeeded in .....

**Hot spot**
> Example: When a hot spot occurs in/at ..... (Name) is the person to see for quick, effective action.

**Hours on end**
> Example: (Name) spend hours on end of off-work time perfecting the ..... This resulted in .....

**Hunger for**
> Example: (Name) has a hunger for knowledge rarely seen in .....

**Ideal conditions**
> Example: The ideal conditions that exist at ..... are the direct result of (Name's) skill and dedication to .....

**Ideal for**
> Example: (Name) is the ideal person for ..... He/She has the requisite skills for/to .....

**Ignited fire in/to**
> Example: (Name) ignited a fire in the spirits of .....

**Illustrious career**
> Example: (Name) illustrious career was recently highlighted when he/she .....

**Immediate impact/success**
> Example: (Name) has had an immediate impact on the operation of .....

**Immediate turnaround**
> Example: Shortly after his/her assignment to ..... an immediate turnaround in ..... was noted.

**Immersed in**
> Example: (Name) is totally committed to and immersed in his/her chosen field. He/She routinely .....

**Impassioned**
> Example: (Name's) impassioned talk to ..... paved the way for. ....

**Impeccable timing**
> Example: (Name) has impeccable timing. He/She always seems to be able to .....

**Impeccably prepared**
> Example: (Name) approaches any task impeccably prepared.

**Impending disaster**
Example: Despite an impending disaster in ..... (Name) was able to .....

**Impetus to/for**
Example: (Name) provided the impetus for the highly successful .....

**Implemented blueprint**
Example: (Name planned and implemented a blueprint for ..... This has been used as a model to/for .....

**Important first step**
Example: (Name) took the important first step in/to .....

**Important point(s)**
Example: (Name) is able to incorporate the important points of ..... into his/her daily work schedule with relative ease.

**Important source of**
Example: (Name) is an important source of ..... in the field of .....

**Impressed with**
Example: I have been totally impressed with the skill and dedication demonstrated by ..... during .....

**Impressive**
Example: (Name) has set an impressive record in/as .....

**Improved lives**
Example: (Name's) ability to ..... has measurably improved the lives and working environment of .....

**Improved quality of**
Example: (Name) efforts to ..... improved the quality of .....

**In a nutshell**
Example: (Name) is, in a nutshell, simply the best ..... in (organization), bar none.

**In face of**
Example: (Name) performance in the face of ..... was admirable.

**In full stride**
Example: (Name) accepts temporary setbacks in full stride and never misses a beat in .....

**In great measure**
Example: The success of ..... was, in great measure, the result of (Name's) boundless .....

**In high gear**
Example: (Name) managed to put his/her organization into high gear recently when the problem of ..... was .....

**In line with**
Example: (Name's) performance was in line with ..... Further, he/she exceeded all expectations in/for .....

247

**In mainstream**

    Example: (Name) clear sighted efforts to ..... were in the
        mainstream with (organization's) goals to .....

**In short supply**

    Example: People the caliber of (Name) are in short supply.
        He/She has the astounding ability to .....

**In spotlight**

    Example: Being in the spotlight or on the hot seat does not
        adversely affect (Name) performance in/as .....

**In step with**

    Example:(Name) is always in step with (organization) policies and
        goals.  In fact, he/she .....

**In the face of**

    Example: (Name's) performance in the face of adversity is without
        equal.

**In the prime**

    Example: (Name) is in the prime of his/her .....

**In touch with**

    Example: (Name) stays in touch with reality.  He/She keeps a
        level head and always stays calm during .....

**In wake of**

    Example: In the wake of disaster in/at ..... (Name) was able
        to .....

**Increased appetite for**

    Example: (Name) continues to have an increased appetite for .....

**Increasing number of**

    Example: (Name) continues to come up with an ever increasing
        number of innovative ideas in/for .....

**Increasingly clear**

    Example: It is becoming increasingly clear that (Name) is one of
        the best ..... in .....

**Incredible level/sense of**

    Example: (Name) has an incredible level of  ..... This was most
        recently demonstrated when he/she .....

**Indebted to**

    Example: (Organization) is indebted to the efforts of (Name).
        He/She has shown a remarkable ability to .....

**Independent thinking**

    Example: (Name's) independent thinking on the subject of .....
        was a major cornerstone for the improvement of .....

**Indispensable to**

    Example:(Name) has been indispensable to (organization)
        because of his/her ability to .....

**Inexhaustible energy**
>Example: The inexhaustible energy (Name) beings to a job has helped (organization) to/in .....

**Inextricably connected**
>Example: This (organization's) success is inextricably connected to the efforts and diligence of (Name).

**Influence on**
>Example: (Name) has been a positive influence on .....

**Influential presence**
>Example: (Name's) influential presence in/as ..... has won merit and praise from .....

**Infuse(d) fresh ideas**
>Example: (Name) infused fresh new ideas into the workplace and is directly responsible for .....

**Ingenuity**
>Example: (Name's) foresightedness and ingenuity led to laudable improvements in .....

**Inherent danger**
>Example: Despite the inherent danger associated with ..... (Name) formulated and implemented .....

**Inherited unsuccessful**
>Example: (Name) inherited an organization largely unsuccessful. However, he/she quickly and efficiently .....

**Injects life**
>Example: (Name) injects life and excitement into others with his/her ability to .....

**Innovative new way/solutions**
>Example: '(Name) found a new and innovative way to ..... This led to dramatic improvement(s) in/of .....

**Inquisitive**
>Example: (Name's) inquisitive nature and ..... lead to the highly successful .....

**Ins and outs**
>Example: (Name) knows the ins and outs of (organization) and uses this knowledge to .....

**Insatiable appetite**
>Example: (Name) has an insatiable appetite for ..... This, coupled with his/her ability to ..... led to .....

**Inspiration to all**
>Example: (Name) talent and work on .....has been an inspiration to .....

**Inspired by**
>Example: Others are inspired by the efforts and ..... of (Name)

**Instinct for**
    Example: (Name) has a certain instinct for finding and fixing .....
**Instituted measures**
    Example: (Name) instituted measures that quickly turned around ..... into an organization that .....
**Integral part of**
    Example: (Name) has become an integral part of (organization) because of his/her multi-talented skills in/as .....
**Intense dedication/work**
    Example:(Name's) intense dedication and work ethics made him/her an overwhelming choice to become .....
**Intense pressure**
    Example: Despite the intense pressure inherent with/to ..... (Name) has been able to .....
**Intimate knowledge**
    Example: (Name's) intimate working knowledge in/of ..... led to ground-breaking advancements in .....
**Intricately involved**
    Example: (Name) has been intricately involved in all facets of .....
**Introduce(d) new life**
    Example: (Name) introduced a new breath of life into a once failing ..... and (results).
**Invaluable contribution(s)**
    Example: (Name's) many invaluable contributions to (organization) have led to .....
**Invested talent/time**
    Example: (Name) invested his/her considerable time and talent on ..... with results that .....
**Investment in future**
    Example: (Name) made an investment in the future of (organization). This investment paid off with interest when/by .....
**Invigorating program**
    Example: (Name) started an invigorating ..... program that completely turned around .....
**Iron will**
    Example: Through sheer iron will and determination (Name) completed .....
**Jolt of adrenaline**
    Example: (Name) provided a much need jolt of adrenaline into (organization) that (results)
**Jump-start**
    Example: (Name) was able to jump start an ailing ..... which quickly won acclaim from .....

**Keen awareness**
> Example: (Name) had a keen awareness of ..... and he/she
> confidently developed a/an ..... that (results)

**Keen grasp of**
> Example: (Name) has a keen grasp of ..... which allows him/her to
> set and achieve clear-cut .....

**Keen observation**
> Example: (Name's) keen powers of observation were instrumental
> in ..... which resulted in .....

**Keep an eye on**
> Example: (Name) managed to keep an eye on ..... while at the
> same time achieving complete success in/by .....

**Kept cool head**
> Example: (Name) kept a cool head in the face of adversity when
> he/she ..... This flawless ..... personifies (Name).

**Kept on toes**
> Example: (Name) is the leading ..... at (organization)  He/She kept
> on his/her toes when .....

**Key element/ingredient(s)**
> Example: (Name) provided the key ingredient to ..... This brought
> about a logical and ..... which won praise from .....

**Key juncture**
> Example: At a key and important juncture (Name) was able to
> infuse .....which led to faultless .....

**Key part of**
> Example: (Name) continues to be a key part of (organization)
> while at the same time demonstrating .....

**Key role in**
> Example: (Name) played a key role in the successful completion
> of ..... which became an overwhelming success.

**Key to success**
> Example: (Name's) work in/as was the key to success in/at .....
> This masterful undertaking led to .....

**Knack for**
> Example: (Name) has a real knack for getting the job done where
> others fail.  This was never better demonstrated than
> when he/she .....

**Know-how**
> Example: (Name) is an ace ..... He/She has the know how to .....

**Labor of love**
> Example: (Name) approaches each and every task with a labor of
> love that is unequalled in (organization).

**Labored hard**
Example: (Name) labored long and hard to complete ..... The successful completion led to a real improvement in .....

**Ladder of success**
Example: (Name) has climbed the ladder of success through personal ..... and .....

**Laid foundation/groundwork**
Example:(Name) laid the foundation for ..... by ..... This multi-talented individual further .....

**Laid to rest**
Example: (Name's) stellar performance in/as ..... laid to rest any questions concerning .....

**Landmark**
Example: (Name's) landmark work on/in/as ..... unquestionably led the way in .....

**Lasting contribution(s)**
Example: (Name) has made significant and lasting contributions to (organization).

**Lasting impact**
Example: (Name's) performance in/as will have a lasting impact on (organization) and will serve as a springboard to/for ....

**Launched new**
Example: (Name) successfully launched a new ..... that will unquestionably surpass .....

**Lead the way**
Example: With unerring accuracy (Name) led the way in/to.....

**Leading the way**
Example: (Name) has an unsurpassed ability in leading the way in/to ..... with his/her versatility and .....

**Learned first-hand**
Example: I was fortunate enough to see first hand (Name's) sterling work/performance in/as ..... This versatile individual is one of the finest ..... in .....

**Least number of**
Example: (Name) had the least number of ..... of anyone in (organization). His/Her well grounded work and vision .....

**Leave no stone unturned**
Example: (Name) will leave no stone unturned in his/her efforts to ..... This unflagging dedication .....

**Left a mark**
Example: (Name) left a mark on (organization) that will not soon be forgotten. His/Her remarkable talent .....

**Left legacy**
    Example: (Name) left a legacy at (organization) that is worthy of
    praise and ..... His/Her sensational work in as .....
    resulted in .....

**Lend a hand**
    Example: (Name) is never too busy to lend a hand to help .....

**Lengthy process**
    Example: The lengthy process of ..... never deterred (Name) from
    his/her goal(s) of ..... He/She with unmatched .....
    achieved .....

**Level best**
    Example: (Name) ability to do his/her level best at any
    assignment demonstrated a remarkable talent for/to .....

**Life-long passion for**
    Example: (Name's) life-long passion for ..... revolutionized the
    way (organization) does .....

**Lifeblood**
    Example: (Name) performance in/as .....has been the lifeblood of
    (organization)

**Lifted heavy weight**
    Example: (Name) lifted a heavy weight off the back of
    (organization) because of his/her ability to .....

**Light the way**
    Example: (Name) was able to light the way for (organization) to
    accomplish .....aided by his/her masterful accomplishment
    of .....

**Lighten the burden**
    Example: (Name) lightened the burden of (organization) by
    personally meritorious service that included .....

**Lightening quick**
    Example: (Name's) lightening quick response to events in critical
    situations resulted in .....

**Like clockwork**
    Example: (Name) completed ..... like clockwork. He/She never
    wavered or missed a step.

**Long and arduous**
    Example: (Name) worked many long and arduous hours
    completing ..... This led to a dramatic improvement in ....

**Long be remembered**
    Example: The work on ..... performed by (Name) will long be
    remembered for his/her skill in/at .....

**Long haul/journey**
    Example: (Name's) invincible determination led the way in the long
    journey from ..... to .....

**Long periods of**
>   Example: There is none better than (Name) during long periods of
>   ..... His/Her superior talent at ..... was instrumental in .....

**Long, hard road**
>   Example: The long hard road to success was orchestrated by
>   (Name). His/Her flawless performance was a level
>   above.....

**Long-lasting/-standing**
>   Example: The long-standing record of ..... was surpassed by
>   (Name) because of his/her .....

**Long-term approach**
>   Example: (Name's) long-term approach to ..... brought about
>   unparalleled success in .....

**Long-term commitment**
>   Example: (Name's) long-term commitment to the improvement of
>   ..... proved him/her to be a top innovator in/at .....

**Looked up to**
>   Example: (Name) is look up to as one of the best ..... in .....

**Looks beyond**
>   Example: (Name) has the ability to look beyond ..... and focus on
>   the more important long-range .....

**Made a difference**
>   Example: (Name) made a difference at (organization) because of
>   his/her ability to .....

**Made good use of**
>   Example: (Organization) made good on its goal of ..... thanks to
>   the super efforts of (Name).

**Made inroads**
>   Example: Significant inroads were made into ..... because of
>   (Name's) unique ability to .....

**Made it easy for**
>   Example: (Name) made it easy for (organization) to ..... thanks to
>   his/her matchless talent in/at .....

**Made short work of**
>   Example: (Name) made short work of the difficult task of ..... and
>   proved himself/herself a shining example of .....

**Made the best of**
>   Example: (Name) made the best possible use of
>   .....demonstrating an unending ability to .....

**Made to order**
>   Example: The difficult task of ..... was made to order for (Name)
>   He/She has the tremendous individual drive necessary
>   to .....

**Made way through**
Example: (Name) made his/her way through the difficult task of ..... by demonstrating a banner performance in/as .....

**Magnitude of situation**
Example: The difficulty or magnitude of a situation never occurs to (Name). He/She cannot be distracted by .....

**Maintained course**
Example: (Name) maintained a steady course during the difficult time of ..... and again proved his/she was .....

**Major challenge(s)**
Example: (Name) faced the major challenge of ..... with skill and ..... The results were .....

**Major contributor**
Example: (Name) made a major contribution to the success of ..... with his/her unerring ability to ...

**Major obstacle**
Example: (Name) overcame all major obstacles in the staggering (area) with a stellar performance.

**Major transition**
Example: (Name) made the major transition from ..... to ..... with his/her customary spotless .....

**Make best of**
Example: (Name) was able to make the best of a bad situation of ..... by his/her revolutionary use of .....

**Make good (on)**
Example: (Name) made good on his/her effort to .....

**Make short work of**
Example: (Name) was able to make short work of the delicate task of ..... despite.....

**Make the grade**
Example: (Name) was able to make the grade in the difficult ..... because of his/her unbelievable ability to .....

**Makes things work**
Example: (Name) simply makes things work better. He/She is the best ..... at (organization)

**Massive undertaking**
Example: The massive undertaking of ..... was successfully completed by (Name) with a seasoned .....

**Master stroke**
Example: (Name's) work on ..... was a master stroke that added ..... to (organization)

**Master the situation/problem**
Example: (Name) was able to master the problem in/of ..... with his/her zealous work and .....

**Mastered details of**
>Example: (Name) was able to master all the intricate details of ....

**Mastermind(ed)**
>Example: (Name) masterminded the most difficult task of ..... with a standout performance and .....

**Masterpiece**
>Example: At the zenith of his/her career field, (Name) was able to ..... with unmatched .....

**Matter of principle**
>Example: As a matter of principle, (Name) refuses to accept anything less than .....

**Maximum capacity**
>Example: (Name) always functions at maximum capacity regardless of the complexity or difficulty of .....

**Measure of success**
>Example: The measure of success demonstrated by (Name) far exceeds(ed) .....

**Meet demands**
>Example: (Name) meets the highest demands of ..... with .....

**Meet new challenges**
>Example: (Name) meets new challenges head-on in a totally impressive way.

**Meet the needs**
>Example:(Name) meets the needs of ..... and is a master at .....

**Memorable event/work**
>Example: The memorable work (Name) did in/on ..... will further the advance of .....

**Mere words fail to**
>Example: Mere words fail to describe the accomplishments of (Name). He/She became the standard-bearer in/as .....

**Merit(s) special praise**
>Example: (Name's) performance in/as ..... merits special praise.

**Met criteria**
>Example: (Name) met all criteria for ..... in less than half the normal/allotted time.

**Meticulous**
>Example: The meticulous attention to detail demonstrated by (Name) went far and beyond .....

**Milestone(s)**
>Example: (Name) passed many milestones on his/her way to .....

**Mission accomplished**
>Example: (Name) has an astounding success rate of getting the mission accomplished during .....

**Modeled after**
    Example: All of the operations of (organization) are modeled after (Name's) extremely successful .....
**Monumental**
    Example: (Name) completed the monumental task of ..... with flawless performance and .....
**More important aspect**
    Example: (Name) completed one of the more important aspects of ..... in .....
**Moved expeditiously**
    Example: (Name) moved expeditiously to correct ..... which had been a long-standing problem in/at.....
**Moved in positive direction**
    Example: (Name) moved in a most positive direction to ..... The results were .....
**Multi-faceted/talented**
    Example: (Name) is a multi-talented individual with a special knack for .....
**Muster up courage/strength**
    Example: (Name) mustered up the courage to tackle ..... with results which/that .....
**Narrow(ed) the gap**
    Example: (Name) narrowed the gap between ..... and ..... He/She was able to do this because of his/her .....
**Natural choice for**
    Example: With (Name's) ability to ....., he/she was the natural choice to .....
**Natural enthusiasm**
    Example: (Name) brings with him/her a natural enthusiasm for ....
**Near perfection**
    Example: (Name's) performance in/as ..... was near perfection.
**Necessary for future of**
    Example: (Name) completed the massive task of ..... which was absolutely necessary for the future of .....
**Needed shot in the arm**
    Example: (Name) gave a much needed shot in the arm to ..... This resulted in .....
**Never gave up**
    Example: (Name) never gave up on his/her quest to ..... The end result was the best .....
**Never wavered/faltered**
    Example: (Name) never faltered in his/her efforts to ..... The results were extraordinary.

**New and challenging**

> Example: (Name) is always looking for new and challenging ways
> to ..... He/She was personally responsible for .....

**New and exciting**

> Example: (Name) brought a new and exciting ..... to
> (organization)  He/She was able to .....

**New approach**

> Example: The new approach of ..... to ..... by (Name) helped
> solve the longstanding problem of .....

**New horizons**

> Example: (Name) has opened new horizons in the area/field of
> ..... with his/her unique ability to .....

**Newfound**

> Example: (Name's) newfound method to/of ..... led the way in the
> resurrection of .....

**Nick of time**

> Example: The serious problem of ..... was discovered and fixed
> by (name) just in the nick of time.

**No end in sight**

> Example: There was no end in sight on the problem of .....
> (Name) was able to fix the problem with his/her multi-
> skills of .....

**No stranger to**

> Example: (Name) is no stranger to hard work.  He/She worked
> ..... hours to fix/repair .....

**Nose to the grind stone**

> Example: (Name) put his/her nose to the grind stone to complete
> the complex task of ..... ahead of time.
> This resulted in .....

**Notable exception**

> Example: (Name) has been a notable exception to an
> otherwise .....  He/She completed ..... using .....

**Nothing left to chance**

> Example: (Name) left nothing to chance in his/her efforts to .....
> The results were nothing less than outstanding.

**Nothing short of**

> Example: (Name's) performance was nothing short of .....

**Nourished**

> Example: (Name) nourished the new idea of .....  The results were
> a marked improvement in .....

**Off to fast start**

> Example: (Name) got off to a fast start on/as ..... and never
> stopped or slowed down.

**On cutting edge of**
   Example: (Name) is on the cutting edge of ….. His/Her ability to
      ….. is far beyond …..
**On guard for/against**
   Example: (Name) always stays on guard for …..
**On the ball**
   Example: (Name) is a person on the ball and on the move
      upward. He/She is always …..
**On-going process/problem**
   Example: (Name) was able to solve the on-going problem of …..
**Once-over**
   Example: (Name) gave the problem a once-over look and
      quickly …..
**Onward and upward**
   Example: (Name) is an "ideas" person, always looking onward and
      upward to/for the next …..
**Opened door/gate**
   Example: (Name's) work in/on ….. revolutionized the way
      (organization) does …..
**Opened new horizon**
   Example: (Name) opened new doors and new horizons with
      his/her recommendation for …..
**Opportunity to create**
   Example: (Name) was given an opportunity to create a new …..
      He/She responded with a/an …..
**Optimistic appraisal/outlook**
   Example: (Name) always maintains an optimistic outlook
      regardless of the circumstances. This helps him/her to …
**Orchestrated**
   Example: (Name) orchestrated a demanding ….. that required
      dexterity in …..
**Outcome never in doubt**
   Example: When (Name) is in charge of a project the outcome is
      never in doubt. This was never more amply
      demonstrated than when he/she …..
**Over and above**
   Example: The work of (Name) is always over and above that of
      ….. He/She has the creative craftsmanship to …..
**Over the top**
   Example: (Name) was able to get (organization) over the top of
      ….. with his/her …..
**Overcame all obstacles**
   Example: (Name) overcame all obstacles with his/her …..

**259**

**Overcame difficulties**
Example: (Name) overcame all difficulties associated with .....
with his/her artful .....

**Overshadowed**
Example: (Name's) work overshadowed that of ..... with his/her
contribution in .....

**Overwhelmingly positive**
Example: (Organization) received an overwhelmingly positive
response to ..... This was a direct result of (Name's) .....

**Paid the price**
Example: (Name) has paid the price for his/her success by .....

**Painstaking work**
Example: With painstaking work (Name) was able to overcome ...

**Part and parcel**
Example: (Name's) work in/on ..... is part and parcel the best ....

**Particularly productive**
Example: (Name) has been particularly productive in the
area/field of ..... because of his/her ability to .....

**Passed with flying colors**
Example: (Name) passed muster on ..... with flying colors.
His/Her noteworthy accomplishments outmatched .....

**Pat on the back**
Example: (Name) deserves a pat on the back for his/her work
on/as ..... He/She personifies what is right about .....

**Path of growth**
Example: (Name) path of growth to ..... included the difficult
job/task of ..... which he/she mastered in .....

**Paved the way**
Example: (Name) paved the way for others when he/she .....
These contributions exceeded .....

**Pay attention**
Example: (Name) always pays close attention to detail especially
when ..... He/She was able to measurably improve .....

**Peak of**
Example: (Name) is at the peak of his/her professional skills.
He/She can only improve by being placed in more
demanding and complex jobs/tasks.

**Perfect blend/choice**
Example: (Name) was the perfect choice to assume ..... because
of his/her remarkable ability to .....

**Perfect example**
Example: (Name) is a perfect example of invincible
determination. He/She has an enormous capacity for .....

**Perfect opportunity**
    Example: (Name) took full advantage of the perfect opportunity to
    ..... His/Her banner performance was highlighted by .....
**Pick the brain(s)**
    Example: Others routinely pick the brain of (Name) because of
    his/her unparalleled expertise in .....
**Pick up the pieces**
    Example: (Name) was able to pick up the pieces of the previous
    disaster of ..... He/She proceeded to discover new ways
    of/to .....
**Picture perfect**
    Example: (Name's) performance in/as ..... was picture perfect.
    He/She provided the cornerstone of/for .....
**Pillar of strength**
    Example: (Name) was a pillar of strength during the entire
    (event/evolution). His/Her exceptional performance
    earned him/her .....
**Pinnacle**
    Example: (Name) is at the pinnacle of his/her profession. His/Her
    sustained superior performance has .....
**Pinpoint accuracy**
    Example: With pinpoint accuracy, (Name) was able to .....
**Pioneer in field/spirit**
    Example: (Name) is a pioneer in the field of ..... His/Her
    unequaled success in ..... led to .....
**Pioneering spirit**
    Example: (Name) has the pioneering spirit needed to assume the
    demanding responsibilities of ..... with his/her .....
**Pitch(ed) in**
    Example: (Name) pitched in to lend a helping hand to ..... which
    proved to be the turning point for .....
**Pivotal situation**
    Example: During a pivotal situation when ..... (Name) enormous
    capacity for ..... carried the day.
**Placed emphasis on**
    Example: (Name) correctly placed the main emphasis of ..... on
    ..... which proved particularly effective in/at .....
**Places high premium**
    Example: (Name) places a high premium on ..... There is none
    better at .....
**Played full part**
    Example: (Name) played a full and active part in the ..... He/She
    personally improved .....

**261**

**Played important role**
>Example: (Name) played an important role in the completion of
>..... Without him/her .....

**Pleased with**
>Example: (Organization) has been more than pleased with the
>performance of (Name). He/She always .....

**Poised for**
>Example: (Name) is poised and ready for increased
>responsibilities now. He/She is the resident expert in/at .....

**Policy maker**
>Example: (Name) has become a policy maker in/at ..... because
>of his/her tremendous .....

**Positive movement**
>Example: The positive movement in/on ..... made by (Name) was
>the centerpiece in ..... that proved a model in/for .....

**Positive response**
>Example: The positive response given by (Name) when asked to
>..... led the way for .....

**Positive thinking**
>Example: (Name's) positive thinking and ..... demonstrated
>unparalleled professionalism in .....

**Positive Feedback**
>Example: The positive feedback on ..... given by (Name) led to
>(organization's) extraordinary ability to .....

**Potent**
>Example: (Name's) potent work on/at ..... brought praiseworthy
>reviews by .....

**Potential crisis**
>Example: (Name) averted a potential crisis in ..... by .....

**Potential risk(s)**
>Example: Sidestepping the potential risk of ..... (Name) was able
>to ..... because of his/her .....

**Pounced upon**
>Example: (Name) pounced upon the opportunity to ....., thus
>demonstrating his/her never ending capacity for/to .....

**Power-packed**
>Example: (Name's) power packed performance in/as ..... His/Her
>never-ending capacity for/to .... was largely
>responsible for .....

**Powerful tool**
>Example: (Name's) use of ..... proved to be a powerful tool in
>improving/controlling .....

**Practical application**
>Example: (Name) upgraded the capacity/capability of ..... with
>his/her practical application of .....

**Precious little/few**
    Example: With precious few resources (Name) was able to .....
**Precious source of**
    Example: (Name) has become a precious source of .....because
    of his/her ability to .....
**Precision**
    Example: (Name's) use of precision ..... made measurable
    improvements in .....
**Presence of mind**
    Example: Fortunately, (Name) had the presence of mind to .....
    which averted a potentially .....
**Press(ed) hard**
    Example: (Name) pressed hard for improvements in .....  He/She
    personally devised a/an ..... that .....
**Press(ing) ahead**
    Example: (Name) continues to press ahead regardless of the
    difficulties.  During one recent problem, he/she .....
**Pressing matters**
    Example: Despite pressing matters in ..... (Name) continued to
    ..... with uncustomary zeal and .....
**Pressure-cooker situation**
    Example: (Name) enjoys being in a pressure cooker situation.
    The immediacy of urgent items brings out the best in
    him/her.
**Priceless**
    Example: (Name's) priceless help as a top ..... was extremely
    helpful in .....
**Pride of accomplishment**
    Example: (Name) takes a personal pride of accomplishment in
    everything he/she does.
**Primary objective**
    Example: (Name) stays focused on the primary objectives and
    does not get sidetracked with matters of minor
    importance.
**Prime mover**
    Example: (Name) is a prime mover of ..... in (organization).  In
    one recent event he/she .....
**Prime reason**
    Example: (Name) is a prime reason (organization) enjoys the
    good standing and reputation it has today.
**Prized position**
    Example: (Name) was offered the prized position of .....  He/She
    responded with his/her customary standard-bearer effort.

**Problem prevalent to**
Example: (Name) overcame the problem prevalent to ..... by developing new procedures that .....

**Problem solver**
Example: (Name) is a real problem solver. He/She is particularly strong in/at .....

**Productivity increased**
Example: (Organization) productivity increased dramatically when (Name) was placed in charge of .....

**Professional triumph**
Example: (Name's) professional triumph in/at ..... demonstrates his/her unending ability to succeed at .....

**Professional vigor**
Example: (Name's) professional vigor is without equal in/at (organization). He/She can always be depended upon to .....

**Profited by/from**
Example: The entire (organization) profited from (Name's) ability to .....

**Profound influence/impact**
Example: (Name's) performance as ..... has had a lasting and profound influence in/on .....

**Profound respect**
Example: (Name) has won the profound respect of ..... by/with his/her measurable improvements in/on .....

**Progressive new**
Example: (Name's) progressive new way of ..... has led to the upgraded capability of .....

**Prominent**
Example: (Name) has become a prominent figure in ..... with his/her exceptional ability to .....

**Proof positive**
Example: (Name's) dependable and innovative nature are proof positive of his/her .....

**Proper balance**
Example: (Name) is able to put a proper balance on ..... and ..... because of his/her outstanding ..... knowledge in .....

**Properly handled/prepare**
Example: (Name's) ability to properly prepare for ....., coupled with his/her ability to ....., has made singularly outstanding contributions to .....

**Proud to serve**
Example: Anyone would be proud to serve with (Name). He/She exhibits a remarkable ability to .....

**Proved fruitful**
Example: (Name's) ability to ..... proved fruitful in the .....
He/She has left his/her mark in .....

**Proved mettle**
Example: (Name) proved his/her mettle when he/she was
assigned to/as ..... by personally .....

**Provided insight into**
Example: (Name) provided valuable insight into ..... This allowed
(organization) to .....

**Prudent balance of**
Example: The prudent balance of ..... was made possible by
(Name) when he/she .....

**Pulled out all stops**
Example: (Name) pulled out all the stops to ..... His/Her
inexhaustible source of ..... led to .....

**Pulled together**
Example: The (organization) all pulled together and completed
..... in time for ..... due to (Name's) .....

**Pursue all avenues**
Example: (Name) pursues all possible avenues and courses of
action when .....

**Pursued with tenacity**
Example: (Name) pursued with unending tenacity the ..... His/Her
admirable ability to ..... led to unsurpassed .....

**Push(ed) forward**
Example: (Name) pushed forward on ..... despite continued
interference/trouble from .....

**Pushed to limit(s)**
Example: (Name) pushed the limits of ..... to ..... and met with
success rarely observed in/by .....

**Put (back) on track**
Example: (Name) was able to put back on track the ..... with a
thoroughly meticulous .....

**Put finger on**
Example: (Name) quickly put the finger on the problem of .....
and .....

**Put in a good word**
Example: (Name) is never too busy to put in a good word for .....

**Put in order**
Example: (Name) put in order the complex and difficult ..... in
dramatic fashion.

**Put lid on**
Example: (Name) put the lid on ..... and ..... The results added a
new dimension to .....

**Put measures in place**
> Example: (Name) put measures in place to ….. This put the
> finishing touches on his/her distinguished record in/as …..

**Put to the test**
> Example: (Name's) talents were recently put to the test when …..
> He/She responded with …..

**Quantum leap**
> Example: (Name) made a quantum leap in the improvement of
> ….. There is none better at …..

**Quest for**
> Example: (Name's) quest for ….. led to …..

**Quick to**
> Example: (Name) is always quick to take the lead in ….. His/Her
> unbeatable ….. distinguishes him/her from …..

**Quickly soared to top**
> Example: (Name) quickly soared to the top of ….. with his/her
> enormous capacity for …..

**Radiates**
> Example: (Name) radiates enthusiasm and ….. in everything that
> he/she does.

**Radical change**
> Example: (Name) brought about a radical change to ….. that
> increased …..

**Raised new issues**
> Example: (Name's) inputs raised new issues that had not
> previously considered.  These inputs contributed to …..

**Raised state of the art**
> Example: (Name') performance in/as ….. raised the state of the
> art in …..

**Range of performance**
> Example: The range of performance in/on ….. demonstrated by
> (Name) far exceeds …..

**Rapid evolution**
> Example: (Name) made the rapid evolution from ….. to …..
> with unusual ease and …..

**Rare insight**
> Example: The rare insight into ….. brought in by (Name) was
> crucial to the success of …..

**Rational expectation(s)**
> Example: (Name's) performance in/as ….. exceeded all rational
> expectations.

**Razor-sharp mind**
> Example: (Name) has a razor-sharp mind and …..

**Reached milestone**
    Example: (Name) reached the major milestone of ..... with his/her unequalled ability to .....
**Reached new heights/summit**
    Example: (Name) reached new heights in area of ..... thanks to his/her excellent ..... and .....
**Reached peak of**
    Example: (Name) is a skilled ..... and has reached the peak of ....
**Readily available**
    Example: (Name) is always readily available to ..... His/Her revitalized ..... has had a profound impact on .....
**Real change**
    Example: (Name) has made real and significant changes to ..... This is one of the most sophisticated ..... in .....
**Realize fullest potential**
    Example: (Name) is one of the few people in ..... to realize his/her full potential in/as .....
**Reasonable solution**
    Example: (Name) always offers a reasonable solution to difficult problems. His/Her tireless, top-quality work in ..... has .....
**Rebounded from**
    Example: (Name) rebounded from a slow start in/as ..... to transform ..... into .....
**Recipe for success**
    Example: (Name) has a simple recipe for success.. He/She always ..... while achieving remarkable .....
**Recognized stewardship**
    Example: (Name's) recognized stewardship in/as ..... is unmatched in (organization) in recent years.
**Record breaking/shattering**
    Example: (Name's) record breaking performance in/ as ..... surpassed .....
**Record of**
    Example: (Name) has a steady and consistent record of ..... His/Her meritorious work furthered .....
**Redeeming qualities**
    Example: (Name) has many redeeming qualities. Among the most notable are .....
**Redefined concept**
    Example: (Name's) work in/as ..... has redefined the traditional concept of .....
**Refreshing thought**(s)
    Example: (Name's) new and refreshing thoughts about/on ..... led to immeasurable .....

**Refuses to accept**
>   Example: (Name) refuses to accept mediocre performance.
>   His/Her meticulous attention to ..... led to .....

**Reinforced action(s)**
>   Example: (Name) reinforced the actions of ..... with a multi-
>   talented ..... and laudatory performance in/as .....

**Rejuvenated**
>   Example: (Name) single-handedly rejuvenated (organization) with
>   the best .....

**Relaxed confidence**
>   Example: (Name) displays a relaxed confidence that .....

**Relentless pressure(s)**
>   Example: Despite the relentless pressures placed on (Name),
>   he/she performed ..... in an exemplary fashion.

**Relentless pursuit**
>   Example: (Name's) relentless pursuit of ..... has led to ..... thanks
>   to his/her exacting .....

**Rendered obsolete**
>   Example: (Name) rendered obsolete the old/previous .....
>   This resulted in a first-rate .....

**Renowned for**
>   Example: (Name) is renowned in (organization) for his/her
>   ability to .....

**Repeated successes**
>   Example: (Name's) repeated successes in any variety of jobs in
>   (organization) are noteworthy and .....

**Reputation**
>   Example: (Name) has earned a top-notch reputation for being able
>   to ..... where others routinely fell short.

**Reservoir of experience**
>   Example: (Name) is a reservoir of experience. This was clearly
>   evidenced during a recent ..... when .....

**Reshaped**
>   Example: (Name) personally reshaped ..... with his/her
>   extraordinary .....

**Resilient**
>   Example: Nothing can keep (Name) down. His/Her resilient
>   personality always .....

**Resounding success**
>   Example: (Name's) efforts in/at ..... were a resounding success.

**Respectable showing**
>   Example: (Name) gave much more than a respectable showing
>   in/as ..... when he/she .....

**Respected figure**
Example: (Name) has become a respected figure in (organization) because of his/her ability to .....

**Responded in full measure**
Example: (Name) responded in full measure to ..... with .....

**Revamped a sagging**
Example: (Name) revamped a sagging ..... and led it to .....

**Revitalized**
Example: (Name) was able to revitalize (organization) from ..... to ..... with his/her .....

**Revolutionary (new) idea(s)**
Example: (Name's) revolutionary new idea on/about ..... led to the immediate improvement of .....

**Revolutionized**
Example: (Name) revolutionized the way (organization) ..... resulting in .....

**Rich past experience(s)**
Example: (Name) brought a rich past experience in/to ..... This quickly became evident when he/she .....

**Rich tradition/variety**
Example: (Name) has a rich variety of talents, including .....

**Richly deserved**
Example: (Name) earned ....., a richly deserved honor for his/her work in/as .....

**Rigorous standards**
Example: (Name's) rigorous work standards led the way in ..... He/She always .....

**Rise to the occasion**
Example: (Name) was able to rise to the occasion recently when he/she was tasked with ..... The results were .....

**Root of problem**
Example: (Name) is able to get to the root of any problem. He/She always finds a way to .....

**Rose from depths of**
Example: (Name) rose from the depths of ..... to ..... because of his/her unique ability to .....

**Rose to the occasion**
Example: Despite the demanding duties of ..... (Name) not only rose to the occasion, he/she also .....

**Run circles around**
Example: (Name) can run circles around ..... with his/her all-around ..... and considerable talent in/as .....

**Run down**
Example: (Name) took a run down ..... and raised it to .....

**Safely weathered**
> Example: (Name) safely weathered the problem of .... thanks to his/her boundless .....

**Saved the day**
> Example: (Name's) experience in ..... saved the day when .....

**Search of excellence**
> Example: In his/her search for excellence, (Name) was able to ..... This innovation saved .....

**Searches for opportunities**
> Example: (Name) continuously searches for opportunities to improve himself/herself.

**Seasoned veteran**
> Example: (Name) is a seasoned veteran at ..... He/She is a valuable addition to .....

**Second to none**
> Example: (Name) is second to none when it comes to ..... He/She served as a role model for .....

**Seed(s) of success**
> Example: The seeds of success to ..... were sewn by (Name) when he/she created a new .....

**Seized the opportunity**
> Example: (Name) seized the opportunity to ..... His/Her sheer willpower and boundless energy .....

**Sensation(al)**
> Example: (Name) is a sensational ..... His/Her performance in/as ..... was totally impressive from start to finish.

**Sense of**
> Example: (Name) takes a great sense of personal responsibility for ..... He/She is a real professional.

**Sense of purpose**
> Example: (Name) takes a real sense of purpose into each job. He/She is a consummate .....

**Serious contender**
> Example: (Name) should be considered as a serious contender for the job of ..... because of his/her .....

**Serious situation**
> Example: The serious situation caused by ..... could have led to problems in ..... Instead, (Name) was able to .....

**Seriously strengthened**
> Example: (Name) seriously strengthened (organization's) ability to ..... His/Her flawless performance resulted in .....

**Served to**
> Example: (Name's) performance as ..... served to strengthen the (organization) in .....

**Set apart**
Example: (Name) set himself/herself apart from ….. because of his/her considerable talent in/as …..

**Set course for future**
Example: (Name) set the course for the future of ….. with a matchless ability to …..

**Set in motion/place**
Example: (Name) set in motion procedures that ….. and should bring uniformly outstanding …..

**Set new precedent**
Example: (Name) set a new precedent in (area) with contributions to ….. that …..

**Set sights on**
Example: When (Name) sets his/her sights on something, it is as good as accomplished. He/She has the unique ability to …..

**Set the stage**
Example: (Name) set the stage for progress in ….. when he/she led a dramatic increase in …..

**Set up and take notice**
Example: (Name's) performance is outstanding. He/She has the ability to make people set up and take notice of his/her talents in/as …..

**Shape(d) the**
Example: (Name) shaped the future of …..by demonstrating considerable talent in/as …..

**Shaped events**
Example: (Name's) performance in/as ….. shaped future events that led to …..

**Sharp increase**
Example: There was a sharp increase in ….. thanks to (Name's) enormous capacity for …..

**Sharply focused**
Example: (Name) always stays sharply focused on the task at hand. He/She has a natural aptitude for …..

**Sheer energy**
Example: Through sheer strength and energy (Name) was able to…..

**Shore up weak points**
Example: (Name) was greatly successful at ….. by shoring up the weak points in/at …..

**Shot in the arm**
Example: (Name) brought a welcomed shot in the arm to (organization) by his/her …..

**Shouldered responsibility**
    Example: (Name) shouldered the awesome responsibility of .....
        by his/her .....

**Significant changes/gains**
    Example: (Name) made significant changes in ..... which resulted
        in unequalled gains in/that .....

**Significant milestone**
    Example: (Name) reached a significant milestone in ..... when
        he/she .....

**Simple and straight-forward**
    Example: (Name's) simple and straight-forward way of doing .....
        has won praise throughout (organization).

**Simply the best**
    Example: (Name) is simply the best ..... at (organization).  His/Her
        performance is underscored by .....

**Sincere honor**
    Example: It has been a sincere honor to serve/work with .....
        His/Her unblemished record .....

**Single-minded purpose**
    Example: (Name) approached the task of .... with a single-minded
        purpose.  He/She is a real go-getter who can .....

**Singled out for**
    Example: (Name) has been singled out for special recognition for
        his/her work in/as .....

**Sink teeth into**
    Example: (Name) was able to sink his/her teeth into the difficult
        job/task of ..... and produce results that were .....

**Sit up & take notice**
    Example: (Name) made others sit up and take notice of his/her
        ability to .....

**Size up situation**
    Example: (Name) was able to quickly size up the critical situation
        of ..... and proceeded to .....

**Solely responsible**
    Example: (Name) was solely responsible for the success of .....

**Solid base/foundation**
    Example: (Name) built a solid foundation of ..... by staying up to
        date on the latest developments of .....

**Solid contributor**
    Example: (Name) has been a solid contributor in/to ..... with
        his/her capacity to/for .....

**Solidified**
    Example: (Name) solidified his/her hold on ..... with a performance
        that .....

**Someone special**
> Example: (Name) is truly someone very special. His/Her knowledge and efficiency in/at ..... is .....

**Sorely needed**
> Example: (Name) brought sorely needed ..... to (organization) with an energetic personality that .....

**Sought after by**
> Example: (Name) is routinely sought after by ..... because of his/her invaluable .....

**Source of knowledge/light**
> Example: (Name) is the resident expert on ..... He/She is considered the main source of knowledge for .....

**Sparked innovation**
> Example: (Name's) knowledge in/of ..... sparked the innovation of ..... and led the way to/for .....

**Spawned new**
> Example: (Name) spawned new frontiers in the effort to .....

**Spearhead effort(s) to**
> Example: (Name) volunteered to spearhead efforts to .....

**Special feel for**
> Example: (Name) is an expert in/at ..... He/She has a special feel for .....

**Special gift**
> Example: (Name) has a special gift for .....

**Special quality(ies)**
> Example: (Name) has some special qualities in the area of .....

**Spirit of cooperation**
> Example: (Name's) spirit of cooperation far exceeds .....

**Splendid record**
> Example: (Name) has built a splendid record of ..... based on his/her performance in/as .....

**Spotless**
> Example: The spotless record of (organization) is due in large part to the work of (Name).

**Spurred action/growth**
> Example: (Name's) response to ..... spurred action on ..... and led to a vast improvement in .....

**Staggering range of talent**
> Example: (Name) has a staggering range of talent. In a recent ..... he/she completely turned around .....

**Stainless record**
> Example: (Name) has a stainless record in all aspects of .....

**Stands tall**
> Example: When it comes to ..... (Name) stands tall. He/She offers the highest caliber performance.

**Started from scratch**
>Example: (Name) started ..... from scratch and built up a/an .....
>that is unprecedented in .....

**State of the art**
>Example: (Name) introduced a state of the art ..... to .....
>His/Her keen technical abilities led to .....

**Stated objective(s)**
>Example: (Name) met all stated objectives and then some.
>He/She was the first person to .....

**Steady stream of**
>Example: (Name) offered a steady stream of new ideas. This
>allowed (organization) to reach new heights in .....

**Step ahead of**
>Example: (Name) is always a step ahead of the action. His/Her
>ability to plan and ..... is totally impressive.

**Stepped forward**
>Example: When the challenge of ..... surfaced (Name) stepped
>forward and, with keen ..... abilities proceeded to .....

**Stick it out**
>Example: (Name) has the ability to stick it out in tough situations.
>He/She has set a benchmark of excellence in .....

**Story of dedication**
>Example: (Name) work habits are a story of dedication. He/She
>springs into action and exerts total dedication when.....

**Straighten up**
>Example: (Name's) efforts to ..... straightened up a previously
>..... and resulted in a smooth and flawless .....

**Strain put on**
>Example: The additional strain put on (organization) because of
>..... was staggering, but (Name) was able to .....

**Strengthened resolve**
>Example: When things go wrong, (Name's) strengthened resolve
>allows him/her to .....

**Strenuous schedule**
>Example: Despite an already strenuous work schedule, (Name)
>still manages to .....

**Stretched boundaries/limits**
>Example: (Name) stretched the limits of ..... because of his/her
>strong technical background in .....

**Stretches the imagination**
>Example: (Name's) ability to ..... stretches the imagination.
>He/She directly contributes to the success of .....

**Striking improvement**
>Example: (Name) has brought a striking improvement to
>(organization) by his/her ability to successfully .....

**Striking results**
> Example: (Name) striking results in/as .....was instrumental in/to .....

**Stroke of genius**
> Example: (Name's) plan to ..... was a stroke of genius. He/She unparalleled productivity has .....

**Strong background**
> Example: (Name) brings a strong background in ..... to (organization). With this he/she was able to .....

**Strong will**
> Example: (Name's) strong will and professional ..... resulted in an exceptionally well/good .....

**Stunning results**
> Example: (Name) was able to achieve stunning results in ..... because of his/her .....

**Substantial impact/number**
> Example: (Name) has had a substantial impact on/in ..... His/Her solid professional performance led to .....

**Substantially improved**
> Example: (Name) has substantially improved the operation of ..... He/She always gives 100 percent.

**Success story**
> Example: (Name's) performance in/as ..... has been a success story from start to finish.

**Supportive fashion**
> Example: The supportive fashion in which (Name) helped ..... led to improvements in .....

**Surge in activity**
> Example: The surge in activity in (organization) can be directly attributed to (Name) and his/her ability to .....

**Surpassed all expectations**
> Example:   (Name's) performance in/as ..... surpassed all expectations and resulted in .....

**Sustained commitment**
> Example: (Name) gave a sustained commitment to the improvement of ..... by his/her .....

**Sweeping changes/reform**
> Example: (Name) brought sweeping changes to (organization). The results of .... were always impressive and .....

**Tackle(s) any**
> Example: (Name) can successfully tackle any and all assignments. He/She is highly proficient and .....

**Take the lead**
> Example: (Name) was able to take the lead in ..... The results were impressive and contributed to .....

**Take to heart**

Example: (Name) takes to heart his/her responsibilities as/of .....
with a dedication rarely observed in .....

**Task at hand**

Example: (Name's) ability to focus on the task at hand is
noteworthy. He/She is exceptionally well
organized and .....

**Temporary setback**

Example: (Name) takes temporary setbacks in full stride. His/Her
resilient and energetic personality .....

**Testimony to**

Example: (Name's) ability to ..... is testimony to his/her .....

**Tests new ideas**

Example: (Name) tests new ideas and ways of doing things. In a
recent action he/she .....

**Thirst for**

Example: (Name) has a thirst for knowledge and can always be
found .....

**Threshold of**

Example: (Name's) ability to ..... has put him/her on the
threshold of .....

**Thrives in/on**

Example: (Name) thrives on ..... His/Her solid professional
competence always .....

**Through thick and thin**

Example: Through thick and thin (Name) can always be
relied upon to ..... regardless of .....

**Thumbs up**

Example: (Name) has earned two thumbs up for his/her
work in/on .....

**Time of transition**

Example: During the time of transition from ..... to ..... (Name)
irreplaceable dedication .....

**Time-tested**

Example: (Name) is highly successful at ..... because he/she
uses time-tested methods to .....

**Tireless efforts**

Example: (Name's) tireless efforts dedicated to the improvement
of ..... was unmatched in .....

**Took advantage of**

Example: (Name) took full advantage of ..... His/Her impressive
.... and dedication were truly impressive.

**Took on added responsibility**
    Example: (Name) took on the added responsibility of ..... despite an already full work load in/as ..... and performed with unmatched .....
**Top speed**
    Example: (Name) proceeded with top speed to ..... using his/her endless energy and .....
**Top to bottom**
    Example: (Name) revamped ..... from top to bottom. The results led to uncommon ..... and .....
**Top-level performance**
    Example: (Name's) top-level performance in/as .....shows an unusually high standard of .....
**Top-notch**
    Example: (Name) is a top-notch ..... demonstrating the energy and resourcefulness .....
**Tough act to follow**
    Example: (Name) is a tough act to follow. He successfully faced the demanding challenge of ..... with .....
**Toward the future**
    Example: (Name) always looks toward the future. He/She continuously seeks to improve .....
**Track record**
    Example: (Name) has a very successful track record in/of ..... He/She is self-motivated and always .....
**Transformed**
    Example: (Name) single-handedly transformer (organization) from ..... to ..... without a single .....
**Tricky business**
    Example: (Name) was able to handle the tricky business of ..... with a great amount of .....
**Tried and true**
    Example: (Name's) tried and true methods of ....., coupled with his/her innate talent to .....resulted in .....
**True pioneer**
    Example: (Name) is a true pioneer in the field of ..... His/Her qualifications in/as ..... are truly first class.
**Trusted completely**
    Example: (Name) can be trusted completely. He/She is a self-starter who can be depended upon to always .....
**Turn the tables**
    Example: (Name) turned the tables on the complex/difficult ..... with the energy and resourcefulness of .....

**Turnaround**
> Example: (Name) engineered a complete turnaround of .....
> which had previously been plagued by/with .....

**Turning point**
> Example: With unusual skill and dexterity, (Name) was able
> to provide the turning point in/for .....

**Ultimate success/test**
> Example: The ultimate success of ..... was a direct result of
> (Name's) performance/work on .....

**Unbeatable combination**
> Example: (Name's) unbeatable combination of ..... and .....
> broke new ground in/on .....

**Unbreakable spirit**
> Example: The unbreakable spirit exhibited by (Name) set
> the stage for the highly successful .....

**Uncharted territory**
> Example: (Name's) work has entered uncharted territory. His/Her
> technical abilities far exceed .....

**Under any circumstances**
> Example: (Name) is the best ..... under any circumstances. No
> one is better at .....

**Under pressure**
> Example: (Name) performs best under pressure. He/She has the
> incredible ability to .....

**Underscore(d) importance**
> Example: (Name) recently underscored his/her importance to
> (organization) by personally .....

**Undertaking**
> Example: (Name's) undertaking of the tremendous job/task of .....
> led to him/her being selected to/for .....

**Unexpected obstacle(s)**
> Example: (Name) overcame many unexpected obstacles on
> his/her way to .....

**Unexpected turn to/for**
> Example: Despite an unexpected turn for the worse, (Name)
> Was able to take ..... and ..... with unparalleled success.

**Unexplored avenues**
> Example: (Name) discovered previously unexplored avenues on
> ways to improve .....

**Unforeseen events**
> Example: The unforeseen events of ..... failed to put a damper on
> (Name's) performance. He/She proved extremely
> proficient in/at .....

**Unglamorous task(s)**
>Example: (Name) was faced with the unglamorous task of …..
>His/Her unique ability to attain quality results, remains …..

**Unique achievement(s)**
>Example: The unique achievements made by (Name) have led to the achievement of ….. by …..

**Uniquely suited**
>Example: (Name) is uniquely suited to ….. with his/her remarkable ability to …..

**Unmistakable**
>Example: (Name's) unmistakable performance in/as ….. led to him/her being selected for/to…..

**Unprecedented**
>Example: The unprecedented success of (Name) in/as ….. demonstrated his/her personal talent for/to …..

**Unreachable goal(s)**
>Example: (Name) sets high standards for ….. and does not consider even the most difficult goals to be unreachable.

**Unrelenting**
>Example: (Name's) unrelenting endeavor to ….. resulted in the most successful ….. in/since ….

**Up and coming**
>Example: (Name) is an up and coming superstar. He/She works zealously to ….. while achieving …..

**Up hill**
>Example: (Name's) up hill battle for/to ….. paid off when he/she ….

**Up to the task**
>Example: (Name) was up to the demanding task of …..
>He/She always adds more to ….. than expected.

**Ushered in new era**
>Example: (Name) ushered in a new era in ….. with his/her totally successful ability to …..

**Valuable insight**
>Example: (Name) contributed valuable insight into …..
>Without his/her knowledge of …. the ….. would have …..

**Vastly different**
>Example: The (organization) is vastly different for the better since (Name) …..

**Versed in**
>Example: (Name) is well versed in the intricate details of …..
>His/Her energetic work habits and ….. have …..

**Very impressive**
>Example: Very impressive indeed was (Name's) performance in/as …..

**Vigorous effort(s)**
>Example: (Name's) successful vigorous efforts to ..... resulted in a substantial gain in .....

**Virtually eliminated**
>Example: (Name) virtually eliminated all ..... while at the same time successfully .....

**Virtue of hard work**
>Example: By the virtue of sheer hard work, (Name) was able to complete .....

**Vital (first) step**
>Example: (Name) took the vital first step in combating ..... The standards he/she set .....

**Vital importance**
>Example: The vital importance of the work (Name) contributed to (organization) cannot be understated.

**Vital role**
>Example: (Name) played a vital role in the successful .....

**Vitality**
>Example: (Name's) vitality and energy are ..... and have .....

**Waged relentless**
>Example: (Name) waged a relentless battle for/against ..... The outcome succeeded in .....

**Way it should be**
>Example: (Name) knows the way things should be done. He/She was instrumental in .....

**Welcomed addition**
>Example: (Name) has proved himself/herself a welcomed addition to (organization) by .....

**Well received**
>Example: (Name) and his/her assistance was well received by .....

**Well suited for**
>Example: (Name) is well suited for difficult jobs consisting of .....

**Well versed**
>Example: (Name) is well versed in all aspects of ..... He/She provides daily valuable solutions to .....

**Went all out**
>Example: (Name) went all out to complete ..... The success he/she achieved is a direct result of his/her .....

**Went far beyond**
>Example: (Name's) performance in/as ..... went far beyond what is normally expected of .....

**Whatever it takes**
>Example: (Name) contributes to the job whatever it takes to be successful.

**Whole-hearted**
>Example: (Name's) whole-hearted support of ….. was instrumental in the successful completion of …..

**Wide range of**
>Example: (Name) has a wide range of talents. One of special note is …..

**Willing to sacrifice**
>Example: (Name) is willing to sacrifice personal ….. for the betterment of …..

**Winning ways**
>Example: (Name's) winning ways have continued. He/She set the standards for/in …..

**Within reach**
>Example: (Name) considers even the most difficult jobs within his/her reach. He/She always/never …..

**Without difficulty**
>Example: (Name) accomplishes the most demanding tasks without difficulty.

**Without reservation**
>Example: Without reservation, (Name) has my highest recommendation for …..

**Won respect of**
>Example: (Name) won the respect and admiration of ….. with his/her …..

**Words cannot express**
>Example: Words cannot adequately express the value (Name) brought to (organization.)

**Work under adversity**
>Example: (Name's) ability to work under adversity without a complaint is praiseworthy.

**Worked frantically**
>Example: (Name) worked frantically to complete ….. ahead of schedule. The result(s) was/were …..

**Worthwhile goals**
>Example: (Name) has accomplished many worthwhile goals. Not the lest of which is/was …..

**Worthy of mention**
>Example: (Name's) ….. is certainly worthy of mention. He/She personally …..

# ADDITIONAL SENTENCE SUBJECTS

Acted swiftly

Addressed the question

Ambitious campaign

At risk

Beneficial to

Brought forces to bear

Captured mood

Clear vision

Commitment to course of action

Concrete form

Covered all bases

Crucial to success

Desired effect

Dynamic force

Embodies qualities of

Feel the energy

Filled vacuum

Focused determination

Frank observation(s)

Full cooperation

Acute sense of

Aggressively enforced

Any number of

Beacon of hope

Best kept secret

Came full circle

Changed course of

Close knit group

Commitment to future

Consummate craftsman

Creative genius

Deeply rooted

Door always open

Eased burden

Entirely new perspective

Fiercely loyal

Firmly committed

Formidable tool

Fueled creative spirit

Full-court press

| | |
|---|---|
| Full speed ahead | Fully committed to |
| Gravity of situation | Glorious effort(s) |
| Healthy source of | Host of challenges |
| In the works | Indescribably |
| Indifferent to | Inescapable reality |
| Infused with spirit | Inherently risky |
| Inner strength | Inspire shared vision |
| Instinctive feel | Integrity |
| Intense personality | Internal fire |
| Intriguing concept/idea | Intrinsic values |
| Intrinsically superior | Intuitive |
| Irreplaceable service | Judicious effort |
| Just in time | Keyed up |
| Keystone | Kindled spirit(s) |
| Landmark decision | Larger than life |
| Lavished praise | Leader's vision |
| Legacy of service | Level playing field |
| Lift(s) people's spirit(s) | Light at end of tunnel |
| Lit fire under | Lively spirit |
| Made good on | Made point of |
| Main ingredient(s) | Mainstream |
| Maintained composure | Make over |
| Marked coming | Marvelous |

Masterwork

Mobilizes others

Moment of truth

Mounted major challenge

Nail down

Never forgot

Nip in the bud

Nourishes spirits

On business end of

Once and for all

Open-handed

Outpouring of

Outward calm

Passed the torch

Passionate defender of

Peacemaker Persona

Personal crusade

Planted the seed

Phenomenal change

Popular belief

Poised on edge of

Powder keg ready to explode

Mind-set

Moderating effect

Moral involvement

Move(d) forward

Nerves of steel

New way of thinking

Not to be forgotten

Nurtured

On hot seat

Open and above board

Open arms

Pass(ed) muster

Overall strategy

Passionate advocate

Peace of mind

Personal agenda

Personal test of courage

Pleasantly surprised

Played out on giant scale

Physical courage

Potentially significant

Power base

| | |
|---|---|
| Power of presence | Pragmatic |
| Pressed forward | Prevail upon |
| Process of discovery | Productive pursuit |
| Profoundly affected | Promise of things to come |
| Provided chemistry necessary | Provided outlet for |
| Proving ground | Pushed envelope |
| Put an end to | Raised spirit(s) of |
| Raised the question(s) | Rare privilege |
| Rarefied atmosphere | Real powder keg |
| Reap consequences | Rebuilt confidence |
| Re-energized efforts | Reflected changes |
| Reform oriented | Reinvigorated sagging |
| Rekindled flame/spirit | Relish with zest |
| Revered for | Revolutionary method(s) |
| Rich in vitality/spirit | Right set of values |
| Right thing to do | Rigorous schedule |
| Risk factor | Road to recovery |
| Rock hard | Rocky road |
| Rooted in history | Run the gauntlet |
| Rush of adrenaline | Safeguard |
| Saw future/light | Second nature |
| Seized the moment | Seized upon idea of |
| Selective field | Sensitive issue(s) |

Sensitive to

Serious crisis

Set world on fire

Sheer willpower/force of

Sight set on

Sign of the times

Singular purpose

Smooth process

Social fabric

Sophisticated role

Spawned rise of

Split-second

Springboard of/for

Square-shooter

Stand on own two feet

Stands alone

Stay(ed) in background

Straight as an arrow

Straightforward response

Strength through unity

Strict conformance/standards

Strident support

Sent clear message/signal

Served the purpose

Shaping the future

Short and sweet

Sign of hope

Significant inroads

Situation of extreme(s)

Social architect

Solid resolve

Soul of organization

Spelled success

Spotlight

Squared away

Squeaky clean

Stand up and be counted

Status symbol

Steered course of

Straight shooter

Strategy aimed at

Strengthens others

Strict control

Strike a blow

| | |
|---|---|
| Strong advocate | Strong influence |
| Strong voice for | Structural change/reform |
| Struggled successfully to | Studied works of |
| Successes mounted | Successfully challenged |
| Summon(ed) up the courage | Sunny disposition |
| Supporting cast | Surge of |
| Sustained effort | Sweep out/aside |
| Sweet victory | Symbol of |
| Sympathetic ear | Systematic approach |
| Take by storm | Take hold of |
| Taste of | Temperamentally suited |
| Tenacious | Tense time(s) |
| Tenuous position | Test of will/character |
| Test willpower/water(s) | Tested to limit(s) |
| Thought-provoking | Thoughtful analysis |
| Throw down the gauntlet | Tight knit group |
| Timeless | Took a stand |
| Took fresh look | Took inventory of facilities |
| Took special interest in | Tore down barrier(s) |
| Total dimension of | Total focus |
| Totally clear | Tough nut to crack |
| Tower of strength | Traditional concept/values |
| Transcends | Treat with courtesy |

| | |
|---|---|
| Triggered response | Triumph |
| True to form | True transformation |
| True visionary | Trusted advisor |
| Turn inside out | Turn over new leaf |
| Turn(ed) the tide | Turned the corner |
| Unassailable performance | Uncluttered thought |
| Uncompromising principles | Undaunted |
| Undeniable appeal | Under best of circumstances |
| Underlines importance | Underwent process of |
| Unencumbered | Unenviable position |
| Unfolding event(s) | Unification of |
| Unifying force | Uninhabited |
| United behind | Unlocked door of opportunity |
| Unshakable character | Unstoppable momentum |
| Up-beat/scale | Upgraded |
| Uplifting experience | Urgent business |
| Valiant gesture | Valid option |
| Vast numbers | Verbal support |
| Verge of | Very special |
| Viable option(s) | Vigilant |
| Vigorous response | Vintage |
| Virtually unchecked | Virtuoso |

| | |
|---|---|
| Vision of future | Vision of substance |
| Visionary | Vital interest/aspect |
| Voyage of discovery | Walk a tightrope |
| Warmly received | Weather(ed) the storm |
| Weed out | Weigh the options |
| Weight of responsibility | Well-founded |
| Went head-long into | Wholehearted endorsement |
| Wide-spread support | Widely accepted/embraced |
| Will power | Win laurels |
| Window of opportunity | Winning game plan |
| With (a) passion | With honor(s) |
| With particular clarity | Without second thought |
| Withstand test of time | Withstood onslaught |
| Won hearts and minds | Wonder work |
| Work ethic strong | Workable solution |
| Workaholic | Worked closely with |
| Worked perfectly | Worked to end |
| Workhorse | World class |
| World of good | Zero in on |
| Zest for challenge | |

# PERSONAL

# AWARDS

# &

# INDIVIDUAL

# RECOGNITION

# INDIVIDUAL RECOGNITION

## Individual recognition includes Letters of Commendation and Letters of Appreciation.

Most organizations encourage maximum use of Letters of Appreciation (LOAs) to recognize deserving personnel. LOAs are relatively easy to write and they do not require excessive research or documentation. Remember, commanding officers are not the only ones who can issue LOAs. Almost any senior can give a subordinate due recognition through a LOA. However, the more noteworthy the performance or accomplishment, the higher the LOA should go for signature.

Most people appreciate being officially recognized for superior performance. Additionally, timely recognition for quality performance gives the person receiving the LOA and others around him/her additional incentive and motivation. LOAs are an effective tool for improving performance and morale throughout an organization. Commanding officers are fully aware of the relationship between positive, timely, and official recognition and improved overall performance. Therein lies a personal benefit to the superior who drafts LOAs for deserving subordinates. That superior has demonstrated to his/her superior that he/she knows effective leadership principles. So, in these terms, the superior drafting the LOAs receives personal recognition. Maximum use of LOAs should be a fundamental part of any organization.

## Letters of Appreciation usually encompass three primary areas:

(1) The event/activity, and date involved;
(2) A listing or notation of personal accomplishments or achievements along with the personality traits displayed; and,
(3) Appropriate closing "thank you" remarks.

In general, a Letter of Appreciation (or Commendation) has three numbered paragraphs, one each covering the above areas. The examples on the following pages are provided to show the kind or type of material that might be used in each paragraph.

From:

To:

Subj: LETTER OF APPRECIATION

1.      I take great pleasure in expressing my appreciation for your outstanding performance while assigned as/to (job) during the period (date) to (date).

2.      While serving in these areas your duties included (list duties). Other duties included (list). Throughout this time frame you executed your duties in an exemplary manner.  You were quick to offer suggestions and viable ideas for improvement.    Several of your ideas have been implemented and have enhanced (area).  You are a very reliable individual who consistently produced superior results.    Your ever present considerate attitude and congenial disposition were positive assets in your day-to-day dealings with others.  Your military appearance and bearing continually reflected your obvious pride in your work and the service.  You approached problem situations intelligently and methodically, always employing the best use of resources at hand in their resolvement.

3.      Your keen sense of responsibility in the performance of your duties reflects great credit upon yourself, and is in keeping with the highest traditions of the United States Army.


/ Signature /


From:

To:

Subj: LETTER OF APPRECIATION

1.      During the period (date) to (date) you were assigned to the (element) of (organization).  You performed your duties as (job) in an outstanding manner and helped contribute directly to the overall mission accomplishments of the command.  Your dedication to duty and constant insistence on error free performance was instrumental in (organization)

earning the following distinctions: (list). Your outstanding efforts, in all areas of responsibility, have resulted in an overall upgrade of (area).

2.      Your (number) years of Army service included assignments to: (list). Your devotion to duty and outstanding support to the Army mission have been evident throughout your career. I commend you for your outstanding professionalism, devotion, and pride that you have exhibited during your Army service.

3.      On the occasion of your discharge from active Army service, I express my sincere desire for your continued success and join with your many friends at (organization) in wishing you and your family the best possible future.


/ Signature /


From:

To:

Subj: LETTER OF APPRECIATION

1.      During the period (date) to (date) you were attached to (organization). You were assigned to the (organizational element) as (job).

2.      With a keen sense of responsibility, you attained a high degree of expertise in your assigned duties. You further enhanced your value by constantly applying yourself to learning the many techniques and procedures used throughout (organization) and became proficient in numerous jobs normally assigned to more senior personnel. Additionally, you performed your additional duties of (list duties) in a manner as to bring credit to (organization) and the United States Army. Your cheerful countenance and easy manner during periods of austere manning and demanding operational commitments were an additional asset to this command.

3.      As you depart (organization) for duty (at) (command) it is with sincere appreciation that I congratulate you on a job well done.

/ Signature /

From:

To:

Subj: LETTER OF APPRECIATION

1.      During the period of (date) through (date) you were assigned as (job), (organization).   Throughout this period you displayed excellent dedication and devotion to duty.

2.      Your knowledge of and experience with ... helped maintain the high state of operational readiness within (organization).  During the time you were assigned, you planned and carried out a wide variety of   ... projects to bring this (organization) to a higher state of material readiness. The overall effect of your performance led to (accomplishments). This was a direct result of your personal leadership and I commend you for this performance.

3.      It is with regret that your tour of active duty with the Army is ending. I am sure that you will continue your interest in the Army in your future endeavors.  On your departure you take with you best wishes for continued success from everyone at (organization).

/ Signature /

From:

To:

Subj: LETTER OF APPRECIATION

1.      It is with great pleasure that I convey my sincere appreciation for your efforts regarding the (event) on (date).

2.      Comments received from   ...   were very complimentary and confirmed my own thoughts pertaining to the professional manner in which the ... was planned and carried out.  I know that it took long, hard hours of work and considerable personal sacrifice to correlate the myriad details necessary to ensure the success of ... Your display of exceptional skill and resourcefulness in coordinating (...) are noteworthy.  Your dependability,

initiative, and talent to surmount difficulties in your path enliven those who come in contact with you.  Your constant dedication and ability to complete tasks in a superior manner is a direct reflection of the respect and support you receive from subordinates and seniors alike.

3.      I applaud your accomplishments and extend to you my personal BEST WISHES.

/ Signature /

From:

To:

Subj:  LETTER OF APPRECIATION

1.      During the period (dates) you were assigned to the (organization) for duty.  As (position), a job normally assigned to (senior pay grade), your performance, across the board, was nothing less than OUTSTANDING.

2.      You were responsible for ... (job highlights).  The tireless hours you devoted to this task were instrumental to the timely (task).  Your contributions enabled (organization) to (list accomplishments).  You consistently demonstrated maturity, persistence, and a "can do" attitude rarely observed among your peers.

3.      My personal thanks for a job WELL DONE.

/ Signature /

From:

To:

Subj:  LETTER OF APPRECIATION

1.      During the period (dates) you were assigned to (organization) for duty.  Your various duty assignments included (list jobs).

2.	Your individual performance and contribution to mission accomplishment in each and every assignment were OUTSTANDING. You were selected over your peers for special recognition as ... Your dedication and performance of duty throughout your tour at the (organization) have been most commendable.

3.	As you prepare for separation from active duty, it is with sincere appreciation that I congratulate you for honorable and faithful service. Having served with distinction in the most powerful Army the world has ever known, you have earned the right to say: "I served my country with pride." I am confident that the excellent traits you displayed at (command) will ensure your continued success in civilian life. Your many friends and I wish you continued success in all your future endeavors.


/ Signature /


# LETTER OF COMMENDATION
From:

To:

Subj:  LETTER OF COMMENDATION

1.	Upon your retirement from active military service, I extend my personal gratitude and appreciation for your continuing faithful service to our country.  You can be justifiably proud of your rewarding and patriotic career.

2.	To aid you in reviewing your (distinguished/successful) career, the below is a listing of commands at which you honorably served.  You entered the service at (location) on (date) and have since served with the following commands:

COMMAND	FROM	TO
(Add commands and dates)

3.	You earned a considerable amount of personal and professional recognition in your career, including the following official awards and decorations:  (Add list of awards)

4.	You, as much as anyone who has ever served, have helped foster and preserve the strong and honorable traditions of a mighty United States

Army that has helped defend and preserve the freedom that you, your fellow countrymen, and others throughout the free world continue to enjoy.

5.      Your professionalism and loyal personal dedication to duty and country reflect great credit upon yourself and the United States Army. On behalf of all of your friends, past and present, I wish you every success and happiness as you depart the Service.


/Signature/


# SPECIAL INDIVIDUAL UNIT/ORGANIZATION RECOGNITION INFORMATION


The criteria for nominating individuals for special unit or organization recognition are as many and varied as there are organizations and individuals involved in the process. In general, a write-up on an individual being nominated for special recognition should include personal and professional performance traits.

The write-up required at an individual command/unit is normally short and brief for two reasons: First, to encourage seniors to take the time and initiative to recommend their top performers. Second, a local nominating or screening selection board usually has the time and desire to personally interview everyone nominated. At this local level of competition the results of the screening board's personal interview usually carries more weight than the write-up.

When local commands/units forward the names of their nominees to higher echelons the supporting write-up must become more and more competitive and comprehensive. Geographic separation of lower echelon commands/units from higher echelons may prevent a personal interview of each individual nominated. As this level of competition is reached a screening board "narrows the field" of nominees, or selects the best candidate, using only the write-up. At this stage, command employment and pride may also come into play.

At the very top levels of competition, public attention becomes a factor and semi-finalists may be individually screened or interviewed by top staff personnel.

When nominating someone for this special recognition, most of the justification should be in terms of what the individual accomplished during the period for which the nomination is submitted.  It may be helpful to briefly note prior performance and accomplishment to show a continuing trend of superior effort and performance.  Some screening board members may not be fully familiar with the particular work load, schedule, or environment of an individual's organization.  If this is the case, be sure to briefly highlight pertinent facts and details.  It is also a good idea to include a few well chosen personal traits (dependable, professional attitude, etc.).

When considering what information to put in the write-up, review the following subjects:

JOB PERFORMANCE
LEADERSHIP
TECHNICAL EXPERTISE
MORALE/TEAMWORK BUILDER
COUNSELING OTHERS
EDUCATION (MILITARY/CIVILIAN)
HELPING OTHERS
SPECIAL RECOGNITION RECEIVED
COMMAND/CIVIC INVOLVEMENT
RESULTS OF INSPECTIONS
NOTEWORTHY OFF-DUTY ACTIVITIES
INNOVATIVE IMPROVEMENTS
SECONDARY/COLLATERAL DUTIES
TRAINING GIVEN/RECEIVED
VOLUNTEER FOR ADDITIONAL DUTIES
MILITARY PROFESSIONALISM
APPEARANCE BEHAVIOR
INDIVIDUAL INITIATIVE
PERSONAL DEVELOPMENT
HELPED MEET ORGANIZATION GOALS


Remember, there is not much difference in the text of a performance appraisal and in the text of an individual award or recognition. It might be helpful to review other sections of this book before writing your first draft.

# INTERVIEW BOARD

If an individual is going to appear before a selection or screening board, it is a good idea for that individual's organization to hold its own selection board screening process. First, this gives the individual some practice at answering questions in a professional but familiar atmosphere. Second, screening board members can critique the individual after the interview and offer ideas and suggestions for improving interview performance.

A person going before almost any interviewing board can be expected to be tense and apprehensive because of the "unknown" elements if for no other reason. If other members of an organization have gone before the same, or a similar, board, get them together with the person who is going to be interviewed. Explaining the routine and process of the interview board can have a very calming effect. Additionally, going over the types of questions that may be asked will increase self-assurance and personal confidence. Those are good qualities to present to a selection board.

The questions board members ask are as varied and diverse as the members who sit on the board. There is no standard question list. Each member is free to venture into any area he may choose. "If you saw a close friend of yours taking drugs, what would you do?" "What do you think about the United States' policy on (whatever)?" Different people might give different answers to questions such as these--and all could be correct. Local interview board members, for the most part, want a candidate's thoughts, ideas, and opinions on subjects. They are not looking for cut-and-dry "right" or "wrong" answers.

# INTERVIEW BOARD HINTS

*Be straightforward, honest, and sincere.

*Don't talk too fast (or too slow).

*Don't talk with your hands (don't wave them around).

*Sit still. Don't squirm around.

*Keep eye-to-eye contact. Use eye-to-eye contact when talking to board members. Do not look at only one individual. You are talking to the entire board, so share your eye contact (and answers) with all members.

*Appearance. Must be above reproach. An excellent appearance always gives a person the inside track to selection.

*World/Military events. Be prepared to discuss world events. Watch the news on TV and read the newspaper--know at least what is behind the headlines.

With the above "ground rules" covered, the following pages are provided to give ideas and examples of how to draft individual recognition write-ups. The first example attempts to show the total range and scope of an individual who is competing for selection at high levels of competition. The remainder of the examples gives a variety of range at the local level.